PLUTARCH'S
LIFE OF ARATUS

PLUTARCH'S
LIFE OF ARATUS

WITH INTRODUCTION, NOTES, AND
APPENDIX

BY

W. H. PORTER

ARNO PRESS
A New York Times Company
New York • 1979

ALLEN COUNTY PUBLIC LIBRARY
FORT WAYNE, INDIANA

Reprint Edition 1979 by Arno Press Inc.

Reprinted by permission of William A. Porter
Reprinted from a copy in the University of
    Illinois Library

GREEK TEXTS AND COMMENTARIES
ISBN for complete set: 0-405-11412-5
See last pages of this volume for titles.

Manufactured in the United States of America

———◆———

Library of Congress Cataloging in Publication Data

Plutarchus.
    Plutarch's Life of Aratus.

    (Greek texts and commentaries)
    Text in Greek; introd. and notes in English.
    Reprint of the 1937 ed. published by Cork
University Press, Dublin and Cork.
    Bibliography: p.
    Includes index.
    1. Aratus of Sicyon, 271-213 B.C. 2. Statesmen
--Greece--Biography. I. Porter, William Holt.
II. Title. III. Series.
PA4369.A75   1979   938'.7'080924 [B]   78-18593
ISBN 0-405-11434-6

PLUTARCH'S

LIFE OF ARATUS

ΠΛΟΥΤΑΡΧΟΥ ΑΡΑΤΟΣ

PLUTARCH'S
LIFE OF ARATUS

WITH INTRODUCTION, NOTES, AND APPENDIX

BY

W. H. PORTER, M.A.

Lecturer in University College, Cork

CORK UNIVERSITY PRESS
EDUCATIONAL CO. OF IRELAND, LTD.
DUBLIN AND CORK
LONGMANS, GREEN AND CO.
LONDON   NEW YORK   TORONTO
CALCUTTA   BOMBAY   MADRAS
1937

LONGMANS, GREEN AND CO. Ltd.
39 PATERNOSTER ROW, LONDON, E.C. 4
6 OLD COURT HOUSE STREET, CALCUTTA
53 NICOL ROAD, BOMBAY
36A MOUNT ROAD, MADRAS

LONGMANS, GREEN AND CO.
114 FIFTH AVENUE, NEW YORK
221 EAST 20TH STREET, CHICAGO
88 TREMONT STREET, BOSTON

LONGMANS, GREEN AND CO.
215 VICTORIA STREET, TORONTO

Amico suo

Iohanni Iosepho Horgan, *qui civitati Corcagiensium suae formam qua nunc utitur praestantissimam elaboravit, hunc libellum*

D. D. D.

Editor

πειρώμενος, *ut ait Plutarchus noster,* ἀνδρὸς ἀγαθοῦ καὶ νοῦν ἔχοντος.

PREFACE.

My thanks are due to the Senate of the National University of Ireland for a generous contribution to the cost of publishing this volume; also to J. B. Metzlersche Verlagsbuchhandlung, Stuttgart, publishers of Pauly-Wissowa, *Real-Encyclopädie der classischen Altertumswissenschaft,* and to Professor F. W. de Waele, of the University of Nijmegen, for their courtesy in permitting me to reproduce the Plan of Ancient Corinth from Suppt. vol. vi (p. 189) of the *Encyclopädie.*

The historical writings of Aratus and his contemporaries have perished; lost likewise is the Latin work which might, in part at least, have filled the gap—the universal history composed by Livy's contemporary, Pompeius Trogus—all except the table of contents (*Prologi*) and an almost worthless abridgement by the unhistorically-minded Justin.

In these circumstances our knowledge of the period 252–220 B.C. depends chiefly on Plutarch's biographies of Agis, Cleomenes, and Aratus. But while three annotated editions of the *Agis and Cleomenes* appeared during the nineteenth century, the *Aratus* has been neglected.

For readers of Dutch, however, this omission is now largely repaired by Dr. W. P. Theunissen's *Ploutarchos: Leven van Aratos met historisch-topographisch Commentaar,* a work of special value from a topographical point of view.

The text of the present edition is based on that of Dr. K. Ziegler, Plutarchi Vitae (iii, 1), Teubner, 1915, which in every respect is far in advance of its predecessors; I have, however, been somewhat less reluctant than Dr. Ziegler to admit conjectural emendations. Of new readings which appear in the text, some are due to my friend, Dr. R. M. Henry; a few are my own.

The *Introduction* may be thought unduly long, but it is to be remembered that the subject, in itself complicated, is further encumbered by much controversial matter; and that the third century B.C. is a period which can hardly be said to exist for our schools and colleges.

Indebtedness to previous writers is acknowledged where it occurs; my chief obligations being to Beloch's *Griechische Geschichte,* to the numerous writings of Dr. W. W. Tarn which directly or indirectly bear upon the history of Aratus, and to an article by Dr. G. De Sanctis (*Klio* ix) which has, I believe, "properly based" the chronology of the secession-state of Alexander, son of Craterus.

Dr. Henry and Dr. H. W. Parke have each read a portion of the book in MS., and have made some suggestions, which I have been glad to adopt. Dr. J. G. O'Neill, author of *Ancient Corinth,* has discussed with me some points of Corinthian topography. Mr. M. Duggan has shared in the correction of proof-sheets. The Librarian of University College, Cork, Mr. T. A. Conroy, has procured me the loan of some books now out of print or otherwise hard to obtain.

W. H. P.

LEHENAGH, CORK,
December, 1936.

CONTENTS.

ABBREVIATIONS.

A. J. A. = American Journal of Archæology.
C. A. H. = Cambridge Ancient History.
C. Q. = Classical Quarterly.
C. R. = Classical Review.
F. H. G. = Fragmenta Historicorum Graecorum (Müller).
I. G. = Inscriptiones Graecae.
J. H. S. = Journal of Hellenic Studies.
L. and S. = Liddell and Scott, Greek Lexicon (new ed.).
O. G. I. = Orientis Graeci Inscriptiones (Dittenberger).
P.-W. = Pauly-Wissowa, Real-Encyclopädie d. class. Altertumswissenschaft.
S. E. G. = upplementum Epigraphicum Graecum.
Syll.³ = ςylloge Inscriptionum Graecarum (Dittenberger).

The following works are cited by the authors' names :—

Beloch, Griechische Geschichte, ed. 2, vol. 4, parts 1 and 2 (1925-7).
Cary, History of the Greek World, B.C. 323-146 (1932).
De Sanctis, La ribellione d' Alessandro, *Klio* ix (1909).
Dinsmoor, Archons of Athens (1931).
Fellmann, Antigonus Gonatas und die Griechischen Staaten (1930).
Ferguson, Athenian Tribal Cycles (1932).
Ferrabino, Arato di Sicione (1921).
Frazer, Pausanias' Description of Greece (1898).
Klatt, Forschungen . . . Quellen und Chronologie des Kleomenischen Krieges (1877).
Kühner-Gerth, Ausfürliche Grammatik d. Gr. Sprache, Part 2 (Syntax, vols. 1 and 2).
Laidlaw, History of Delos (1933), ch. 3 and App.
O'Neill, Ancient Corinth, part 1, ch. 2 (1929).
Perrin, Plutarch's Lives, vol. 11 (Loeb transl.), (1926).
Schulz, Quibus ex fontibus fluxerint *Ag. Cleom. Arat.* vitae Plutarcheae (1886).
Shuckburgh, Polybius (transl.), (1889).
Skalet, Ancient Sicyon (1928).
Stagl, Plut. in Verhältnis zu Polybios in der vita des Aratos (1904).
Susemihl, Geschichte des Griech. Literatur in der Alexandrinerzeit (1892).
Tarn, Antigonos Gonatas (1913).
*Theunissen, Ploutarchos Leven van Aratos (1935).
*Walbank, Aratos of Sicyon (1933).

---

* Both of these books contain valuable historical biographies, to which, however, the works of Cary, Ferguson, and Laidlaw, cited above, should be added.

CORRIGENDA

P. xviii, *line* 21, *for* third *read* second.

P. xxxix, *line* 17, for *Arat.* 4 read *Arat.* 9.

P. 10, *line* 10, *for* τὴν *read* τὴν.

P. 23, *line* 9. *for* πὰρ' *read* παρ'.

P. 45, *line* 7, *for* ἐνηνοχὼς *read* ἐνηνοχὼς.

P. 48, *line* 16, *for* ἀτὸπων *read* ἀτόπων

INTRODUCTION.

Section I.—*The biography and its sources.*

There were descendants of Aratus still living at Sicyon and Pellene some three hundred years after the death of their famous ancestor. To one of these, Polycrates of Sicyon, the biography is dedicated, and Plutarch expresses the hope that it may inspire his sons to maintain the honourable traditions of the family. The work accords well with its avowed object. More than a third of the whole consists of lively narratives of Aratus' achievements—his liberation of Sicyon, his journey to Egypt, his capture of Acrocorinth, his rout of the Aetolians at Pellene, his victory over Aristippus, tyrant of Argos, his outwitting of the insurgents at Corinth, his encounter with King Philip at Mount Ithome.

But the *Life* is not a mere panegyric. The failings of the hero are not concealed; his incapacity as a general, his want of spirit on the field of battle, his ungenerous treatment of Lydiades, his ruthlessness towards Aristomachus and the Mantineans; and Plutarch cannot restrain his indignation when he tells of the recall of the Macedonians to Peloponnesus.

The *Aratus* is not one of the series of *Parallel Lives,* but seems to have been composed while the material collected for the *Lives of Agis and Cleomenes* was still fresh in Plutarch's mind. This is at any rate suggested by three rather striking coincidences.

The comparison of Aratus to a steersman abandoning the helm during a storm is found both in *Cleom.* 15, 1, and *Arat.* 38, 5.

Again, we are told in both *Cleom.* 16, 2, and *Arat.* 41, 2, that at the nadir of his fortunes, when the Achaean resistance to Sparta had collapsed (225–4 B.C.), Aratus had been in public life for thirty-three years. This is a manifest error. Plutarch apparently made a miscalculation when writing the *Cleomenes,* and repeated the figure afterwards in the *Aratus* without taking the trouble to verify it.

c

Finally, most significant of all is the reference to the Dorian mode in music. In *Cleom.* 16, 6, it is applied by way of metaphor to the Dorian constitution of Sparta. In *Arat.* 2, 1, it appears as a simile, in abbreviated form, to illustrate the much less Dorian constitution of Sicyon. In this connection it would hardly have suggested itself to Plutarch unless the *Cleomenes* passage, probably borrowed from the historian Phylarchus, had already been written.

The task of writing the biographies of the Spartan kings was an easier one than that of recounting the multifarious activities of Aratus, whose public career covered nearly forty years. The mass of material was vast, and the problem one of selection. Plutarch dealt with it by omitting almost all the background. For the modern reader who has no means of supplying the deficiency, the result has been to make the work something of an enigma.

To cite some of Plutarch's more obvious sins of omission: the relations of Aratus to Antigonus Gonatas, and of both of them to Antigonus' nephew, Alexander of Corinth, are left in obscurity; and the same obscurity veils the relations both of Antigonus and Alexander with Ptolemy Philadelphus. The reader is told nothing of political conditions in Peloponnesus at the time of the liberation of Sicyon; of the causes which involved the Achaeans in the Aetolo-Boeotian war; of the Aetolian intervention in Western Peloponnesus; of Lydiades' usurpation of power at Megalopolis and his subsequent relations with Macedon. No light is thrown on the vacillating policy of Orchomenos and Mantinea before the outbreak of the Cleomenic War, or on the social problem in Peloponnesus at the same epoch, or on the nature of the hegemony demanded by Cleomenes. The account of the collapse of the negotiations between Cleomenes and the League is entirely superficial; Aratus' private negotiations with Antigonus Doson are dismissed with a brief reference, as is the extraordinary *strategia* conferred upon Aratus about the same time. Finally, the story of Aratus' career after Sellasia would be almost unintelligible without the aid of Polybius.

Dates in the *Aratus* are few and far between. We are not told the year of Aratus' birth or death, of his triumphs at Sicyon

or Corinth, or of the battle of Sellasia. Of the scanty indications
of time two are certainly wrong (35, 7; 41, 2). The Aetolian
invasion of Achaea, the battle of Hecatombaeum, and Aratus'
appointment as *strategos autocrator* are all mentioned out of
chronological order.[1] In fact were it not for information derived
from Polybius (especially Book ii, 37–70) and very occasionally
from the *Agis and Cleomenes* the chronology of Aratus' career
would have remained a field for futile and unending speculation.

Sources. Plutarch's principal source is Aratus' own *Memoirs*;
next in order, Phylarchus' *Histories* and the *Argolica* of Deinias.
From chapter 46 to the end the only known source is Polybius.

The *Memoirs* were still extant in the fourth century A.D.; they
are mentioned by the patriarch Photius as used by Sopater in his
Eclogues. As to their character we have the following information : —

(1) In the first (anonymous) *Life of Aratus of Soli* we read
that among historians named Aratus was a most distinguished
(ἐπισημότατος) Sicyonian, to whom belongs the comprehensive
(πολύβιβλος) history in more than thirty books (ὑπὲρ τὰ λ′
βιβλία ἔχουσα). (See F.H.G. iii, pp. 21–23).

(2) Polybius (1, 3, 1; cf. 4, 2, 2) began his own history with
the 140th Olympiad (B.C. 220), "which is continuous with Aratus'
narrative."

(3) In 2, 40, 4, Polybius writes : "A brief record will, I think,
suffice both here and afterwards of Aratus' measures, for the
memoirs left by him are exceedingly truthful and clear (λίαν
ἀληθινοὺς καὶ σαφεῖς ὑπομνηματισμούς)": cf. also 2, 56.

(4) In *Arat.* 3 the *Memoirs* are said to have been written as
a side issue (παρέργως) and hastily (ὑπὸ χεῖρα) in the first words
that occurred.

---

[1] Also in chapters 25–34 we find treatment by topics substituted
for chronological arrangement. The subject-matter of these chapters
is as follows : —

25–29. Aratus' assaults on the Argive tyrants, 243–235 B.C.

30. Aratus' relations with Lydiades, 235–230 B.C., with an account
of the antecedents of Argos' accession to the League in 229.

31–32. The Aetolian invasion of Achaea (241 B.C.).

33–34. Aratus' relations with Athens in war and peace, 242–229 B.C.

It would appear that Aratus wrote of his career in minute detail. If his work contained more than thirty books and ended with the battle of Sellasia, there must have been on the average more than one book assigned to each year from the liberation of Sicyon onward. Assuming that the books were of ordinary length we might conjecture that the work was at least twenty times as long as Plutarch's biography. Plutarch at any rate did not suffer from shortage of material.

It is probable that Aratus kept some sort of diary, from which he put the memoirs together during the last years of his life. Plutarch says that the book was filled with abuse of the Macedonians; and Klatt has hence inferred that it was completed by Aratus after his estrangement from Philip, about two years before his death. Lack of revision would account for the negligent style on which Plutarch remarks. It is probable also that the *Memoirs* included some of Aratus' public speeches, for Polybius, who has protested against the practice of composing fictitious speeches, gives (2, 50) a quotation or summary from a "long speech" of Aratus. As Aratus was a practising politician all his days, the *Memoirs* were evidently composed less for the enlightenment of posterity than for the vindication of his conduct and policy among contemporaries. Aratus seems to have been, in fact, the first Greek statesman to write autobiography on a large scale,[2] and the book must have been of absorbing interest in a community not blessed (or cursed) with a newspaper press. Had Aratus lived a little longer—he was but fifty-nine when he died—the labours of the autobiographer would have rendered no small service to the cause of the politician. The book was said to lack literary grace, but we have Polybius' testimony to its clarity, and clarity is the first essential in a work intended to influence the community at large.

Polybius said also that the *Memoirs* were "exceedingly truthful." But in this matter Polybius is a witness not above suspicion; what he has himself written about the fate of

[2] It is difficult to draw the line between political autobiography and contemporary history. To which department are we to assign the περὶ τῆς δεκαετίας of Demetrius of Phalerum (Diog. Laert. v. 80–81, Strabo ix, p. 398)? This treatise in any case according to Diog. consisted of but one book. King Pyrrhus also wrote ὑπομνήματα (Dionys. Hal. *Ant. Rom.* xix, 11), but nothing is known of the scope of the work.

Aristomachus of Argos or the Achaean treatment of the Mantineans shows that he was capable of special pleading. And
Polybius admits that these "exceedingly truthful memoirs" did
not contain the whole truth about the negotiations between Aratus
and Antigonus Doson.

Again, we find in Plutarch a scornful criticism—was it his
own or Phylarchus'?—of Aratus' disclaimer of responsibility for
Erginus' assault on Piraeus in time of peace; and it cannot be
denied that the criticism is justified (*Arat.* 33, 4).

Again, it is somewhat discomposing to find Plutarch claiming
for Aratus the chief credit for the evacuation of Piraeus
(*Arat.* 34, 5–6) by Diogenes, the commander of the Macedonian
garrison; for the Athenians conferred every imaginable honour on
Diogenes, while among the numberless honorific decrees discovered
at Athens, none has so far been found recognising the services of
Aratus. (This point was emphasised and indeed over-emphasised
by Klatt.) We have reason enough, then, to suspect that the
Memoirs were tainted with *suppressio veri* and *suggestio falsi.*

When Polybius calls the *Memoirs* "exceedingly truthful"
he is evidently contrasting them with Phylarchus' *Histories.*
Like Polybius himself, Aratus, we must suppose, was a 'prag-
matic' historian, who did not indulge in flights of imagination,
and was generally sound on facts and figures. But the *Memoirs*
were an apologia not exempt from bias, both conscious and
unconscious.

In the absence of explicit evidence we must assume that
Plutarch, when he records events within Aratus' purview, and
records them without unfavourable comment on Aratus or the
Achaeans, is using the *Memoirs* as his authority.

The *Memoirs* are, however, actually cited only three times—
in connection with (1) the Aetolian attack on Pellene (ch. 32),
(2) Erginus' attempt on Piraeus (ch. 33), and (3) Aratus' attitude
to the Macedonians (ch. 38).

Of much less importance for the biography is the work of
Phylarchus,[3] a contemporary of Aratus (*Polyb.* 2, 56), and, it
would seem, a metic of Athens. His *Histories* in twenty-eight
books began with Pyrrhus' invasion of Peloponnesus and ended

[3] F.H.G. i, p. 334.

with the death of Cleomenes, to whose career, as appears from the fragments, the last four books were devoted. Polybius, in justifying his preference for the *Memoirs,* has made a long and vehement attack on Phylarchus' historical methods (2, 56–63), accusing him of carelessness, exaggeration, sensationalism, failure to relate events to their causes, and in particular of reckless partiality towards Cleomenes (in the last of which charges Plutarch concurs). It is plain that Phylarchus was a dramatic historian, more concerned to startle and impress the reader than to record facts with accuracy, but his accounts of Agis and Cleomenes, which have reached us through the medium of Plutarch, reveal a touch of genius. His work was marked by frequent and sympathetic references to women.

He is cited once in the *Aratus* (ch. 38), where we are told that he agreed with Polybius about the incompleteness of Aratus' account of his negotiations with Antigonus Doson.[4]

In telling of Aratus' conflict with the Argive tyrants Plutarch has used the *Argolica* of Deinias (cited in ch. 29), whose influence may be detected in occasional criticisms of Aratus' conduct.

Polemon of Ilium is cited (ch. 13) by Plutarch in his digression on Sicyonian painters. He lived in the first half of the third century.[5]

Plutarch has also used collections of anecdotes and accounts of discussions in the philosophical schools.

The *Aratus* naturally falls into four sections:

The first (chapters 1–23) carries the story down to the capture of Corinth. In this section the historical material is obviously taken from the *Memoirs,* except for one incident— Antigonus Gonatas' recovery of Acrocorinth (ch. 17)—which may reasonably be attributed to Phylarchus.

The second (24–35) ends with the admission of Argos to the League. Here Plutarch has supplemented the *Memoirs* by the *Argolica* of Deinias; while a portion of the account of the Aetolian invasion and its repulse (31–32) seems to be derived from Phylarchus.

---

[4] Polybius himself occasionally uses Phylarchus; e.g., his account of the death of Antigonus Doson, when compared with Plutarch's in *Cleom.* 30, reveals Phylarchus as the common source.

[5] Deinias, F.H.G. iii, p. 24 ff.: Polemon, *Ib.* iii, p. 166 ff.

The third (35–46) deals with the Cleomenic war. Here the facts appear to come from the *Memoirs*, the criticisms from Phylarchus' *Histories*.

The fourth (46–54) gives a brief and unsatisfactory account of Aratus' career after Sellasia. Here Plutarch follows Polybius, supplemented perhaps in the last chapter by traditions still current in Aratus' family.

Plutarch's use of his sources. Comparing Plutarch's two narratives of the Cleomenic war we note that in general he confines his detailed accounts—whether drawn from Aratus or Phylarchus—to matters of direct importance for the hero of the biography.

Thus, although the *Cleomenes* is almost entirely derived from Phylarchus, Plutarch is at pains to excerpt from Aratus' *Memoirs* the account of the two embassies sent to Aratus by Cleomenes, so important does he consider these embassies for *Cleomenes'* career. But in the *Aratus*, though this biography is based on the *Memoirs*, a careless summary is deemed sufficient, because Plutarch does not regard the embassies as important for *Aratus'* career (cf. *Cleom.* 19 and *Arat.* 41).

For the same reason, doubtless, whereas in *Cleom.* 15–16 we have a clear account of the two occasions on which the Achæans arranged to meet Cleomenes in conference, we find that in the *Aratus* the first of these occasions is passed over in silence (ch. 39).

But even matters of outstanding importance for the reader's grasp of the career or character of the hero himself may receive from Plutarch the most casual treatment, as, *e.g.*, Aratus' private negotiations with Antigonus Doson, for the details of which Plutarch practically refers his reader to Polybius (ch. 38).

In fine, Plutarch's method of selecting his materials, though not altogether arbitrary, is neither scientific nor systematic.

It is of less consequence that when Plutarch appears to be enunciating opinions of his own, he is more probably echoing one of his authorities. Thus, the unfavourable references to Lydiades (ch. 30) are almost certainly echoes of Aratus' *Memoirs*, while the denunciation of Aratus for recalling the Macedonians (ch. 38), like the corresponding passage in the *Cleomenes*, is little more than *crambe repetita* from Cleomenes' devotee, Phylarchus.

Only for chapters 47–54 (the period after Sellasia) can we bring Plutarch face to face with his source—Polybius in this instance—and even here without complete certainty, as only the first five books of the historian are extant in full. For a close examination of Plutarch's methods we are confined in fact to a comparison of *Arat.* 47–48 with the appropriate parts of the fourth and fifth books of Polybius. This close examination was made by Schulz, whose conclusions are worth recording:

" Sometimes Plutarch copies his source word for word; sometimes reproduces the material in words of his own; sometimes gives the sense in a brief summary; sometimes omits important facts; sometimes by his epitomising falls into actual mistakes; sometimes in judging events or persons inserts an opinion independent of his source without even an introductory δοκεῖ μοι."[6]

Section II.—τὰ πρὸ ᾿Αράτου.

In 280 B.C., that is, nine years before Aratus was born, the Greeks almost succeeded in achieving their freedom from Macedon. At that time, over the greater part of the country, south of Epirus and Thessaly, the dominant power was Antigonus Gonatas, son of Demetrius the Besieger. Within Peloponnesus only Laconia and Messenia, north of the isthmus only Aetolia and the unimportant Acarnania were entirely independent of his control. He held the fortress of Demetrias on the Pagasaean Gulf, Chalcis, Piraeus, and Corinth. He was master of an efficient mercenary army and a fleet that had never been vanquished. If he did not, like his father, impose conscription on the Greeks, he compelled them to pay the cost of the armed forces that held them in subjection. Naturally, he was unpopular, more unpopular in fact than any of the Macedonian dynasts except Cassander. The richer classes may have preferred to exercise power under the eye of his garrison-commanders rather than endure the domination of their own masses, but Antigonus must have realised that the suzerainty of a king who had no kingdom of his own was not likely to continue permanently. He was only waiting, however, for an opportunity to make good the deficiency.

Macedon, once his father's realm, was now held by Ptolemy Ceraunus (the disinherited son of Ptolemy Soter, the late King of Egypt), who after a particularly atrocious murder had just

---

[6] In the notes I have discussed the sources chapter by chapter.

been accepted as king by the army (280 B.C.). Antigonus thought the time had come to assert his own claims to the Macedonian throne, and accordingly set sail for the North, but his fleet was severely defeated in battle with Ceraunus and his allies, and the defeat was followed by an upheaval in Greece.

It is true that the confederation of Peloponnesian States organised by Areus, king of Sparta, became involved (in circumstances which our tradition did not properly understand) in a disastrous conflict with the Aetolian League, and disbanded without effecting anything; but none the less Antigonus' system of government in Greece suddenly broke down. In 279 he retained nothing but Demetrias in Thessaly, Corinth, and a few small towns in Peloponnesus,[1] and despairing of his fortunes carried off the best part of his army for a campaign in Asia Minor against Antiochus I.

Greece, however, was not to be quit of Antigonus for very long. He returned by way of Macedon. There an invasion of Celts from the North had brought the career of Ceraunus to a sudden end (279 B.C.). After some two years of anarchy Antigonus, who had returned to Europe, inflicted a decisive defeat on a body of Celts at Lysimacheia in the Gallipoli Peninsula, which paved the way for his accession to the throne in 276. Four years later the death of his rival Pyrrhus at Argos in a street fight left him in Peloponnesus at the head of an army with no one to oppose him.

He might now have recovered all that his father had held in Greece, but he was content with a more moderate programme. In the course of the next few years he annexed certain places in Northern Greece—Chalcis, Eretria, Piraeus, Megara[2]—thus linking up Demetrias with Corinth, but he left the Boeotians

---

[1] Tarn, J.H.S. LIV (1934), p. 22, adduces fresh and convincing evidence for assigning the recovery of Piraeus by the Athenians under Olympidorus to the year 280–279. Some of the Achaean towns were still held for Antigonus, as was Troezen in Argolis until, some time before the Pyrrhic war, it was captured by the Spartan Cleonymus who installed a harmost in the town (Polyaen. 2, 29).

[2] Tarn (J.H.S. LIV (1934), p. 36) has argued very convincingly that Antigonus recovered Piraeus in 271–270. The annexation of Eretria came somewhat later, as Tarn infers from Diog. Laert. ii, 127, where we are informed that Hierocles, Governor of Piraeus, gave the exiled Menedemus an account of the capture of Eretria. Megara may have remained independent till the Chremonidean War.

alone, and cultivated friendly relations with the Aetolians, who controlled Delphi, and whose territories extended from the Adriatic to Thermopylae on the Aegean Sea.

But south of the isthmus he pursued a different policy.

The disturbance in Peloponnesus excited by Pyrrhus' activities did not immediately subside. According to Justin, some States began to ally themselves with Antigonus, while others were on the verge of civil war.[3] We must suppose that Justin is referring to Elis, Argolis, and Arcadia. The Achaean League, which had been formed in 280 by the four cities, Dyme, Pharae, Patrae, and Tritaea, and enlarged in 275 by the accession of Cerynea, Bura, and Aegium, does not come under either of Justin's categories, any more than Laconia or Messenia.

What Antigonus did was to establish a 'dominatio'[4] in a number of cities. This word does not *necessarily* mean, as Beloch supposed, "government through the medium of tyrants." Justin, Trogus' excerptor, states that the Peloponnesians suspected Sparta in 280, *dominationem non libertatem Graeciae quaerere* (24, 1, 8). But Sparta's traditional instruments of government were not tyrants, but harmosts and oligarchies. Antigonus' *dominatio* doubtless assumed different forms in different places. What places were affected we do not know, for Trogus' history is not extant. Justin confines himself to the melodramatic story of Aristotimus, who (*c.* 270) seized power in Elis, but lost his life at the hands of returned exiles from Aetolia. Aristotimus was indeed a tyrant and a partisan of Antigonus, but he was not part of a 'system' (as commonly supposed), for when the viceroy Craterus arrived in Elis too late to save him he imposed no new tyrant in his place, but left the Eleans to themselves.[5] In reality the *system* of tyrants, so far as it existed at all, belongs to a later period. (See Addendum A at end of this section.)

---

[3] Justin 26, 1–2: Peloponnensii per proditionem Antigono traditi: et . . . prout singulae civitates aut auxilium de Pyrro speraverant aut metum sustinuerant ita cum Antigono societatem iungebant aut mutuis inter se odiis in bellum ruebant.

[4] *Prol. Trag.* 26: Quibus in urbibus Graeciae dominationem Antigonus Gonatas constituerit (narratur).

[5] Plut. *Mor* 251, Justin 26, 1, also Paus. 5, 5, 1: 6, 14, 11, by whom the tyrant is connected with Antigonus.

Viewing the king's policy in the light of the event we recognise that Antigonus would have consulted the true interests of Macedon and saved himself from much futile labour and anxiety if he had, upon the death of Pyrrhus, withdrawn altogether from Greece south of Demetrias. Once and again, after what seemed to be a decisive victory, some incalculable event occurred to humble his pride and rob him of the fruits of victory.

In 272 Antigonus was all-powerful in Greece: in 267 a considerable part of the Greeks were up in arms against Macedon once more. In the "Chremonidean War," which seems to have lasted from 267[6] to 263–2, we note the emergence of certain factors which remain constant or recur during the next half-century.

First among these is the enmity of the house of Ptolemy to the house of Antigonus. The personal animosity of Philadelphus and still more of Arsinoë, his sister, whom he married about 276 B.C., was the original cause of the war; but right on to the battle of Sellasia in 222, hostility to Macedon and support of her enemies appears as the guiding principle of Egyptian policy.

The second factor is the attitude of Sparta. It was not merely that Areus, her king, was a man of large ideas, who wished to be as kingly as any of the Macedonian upstarts. The choice for Sparta was between hegemony and death. Short of a complete reorganisation, the only chance the Spartans had of recovery from the creeping paralysis of the last hundred years was to become once more the dominating power in Peloponnesus.

Areus had made a bid for domination thirteen years before. He had failed then; now the odds seemed in his favour when the King of Egypt sought the alliance of Sparta. The issue, however, proved fatal to himself, and merely accelerated the decline of his country. It was the last attempt of the old Spartan régime to renew its strength; but Cleomenes, forty years later, when reorganising the State, still felt the ideal of Spartan supremacy in Peloponnesus to be the one thing worth living for.

Finally, both in the Chremonidean and Cleomenic wars, we find Elis on the side of Sparta, as well as the four Arcadian cities, Tegea, Mantinea, Orchomenos, and Caphyae, whose

---

[6] Dinsmoor (p. 81) writing in 1931 argued very persuasively for beginning the war in 270, but his case, to my mind, has been refuted by Tarn, *op. cit.*, pp. 26–39.

territories formed a corridor stretching northwards from the Laconian border. With these in 267 were associated the Arcadian Phigalea, the Achaeans,[7] and some towns in Crete.

In the autumn Athens, chafing under the loss of Piraeus, joined the Egypto-Spartan coalition. Chremonides' decree declared that Ptolemy, following the policy of his father and sister (Arsinoë had died in July, 270), was manifesting an earnest resolve to free Hellas.

Into the details of the conflict we need not enter, but we may note the extraordinarily feeble part played by Egypt. For Sparta the result was (1) a defeat near Corinth, where king Areus fell, (2) the disruption of the League, and (3) the defeat and death of Acrotatus, son and successor of Areus, in battle with Aristodemus of Megalopolis, who already was, or soon afterwards became, tyrant of the city.

Antigonus had reduced the Spartans and their Peloponnesian allies to a state of quiescence; and with this he was content.

To Athens the war brought a Macedonian garrison, which was installed in the Museum fort, to remain there for the next seven years. The spirit of the people was broken. In later days Aratus learnt to his sorrow that the Athenians had abandoned for good all ambition to play a part in the affairs of Greece.[8]

After the Chremonidean war there was no further activity in Greece till Aratus liberated Sicyon.

Of the history of Sicyon since its reconstruction by Demetrius in 303 we have no information, but from Plutarch's statements in *Arat.* 2 we infer that the city was generally subject to tyrants. We infer also that between these tyrants and the Macedonian king a spirit of mutual toleration prevailed. Both parties had the same enemies.

In the year 272, however, Sicyon was represented on the Amphictyonic Council (Syll.[3] 1, 417–418), and this points to a period of popular government. Was this period merely a momentary interlude between two tyrants, or were Cleinias and Timocleidas already in office? In the latter alternative Cleinias'

---

[7] Leontium, Aegira, Pellene, Olenus probably joined the League during the Pyrrhic War. For Olenus see S.E.G. 74 with Wilhelm's comment in *Anz. Ak. Wien*, 1922.

[8] Authorities: I.G.[2] ii, 687; Paus 1, 1, 1; 1, 3, 6; 1, 4–6: *Prol. Trog.* 26: Justin 26, 2: for the career of Aristodemus of Megalopolis Paus. 8, 27, 11; 8, 30, 7; 8, 36, 5: Plut. *Agis* 3.

régime must have lasted some nine years, for he was murdered in 264. But from Plutarch one does not derive the impression of so long a period; and Geyer's view, that Cleinias' rule and Cleon's tyranny, which preceded it, both came after 272, is more likely to be correct.

After the liberation of Sicyon Aratus recalled a number of exiles who had been in banishment for some fifty years. If these persons were not restored by Cleinias it must have been because they were enemies of Cleinias' friend, Antigonus.

Antigonus had been Cleinias' friend, but for some twelve years he allowed his murderer Abantidas to rule in Sicyon. When Abantidas' crime was repaid in kind his old father, Paseas, seized power, but was speedily despatched by one Nicocles. It has been held on quite inadequate grounds that Nicocles was an enemy of Antigonus. To me the evidence (which will be discussed in the next section) suggests that the king's attitude to Nicocles was one of provisional acquiescence—"Wait and see."

Antigonus' first war with Egypt. We have no narrative of this war, but a study of certain isolated references in ancient authors combined with the evidence of inscriptions supplies the following data[9] : —

(1) Peace was made in 261 between the Powers.

(2) Within three years the war was renewed, probably by Antigonus.

(3). In 258 (or possibly 256) the Macedonian defeated the Egyptian fleet off the island of Cos.

(4) In 255 a new peace was concluded.

(5) The Cyclades, which had been under the suzerainty of Egypt, now came under the control of Macedon.

So it happened that Aratus, on his voyage to Egypt, when compelled by stress of weather to seek refuge in an Aegean harbour, came near being arrested by the commander of a Macedonian garrison.[10]

ADDENDUM A: *Antigonus' "System of Tyrants."* Polybius definitely asserts that Antigonus seems to have planted more

---

[9] See Addendum B at end of the section.   [10] *Arat.* 12.

tyrants among the Greeks than any other king.[11] Two questions arise : —

(1) Can we, with our fragmentary information, justify Polybius' statement regarding the number of tyrants?

(2) Can we suggest to what period in Antigonus' career the policy of planting or supporting tyrants particularly belongs?

We have no data in any single instance to distinguish tyrants established by Antigonus from those merely supported or countenanced by him.

But conditions in Peloponnesus were such that even if a tyrant started independently, he was bound to gravitate into the Macedonian faction.

The following is a list of tyrants contemporary with Antigonus or his son Demetrius (they are all Peloponnesians) : —

Before the War with Pyrrhus.

At Bura—'Anonymous'; slain, 275.

At Cerynea—Iseas; resigned, 275.

At Sicyon—Cleon and predecessors.

Between the Pyrrhic War and the Death of Alexander of Corinth.

At Elis—Aristotimus; slain, *c.* 270.

At Sicyon—Abantidas (seized power, 264), Paseas, Nicocles.

At Argos—Aristomachus I (first mentioned about 250).

At Megalopolis—Aristodemus (slain, 252–1 B.C. : see next section).

After the Death of Alexander of Corinth.

At Argos—Aristomachus I; killed, 241; Aristippus, killed, 235; Aristomachus II, resigned, 229.

At Megalopolis—Lydiades, resigned, 235.

At Orchomenos—Nearchus, resigned, (?) 235.

At Hermione—Xenon, resigned, 229.

At Phlius—Cleonymus, resigned, 229.

---

[11] Pol. ii, 41, 10 : πλείστους γὰρ μονάρχους οὗτος ἐμφυτεῦσαι δοκεῖ τοῖς Ἕλλησι : 9, 29, 6 (the Aetolian Chlaeneas is speaking of Demetrius Cassander and Antigonus Gonatas) : ὧν οἱ μὲν φρουρὰς εἰσάγοντες . . . οἱ δὲ, τυράννους ἐμφυτεύοντες οὐδεμίαν πόλιν ἄμοιρον ἐποίησαν τοῦ τῆς δουλείας ὀνόματος.

But it must be remembered that Greeks saw no essential difference between an unconstitutional ruler, lording it over his fellow-citizens, and a royal officer wielding power equally unconstitutional as the agent of his master. Both were tyrants. Thus the historian Pythermus[12] speaks of οἱ τυραννεύοντες Πειραιῶς, meaning garrison-commanders there. Hence, every Macedonian governor from Craterus to the humblest jack-in-office that bullied the inhabitants of some small town or island was to the Greeks a τύραννος. To all such, the word ἐμφυτεύειν can, in strict propriety, be applied; even though among the rest we have no means of distinguishing the 'planted' from the merely 'countenanced.'

There is no evidence, as I have already stated, that the tyrants before the Chremonidean war belong to a system. Fellmann (pp. 49, 50) has further observed that Aratus in the next decade would not have appealed to Antigonus to free Sicyon if the king himself at that time was building up a system of tyrants in Peloponnesus. The same scholar has made a happy suggestion respecting the time when the system, if system it can be called, actually originated. *It developed only after the death of Alexander of Corinth.* In the reign of Antigonus' successor, Demetrius, we have two incidents recorded of Macedonian generals operating in Peloponnesus. One, Agias, we find in command of the garrison at Argos; and another, Bithys, apparently using Argos as his base. But our tradition records not a single instance of tyrants co-operating with one another against an enemy of Macedon.

ADDENDUM B.—*Egypto-Macedonian relations, 261–245 B.C.* For the chronology we are dependent in large measure on inscriptions from the temple of Apollo at Delos. Between 314 and 168 Delos was independent of Athens, and for a large part of this period the names of the Delian archons are known, and can be arranged chronologically, with a possible "margin of error" of one year in the list from 307–218. [Thus Dinsmoor's list differs from Durrbach's (IG. xi, 2) in postdating by one year all archons from 307 to 219. My references here are to Durrbach's list, which will be found also in Laidlaw, p. 275.]

The Delian year (unlike the Attic, which started in August) began with a month, Lechaion, corresponding to our January.

[12] Of Ephesus, a contemporary of Aratus (F.H.G. 4, p. 488).

In the choragic inscriptions the prescript, where preserved, usually contains the formula,

$$\text{ὑγίεια καὶ εὐετηρία ἐγένετο,}$$

but for the year 261 the formula runs

$$\text{ὑγίεια εὐετηρία εἰρήνη ἐγένετο,}$$

(IG, xi, 2, 114), and similarly for the year 255 (IG. xi, 2, 116).

Such formulae may refer to real events. In C.A.H. vii, p. 708, Tarn cites a considerable number of examples. In the present instances the year 261 is a likely date for a peace between the powers, for the Chremonidean war had ended with the capture of Athens in 263–2. But the mention of εἰρήνη in 255 shows that a new war had broken out in the interval.

Antigonus' First War with Egypt. A naval battle off the island of Cos is mentioned in Plutarch, *Mor.* 545; it was won by "Antigonus the Second," who before the engagement remarked to a friend who expressed alarm at the number of the enemy's ships, "But how many ships do you think *I* count for?" In *Mor.* 183 the same remark is attributed to "Antigonus the Second" before a battle against "Ptolemy's generals"; and Athenaeus (v 209 e) speaks of the "sacred trireme," in which Antigonus conquered "Ptolemy's generals" off Leucolla in Cos. This battle has been identified by Beloch and others with that alluded to in Diogenes Laertius' life of the philosopher Arcesilaus (iv 39), and, since the flagship is said by Athenaeus (*loc. cit.*) to have received the name *Isthmia*, we may date the battle in one of the Isthmian years (i.e., the even years B.C.) between 261 and 255. Tarn (C.A.H. vii, p. 862) gives reasons for preferring the year 258. Evidently Antigonus intervened in the "Second Syrian War" which his nephew, Antiochus II, in alliance with the Rhodians was waging against Ptolemy Philadelphus.

Results of the War. For Antigonus the war (which ended in 255) resulted in the acquisition of the Cyclades, as may be inferred (1) from the reference to King Antigonus in some seven insular inscriptions;[13] (2) from the dedication of his flagship on Delos and of a portico [*Bull. Corr. Hellén.* xxxviii, p. 299] dated 254–2, which shows that he was well pleased with the

---

[13] Beloch has shown the unlikelihood of "King Antigonus" in these inscriptions being Doson. Some of them, however, may refer to a second Antigonid supremacy after 245 B.C.

results of the war; (3) from the story in Sext. Empir. *adv. Gramm.*, 276, that Ptolemy on some occasion sent one Sostratus, who obtained better terms for his master by an apt quotation from the *Iliad*. If this was the Sostratus who built the Pharos at Alexandria he would have been towards seventy in 255, which makes it unlikely that the reference is to the later war between the powers; and in any case the most likely occasion for such an embassy from Ptolemy to Antigonus was after a naval defeat in the Eastern Aegean.

Finally, we must refer to the 'Antigoneia' and 'Stratoniceia' (the latter a festival founded by Antigonus' niece, the sister of Antiochus II), in connection with which the "first vases" were dedicated in 252. It was the custom to deposit a capital sum with the temple authorities, from the interest on which the cost of the dedications was defrayed. Hence the dedication of a "first vase" in 252 implies the establishment of the festival in 253. About this time, as we know, Demetrius, son of Antigonus, married his cousin Stratonice, an appropriate occasion for the festival founded by her.

But was the establishment of a Delian festival by a king of Egypt or Macedon an indication of sovereignty over Delos? This is a question on which opposite opinions are still held. But, whatever be our answer, the cumulative effect of the evidence given above points to the conclusion (as Beloch 4, 2, p. 512, has recognised) that before 253 power in the Aegean shifted from Egypt to Macedon.

But from the Adulis inscription (O.G.I. 54) it appears that the Cyclades were inherited by Ptolemy Euergetes from his father, Philadelphus (who died at the beginning of 246 B.C.). They must have been won back by the end of 247. When, therefore, we find the first vase of a Ptolemaic festival on Delos catalogued in 248 (Badros' archonship), we may fairly conclude that Egypt's recovery in the Aegean dates at latest from 249.

How this recovery came about we are not informed; but we have evidence [see next section] that Alexander, son of Craterus, viceroy of Corinth and Euboea, revolted from his uncle Antigonus about 250; and Beloch's view that the revolt and Egypt's recovery of sea-power are connected has met with general acceptance, for Corinth and Chalcis were the headquarters of the Macedonian fleet.

Second Egyptian War. In *Pelop.* 2 Plutarch speaks of a

d

battle at Andros in which a king Antigonus was concerned. He does not tell us whether he means Gonatas or Doson, but he tells the same story of Antigonus at Andros, as elsewhere he has told of "Antigonus *the Second*" at Cos. It is probable that in *Pelop.* 2 he had Gonatas in mind. This is confirmed by *Prol. Trog.* 27, of which, thanks to Pozzi, we now know the MS. reading to be: ut Antigonus Andro proelio navali *prona* vicerit. For *prona* Müller's *Sophrona* may be regarded as a certain emendation. From Phylarchus (F.H.G. i, 339) we know that Sophron, governor of Ephesus, betrayed the city to Euergetes, whose service he entered (at earliest in the latter half of 246). This fits in well with the festivals established on Delos by Antigonus in 245 (first vase 244)—the Soteria and Paneia.

The names of these festivals, as Fellmann has observed, have a particular significance, for Pan was Antigonus' "patron deity," and Soteria implies 'recovery.' About this time the rebel Alexander died, and Antigonus recovered Corinth.

Tarn, who in J.H.S., 1909, proved to the satisfaction of most critics that the Antigonus of *Prol. Trog.* 27 is Gonatas, not Doson, has urged very convincingly that the two festivals were instituted to celebrate the recovery of (1) Corinth and (2) Macedonian power (if not suzerainty) in the Aegean.

From the Delian evidence, then, it seems that the following information can be derived: —

255 B.C. Peace between Egypt and Macedon: Antigonus dominant in the Aegean.

253. "Antigoneia," thank-offering for victory.

249. "Second Ptolemaieia," recovery of Egyptian control of the Aegean (confirmed by the Adulis inscr.).

246. "Third Ptolemaieia," accession festival of Ptolemy Euergetes.

245. Antigonus' "Soteria and Paneia," thank-offerings for the defeat of Egypt and the recovery of Corinth.

We may note in conclusion that nothing in the evidence from Delos forbids us to suppose that Macedon remained dominant in the Aegean and at peace with Egypt from 255 till 249 B.C.

[It is clear, as Tarn (p. 459) has observed, that if the founder of a festival chose along with the capital sum to deposit the equivalent of one year's interest, the first annual vase-dedication might be made at the time of founding the festival. Hence the 'Paneia' and 'Soteria' may have been *founded* in 244, when the first vase was dedicated; and the successes at Andros and Corinth, which the festivals presumably commemorated, *may* belong, one or both, to this same year.]

SECTION III.—*The first period of Aratus' career: Sicyon and Corinth.*

Plutarch tells us nothing directly of political conditions in Peloponnesus at the time of the liberation of Sicyon. It is not, however, disputed that peace, internal and external, had been maintained throughout the greater part of the peninsula since the close of the Chremonidean war. But scholars differ in their views of the political situation in the late 'fifties at Corinth, Argos, and Megalopolis.

Corinth. In the latter part of the present section I discuss in detail the chronology of Alexander's secession. Here I need only state the conclusion I have reached: *Plutarch's narrative presupposes that Corinth was still in Antigonus' hands when Aratus returned to Sicyon after his visit to Ptolemy.*

This conclusion leads to the further inference that the peace of 255 B.C. was still in being when Aratus freed Sicyon; for, as Beloch[1] has seen, the secession of Alexander is required to explain Ptolemy's recovery of ascendancy in the Aegean.

Argos. Tarn writes (p. 361):

" In the course of the year 264 Abantidas slew Kleinias and made himself master of the city (Sicyon). The little Aratos escaped . . . and was sent to Argos. Abantidas could not reach him there under the strong rule of Aristomachos, and there he grew to manhood to reward Aristomachos in after years by trying to assassinate him."

But our earliest notice of Aristomachus is IG. ii² 774, which speaks of him as co-operating with Athens against Alexander of

[1] 4, 1, p. 612 n.

Corinth in a war which may be placed in the year 249 or even later. Tarn adduces no evidence to prove that he was tyrant in 264 or even in 252–1; and what we know of Argos on the eve of Aratus' march to Sicyon renders it highly improbable. Plutarch, it is true, when he writes of the year 243–2, recognizes plainly enough the strong government of which Tarn speaks:

> "Aratus, grieved at the servitude of the Argives, planned to slay their tyrant Aristomachus. Men were found bold enough to undertake the task but they had no swords, the possession of which had been forbidden by the tyrant under severe penalties."[2]

But a decade earlier a very different state of things prevailed in Argos. Abantidas of Sicyon was murdered by two men, Deinias and Aristoteles.[3] Deinias seems to be the Argive historian of that name, and Aristoteles the Argive friend of Aratus mentioned in *Arat.* 43 and *Cleom.* 20. It would appear then that the plot against Abantidas was hatched in Argos. But this is just the sort of activity which a strong government, especially the government of a tyrant, would regard with stern disapproval. Further, in describing Aratus' preparations for the attack on Sicyon, Plutarch remarks:[4]

> "The provision of arms was nothing out of the way, for most people at that time were engaged in robbing and raiding one another; and the scaling-ladders were made by the engineer Euphranor without concealment since his trade diverted suspicion, though he was himself one of the exiles."

To exiles from Sicyon or elsewhere Argos was evidently a land of liberty. Aratus is even able to hire "a few soldiers" from a brigand-captain in the neighbourhood, and while at pains to conceal his intentions from Nicocles' spies does not trouble about the authorities at Argos.

All this suggests that Argos was not yet under "the strong rule of Aristomachus," who probably seized power when Alexander of Corinth threatened the city with war.

---

[2] *Arat.* 25.   [3] *Arat.* 3.   [4] *Arat.* 6.

Megalopolis. In *Arat.* 5 we read:

> " The first persons to whom Aratus revealed his plan
> (for the surprise of Sicyon) were Aristomachus, a Sicyonian
> exile, and Ecdelus, an Arcadian from Megalopolis . . .
> These adopted his proposals, and he began conversations
> with the other exiles."

The turn of phrase seems to imply that Ecdelus like Aristomachus was an exile living at Argos. At some unspecified date
Ecdelus, as we learn from *Philop.* 1 and Polyb. 10, 22, took part
in the assassination of Aristodemus the Good,[5] who had held
power at Megalopolis—as strategos or as tyrant—ever since the
Chremonidean war. It might seem, then, that Ecdelus had been
expelled from his home by Aristodemus, and was now awaiting
an opportunity to strike a blow for liberty against the tyrant;
and we have seen that conditions in Argos at the time made it a
convenient city of refuge.

Tarn indeed argues that the blow had already been struck;
but, if so, Ecdelus would have been back in Megalopolis, and
Plutarch would have had no obvious reason for coupling his name
with the Sicyonian exile, Aristomachus. A more important consideration is that Ecdelus would have been a leading personage
in his native city, and instead of merely sharing in the enterprise
as an individual, might have been expected to present himself at
the head of a Megalopolitan contingent. But we know how
Aratus' force was made up. There were exiles from Sicyon,
slaves from the households of Aratus and his friends, and a few
soldiers hired from the klepht Xenophilus. As no Megalopolitan
force is mentioned we may assume that Ecdelus was an exile and
the tyrant Aristodemus still reigning at Megalopolis.

Up to the moment of Aratus' seizure of Sicyon the Macedonian
king might think he had reason to congratulate himself on the
stability of conditions in Peloponnesus. Except to the persons
immediately concerned it mattered little if one Sicyonian tyrant
was slain and his place taken by another, but Aratus' exploit
marked the beginning of a new epoch.

Chronology of the liberation of Sicyon. Aratus freed the city
in the month Daisios (*Arat.* 53), but in what year we do not
know: Sicyon joined the Achaean League in the year May 251—

---

[5] ὁ χρηστός, Paus. 8, 36, 5.

May 250, but we do not know in what month: Aratus at the
time of the union was under twenty-one (ἔχων εἴκοσι ἔτη)[6].
From these data it cannot be determined whether the city was
freed in 252 or 251; on the other hand they provide no reason
for pushing the event back beyond May 252.

Between liberation and union with Achaea there was an
appreciable interval of time.

(1) Referring to the union Polybius remarks that from the
very start (ἀρχῆθεν εὐθύς) Aratus had been an admirer of the
League's policy.

(2) One of Aratus' chief reasons for promoting the union was
the internal condition of the city.   The five hundred returned
exiles had engaged in violent disputes with the holders of their
confiscated property, and the city was almost involved in civil war.
It must have taken a considerable time for such a state of dis-
order to develop.

(3) In the interval between liberation and union Sicyon, it
appears, took part in a military campaign in Arcadia. Of this there
is nothing in Plutarch, but Pausanias (8, 10, 5) records a battle at
Mantinea in which the Spartans "under King Agis" were defeated
by a combination of Arcadians, Achaeans, and Sicyonians under
Aratus.   In this battle " King Agis" fell.   Pausanias' allusions
to historical events are frequently very wide of the mark, and
the present notice is no exception, for King Agis was executed
at Sparta in 241 B.C.   Beloch, however, has shown (4, 2, p. 523 f.)
that if, instead of " King Agis" we assume the Spartan commander at Mantinea to have been the king's eldest paternal uncle

---

[6] Polyb. 2, 43, Aratus was therefore born in 271.   Beloch, however
(4, 2, p. 518), refuses to take Polybius' statement at face value; he
was merely ''speaking in round numbers''; for Aratus was Achaean
strategos in 245, for which office Beloch assumes the minimum age to
have been 30.   Hence, he concludes, Aratus was born in 275.   But
while we may grant the minimum legal age for a strategos to have
been 30, as it was for the office of ambassador (Polyb. 24, 6, 5) and
for membership of the Syncletos (see *infra* Sect. 7), it is not likely
that Polybius talked loosely on a matter so familiar to him as Aratus'
age. The statement that Aratus was 20 when Sicyon joined the League
fits in with Plutarch's statement (derived from the *Memoirs*) that he
was a μειράκιον when he freed Sicyon (i.e., 19–20, see note on *Arat.* 4, 1).
Beloch in fact has nothing to urge against the hypothesis that Aratus
for his strategia, like Polybius for his ambassadorship, was dispensed
from the law requiring a minimum age.

and namesake, acting as regent during his minority, the other data of Pausanias suit a date about the middle of the century. We may, therefore, with Bölte[7] assign the battle to the period when under Aratus Sicyon was an independent state.

Pausanias does not record the antecedents of the battle, but we may presume that the Spartans, after the assassination of Aristodemus (their doughty adversary in the Chremonidean war), seized the opportunity to assert themselves in Arcadia, but were defeated by the re-formed Arcadian League and its allies.

Not long after the union of Sicyon with the League Aratus set out for Egypt to crave financial aid from Ptolemy, and not long after his return Alexander established his secession state. For this latter event the latest possible date is 249. Assuming that Sicyon was freed in May 251 we may draw up an hypothetical time-table of events as follows:

251 (early summer), Assassination of Aristodemus.
(late summer), Spartan invasion and battle of Mantinea.
(late autumn or winter), Sicyon attached to the League.
250 (spring), Aratus' voyage to Egypt.
(autumn), Aratus back in Sicyon.
249 (spring), Revolt of Alexander.
(summer), Ptolemy's recovery of the Cyclades.
(autumn), Ptolemy's festival on Delos.

But it is also possible to date the liberation of Sicyon in May 252; the battle of Mantinea in the following summer; the union of Sicyon with the League, and Aratus' departure for Egypt in the year 251; Aratus' return, late in 251 or early in 250, followed at no long interval by Alexander's revolt.

An argument for 252, to be found in an article written many years ago by Ferguson, is worth disinterring from the footnote to which he consigned it. To the question, " From what point of time was the entry of a city into the League calculated?" he suggests the answer, " From the entry into office of the first batch of officials at whose election the citizens of the city in question

---

[7] P.-W., Sikyon. The authenticity of the battle has been denied on different but in my opinion equally inadequate grounds by Hiller von Gaertringen, *Klio* xxi (1926), p. 10, and Tarn, *C.R.* xxxix (1925), p. 104.

had an opportunity of voting." On this hypothesis the Sicyonians would be counted as entering the League in 251–250, if they voted at the election of officers who entered upon their duties in May 251. Hence the date of the liberation could not be later than Daisios (May–June) of 252.[8]

On the whole, the balance of evidence seems to favour 252.

The Problem of Alexander's Revolt. The period of Alexander's independence comes, at any rate, within the decade 253–243. He was still his uncle's viceroy in 253, when Antigonus established his festivals on Delos; he was dead some time before 243 (mid-summer), when Aratus took Corinth from Antigonus.

The sources of our information — such as it is — about Alexander are partly literary, partly epigraphic.

(1) In the Prologue to Book 26 of Trogus' History, we find Alexander's revolt catalogued between the death of Areus, King of Sparta (264 B.C.), and the liberation of Sicyon.[9] But the arrangement of events in these prologues, as De Sanctis has shown, deviates so often from the chronological that no conclusion can be drawn from this.

(2) In *Arat.* 17 we learn of the ruse by which Antigonus regained Corinth after Alexander's death, attributed by rumour to poison administered at the king's instigation.

(3) In *Arat.* 18 we read that Aratus at some unspecified time unsuccessfully attempted to take Corinth from Alexander.

(4) From Suidas, *Euphorion,* we learn that Alexander's kingdom included Euboea; which is confirmed by IG. xii, 9, 212 (Eretria).

(5) In Syll.[3] 454, which cannot be precisely dated, Heracleitus of Athmonon is honoured by the Salaminians "because during the war with Alexander, son of Craterus, when pirates sailed from Epilimnius (probably a port in Crete, in possession, as Cary has suggested, of Ptolemy) he used his best endeavours to save the country from injury."

---

[8] J.H.S. (1910), p. 197.

[9] A glance at the Prol. will show that it is arranged by personages. We find reference to (1) the actions of Antigonus, (2) Aratus, (3) Antiochus, (4) Ptolemy "the Son," (5) Demetrius "the Fair," (6) Seleucus Callinicus.

(6) In IG. ii² 774, Aristomachus (the tyrant) and the Argives are honoured for refusing to make a separate peace with Alexander, and for advancing money to the Athenians.

From none of these sources can the date of the revolt be fixed beyond a vague *"circa* 250 B.C."

The Attic inscription IG. 791 (Syll.³ 491), had it reached us intact, might have thrown some light on the matter. It refers to a time when Attica was in danger of invasion. But the present condition of the stone makes it impossible to decide whether the archon Diomedon, in whose year the particular decree was carried, belongs to 253–2, in which case the enemy would almost certainly be Alexander (who, as we have seen, was engaged in war with Athens after his revolt); or to 232–1, when the enemy was Aratus.[10]

Neither can the date of the revolt be settled by reference to the Delian festival-lists.

Tarn writes[11] : —

" In 253 Antigonus founded two vase-festivals at Delos, the Antigoneia in connection with the dedication of his portico that year; and the Stratoniceia, instituted on behalf of Stratonice, to celebrate the marriage of his son Demetrius with Stratonice, Antiochus' sister. He did not much longer enjoy his sea-command undisturbed; *late in 253 or in 252 Ptolemy instigated or supported the revolt of Alexander of Corinth,* which deprived Antigonus of his naval bases in Greece, Corinth and Chalcis, and probably of his squadrons there, and left him partially crippled. What happened at sea is obscure. Possibly in 250 Antigonus held Delos; and though *Ptolemy recovered the island in 249,* when he founded the vase-festival known as the second Ptolemaieia, the Island League broke up about this time, which suggests that Antigonus managed to retain certain islands, and that Ptolemy's success at sea was perhaps somewhat indeterminate."

Of the two passages which I have italicised, the second is a statement of fact[12]; the first is a mere hypothesis. The recovery

of Delos in 249 does not presuppose a revolt of Alexander in
253–2. If Alexander was in league with Ptolemy, his revolt in
any year between 253 and 249 would have enabled Egypt to
re-assert herself in the Aegean before the year 249 had closed.

Our problem is then: Of the two hypotheses about the date
of the revolt—that it preceded or that it followed Aratus' liberation
of Sicyon[13]—which harmonises better with the evidence derived
from the *Aratus?*

Beloch's interpretation of Plutarch's evidence. Beloch maintains (1) that Antigonus' neglect to liberate Sicyon as he promised
Aratus[14] can be explained only on the assumption that Alexander
had already revolted. The liberation by Aratus was at first
nothing but an intervention in Antigonus' interest:

(2) that the Sicyonian tyrants, Abantidas and Paseas[15] (the
latter of whom Nicocles assassinated), had been Antigonus'
partisans. Nicocles on the other hand was "on the best terms
with Alexander," since, when the Sicyonians fired the tyrant's
house on the night of the liberation, people in Corinth (οἱ ἐν
Κορίνῳ) seeing the flames almost decided to go to the rescue:[16]

(3) that Sicyon under Aratus took part in Antigonus' war
against Alexander:[17]

(4) that Antigonus' later ill-will towards Aratus[18] was due to
his refusal to make himself tyrant. Aratus' attachment of Sicyon
to the League is evidence that Antigonus held Corinth no longer.
The League could not have protected Sicyon from Macedon,
though it could from Alexander.

Criticism of Beloch's interpretation. In reply to (1), it might
be urged that Aratus' appeal to Antigonus to liberate Sicyon
implies that Antigonus still held Corinth. Plutarch distinguishes
the Macedonian king, to whom Aratus appealed, from the Egyptian
king, who was too far away to justify hopes of his intervention
(*Arat.* 4, *ad fin.*). But if Antigonus, in losing Corinth and
Euboea, had lost command of the sea (as he certainly had, for
Athens and Argos were left to themselves when they became
involved in war with the rebel), Aratus might have postponed hope
of help from him to the Greek Kalends. Antigonus' inaction

---

[13] Beloch following Sokelow dates the revolt 253–2; De Sanctis places
it about 248, which, however, in view of the second Ptolemaieia on Delos
in 249 is too late.

[14] *Arat.* 4.   [15] *Ib.* 2.   [16] *Ib.* 8.   [17] Cf. *ib.* 18.   [18] *Ib.* 9.

needs no explanation; he found it inconvenient to keep his word, just as he had found it inconvenient years before to keep his word with Pyrrhus, whom he promised to send reinforcements for his Italian campaign.[19]

As for (2), we know nothing of Abantidas except that Antigonus tolerated his tyranny at Sicyon for nearly twelve years. If that suffices to qualify him as a Macedonian partisan, Beloch's statement is justified. But in any case Tarn (p. 395) is correct in saying that "there is no evidence that Abantidas or any other Sicyonian tyrant had ever been a nominee, an ally, or a friend of Antigonus."

In fact, the history of Sicyon during the previous quarter of a century suggests that Antigonus at no time cared two straws who governed it provided it was governed in a manner that would cause no embarrassment to himself. When Aratus broke this condition by admitting the exiles, the king's ill-will ($\phi\theta\acute{o}\nu\upsilon\varsigma$) at once became apparent (*Arat.* 4): Abantidas and Paseas had been tolerated or recognised because they respected Antigonus' wishes. That Abantidas had obtained power by murdering Antigonus' friend Cleinias, made no difference. This view is confirmed by the passage (*Arat.* 4) in which Plutarch refers to the fears entertained by Nicocles, who had a watch set upon Aratus at Argos, "because he suspected that Aratus was in communication with the kings who had been his father's guest-friends." Note the plural. Nicocles, if he was really a protégé of the rebel Alexander and Alexander of Ptolemy Philadelphus, would have had nothing at all to fear from Ptolemy. But it is plain from the passage cited that Nicocles' fears arose not from consciousness of pursuing an anti-Macedonian policy, but from a suspicion that *one or other of the kings* might be induced by Aratus to take up his cause, and abolish the tyranny at Sicyon.

The story of the effect produced at Corinth by the fire at Nicocles' house in Sicyon, which Beloch relies on to prove that

---

[19] In *Arat.* 4 it is said that Nicocles was likely to lose Sicyon ὑπ' Αἰτωλῶν ἐπιβουλευομέν_{ην}. Tarn remarks, "The Aetolian assault was Antigonus' way of redeeming his promise, the only way in which he could do so." But the action of the Aetolians c. 270 in aiding the Elean refugees against Aristotimus and c. 240 in seeking to restore Agis' partisans to Sparta suggests that their present intention in threatening Sicyon was to restore the eighty Sicyonians banished by Nicocles.

already Alexander was in rebellion, may just as well be regarded as evidence of peaceful relations at the moment among all three parties—Nicocles, Alexander (still viceroy of Corinth), and Antigonus. What Plutarch tells of the fire is this. Day was already dawning when the Sicyonians met in the theatre to hear from Aratus that the city was free. After this, they hurried to the tyrant's house and set it on fire; but on discovering that the tyrant himself had escaped by an underground passage, they put out the flames and started looting the house instead. Hence, all that "the people in Corinth" saw was the fire from a single house blazing for a little while; the cause remained unknown. It might be argued that if Corinth was at war with Macedon as a result of Alexander's revolt, the fire at Sicyon would have appeared a suspicious occurrence requiring actual investigation, whereas, if a general peace still prevailed[20] "the people in Corinth" might naturally think at first of going to render aid, and later, as the flames died down and daylight increased, decide that the Sicyonians could deal with the fire themselves.

As to (3), the statement in *Arat.* 18 : "Aratus even while Alexander was still alive had set his hand to the enterprise (of capturing Acrocorinth), but when an alliance was made between the Achaeans and Alexander he desisted," seems to imply that the abortive attack is to be referred to the period after Sicyon joined the League. A bit of guerrilla warfare, involving the forces of Sicyon only and liable to be disavowed by the Achaean government in the event of failure, would be quite in Aratus' style.

Aratus may have intervened in the war between Alexander and the cities of Athens and Argos (*c.* 249–8). It is true that he was receiving money from Ptolemy, who, it is generally admitted, had instigated or supported Alexander's revolt. But Aratus, if successful, would not have found it hard to convince the king that Acrocorinth was safer with the Achaeans than with Alexander.

As to (4), Beloch evidently thought that the main reason for the attachment of Sicyon to the League was Aratus' fear of Alexander, Antigonus' displeasure being but a secondary consideration. But if Plutarch was aware that Antigonus' direct authority in Peloponnesus had been swept away by the revolt of Alexander, why has he so much to say about Antigonus and not

---

[20] As evidence of a general peace, Kolbe refers to Antigonus' stud-farm in Sicyonia (*Arat.* 6); De Sanctis, to the freedom with which Nicocles' spies promenade in the Argive agora (*Ib.*).

a word about Alexander, who on Beloch's own hypothesis had
ample grounds for offence against Aratus for his recent gratuitous
attack on Acrocorinthus? Alexander in his impregnable citadel
would have been a real enemy; Antigonus, far away in Demetrias
or Pella, at worst an inimical influence, whose ill-will could have
meant little in actual fact. And Beloch's argument that Aratus
would never have thought of attaching Sicyon to the League while
Antigonus was still lord of Corinth is a piece of à priori reasoning
that does not require refutation.

The King's gift to Aratus. In *Arat.* 11, 2 Plutarch writes: —

> " Now there had come to him a gift of money from
> the king, twenty-five talents. These he took and bestowed
> on his fellow-citizens who were lacking in means for the
> ransom of captives and other purposes. But since the
> returned exiles were implacable in harassing those who held
> their property and the city was in danger of destruction,
> Aratus, seeing his only hope in Ptolemy's generosity, made
> up his mind to take ship and ask the king to contribute
> funds for the settlement of the dispute."

Who is the king mentioned in the first sentence? It was generally
supposed to be Ptolemy (Philadelphus), until in 1906 Holleaux
in *Hermes* tried to prove that Plutarch was referring to Antigonus.
It is true that Antigonus is the last king mentioned; as far back
as chapter 9 we learn that his disagreeable attitude ($\phi\theta\acute{o}\nu os$) was
one of the factors which decided Aratus in attaching Sicyon to
the League. But if Plutarch had this passage in mind, how could
he have avoided an explanation of the apparent inconsistency
attributed to the Macedonian king? Another thing which calls
for explanation is why, if Aratus had already received twenty-five
talents from Antigonus, he should be described as " seeing in
Ptolemy's generosity his only hope." Again, would it not be
strange if in the first sentence of the passage cited " the king "
means the Macedonian, in the third the Egyptian king?
    It must be admitted that some explanation is required of
the ambiguous and unworkmanlike composition of the passage.
My own suggestion is that this is one of the passages in which
Plutarch has lightened his labours by "cribbing" from his source,
Aratus' *Memoirs*, careless of the fact that the passage transcribed
did not adjust itself very happily to its new context.

To sum up: it appears that the 253–2 dating of Alexander's revolt fails to explain why Plutarch refers so frequently to the *ex hypothesi* dispossessed Antigonus while persistently silent about the man on the spot, Alexander; or why Aratus appealed for Antigonus' intervention at all; or why he subsequently incurred the king's displeasure; or why that displeasure was of such consequence as to induce him to merge the independence of Sicyon in the Achaean League. As we proceed, we shall find further difficulties implicit in this hypothesis.

Aratus' shipwreck on the way to Alexandria. In Chapter 12 we read that Aratus " put out from Methone beyond Malea intending to take the regular passage." A storm, however, forced him into the Aegean, and the steersman with difficulty put in at "Adria" (*sic*)

> " which was enemy territory, for it was held by Antigonus and had a garrison. Aratus anticipated arrest by landing, abandoning the ship, and retiring a long distance from the sea. A little later the garrison-commander came to the ship looking for Aratus, but was deceived by his servants, who had been directed to say that he had immediately started off to Euboea."

The word "Adria" is certainly corrupt, for there is no such place in the Aegean area. But wherever we locate the shipwreck (or, more accurately, forced landing), the difficulty remains that Antigonus is not likely to have held any Aegean islands with garrisons two years after Alexander's revolt. Again, one may ask, from whom would the garrison-commander have received orders to look out for Aratus? Antigonus himself was in Demetrias or Pella, where he was hardly likely to hear of Aratus' proposed journey in sufficient time to enable him to arrange for his arrest; and while Alexander held Corinth, Aratus was a person of minor importance.

For the corrupt "Adria" we may choose between Bergk's " Hydria " or Palmerius' "Andria," i.e., the territory as opposed to the town of Andros.[21]

Hydria, famous though " Hydra's isle " became in Byron's days, was of no account in antiquity, and is mentioned only three times by classical writers; why should Antigonus have kept a

---

[21] See note on *Arat.* 12, 2.

garrison there ? Further, we are told that the garrison-commander was thrown off the scent by being informed that Aratus had sailed off to Euboea. A falsehood, to be believed, must wear the mask of truth, and this falsehood *was* believed. But a story to the effect that Aratus at Hydria had found a ship at a moment's notice in stormy weather to take him to Euboea, as far away from Hydria as Dublin is from Holyhead, does not wear the mask of truth.

But let the scene of the shipwreck be transferred to Andros, and Plutarch's narrative becomes intelligible. To cross from Andros to Euboea—a distance of some six miles—Aratus might simply have commandeered the ship's boat[22]; and Euboea is a big island where a fugitive could easily elude capture.

For Beloch, the difficulty is this: if Alexander was already in revolt and holding Euboea, the scene of the shipwreck (as he himself has seen) cannot be Andros, for Andros is too near Euboea to have been still garrisoned by Antigonus; but neither can it be Hydria in any case, for Hydria is too far from Euboea for the servants' tale to have been believed by Antigonus' officer.

On the other hand, if Alexander was still Macedonian viceroy at Corinth, he was bound to hear of Aratus' approaching departure for Egypt, which must have been the chief topic of conversation at Sicyon for weeks beforehand. Captains of Macedonian warships and garrison-commanders on Aegean islands held by Antigonus would be instructed to arrest Aratus if his ship should come within their reach. Aratus thought to outwit his enemies by starting from Methone and avoiding the Aegean altogether, but the storm upset his calculations.

Antigonus would doubtless have justified the attempt to seize Aratus on the ground that he had been responsible for attaching Sicyon to a state which did not acknowledge the king's authority. Plutarch's reference to the ill-will evinced by Antigonus at Aratus' proceedings even before Sicyon joined the League is evidence that he claimed some degree of control over the city. The union with Achaea he regarded as a hostile act. Imagine the attitude of the British Government if the sovereign state of Afghanistan were to negotiate its entry into the Soviet Union!

We had already seen the difficulties involved in the assumption that Alexander's revolt came before the entry of Sicyon into the

---

[22] This point was made by De Sanctis.

League. Now, an examination of Plutarch's account of Aratus'
shipwreck has led to the conclusion that at the time of the voyage
Alexander had not yet revolted from Antigonus.

There is no evidence in Plutarch to fix the date of the voyage,
but it followed quickly upon the union of Sicyon with the Achaeans,
for the internal difficulties of the Sicyonians called for immediate
settlement. We may place it in the autumn of 251, a time of
year when storms at sea are to be expected. Aratus may have spent
the winter at Alexandria, returning home in the early spring
of 250.

In view of the "second Ptolemaieia," which belongs to the
year 249, we may date Alexander's revolt shortly after Aratus'
return home.

The date of Alexander's death and Antigonus' recovery of
Corinth. After his return from Egypt Aratus was for a long time
occupied with the economic problems of Sicyon. We do not hear
of him again till 245, when he became Achaean strategos for the
first time.[23] He began his official career by engaging in the war
which had broken out between Aetolia and Boeotia.

The war had already been going on for some time. According
to Polybius,[24] the instigators were the Achaeans themselves.
Aratus began by sailing across the Gulf and ravaging the Aetolian
territories of Locris and Calydon. But when the Aetolians
threatened Boeotia the Achaeans had to make a more serious
effort. An army of ten thousand men was raised, with which
Aratus marched to the assistance of the Boeotians, but they,
without waiting for his arrival, joined battle with the enemy at
Chaeronea, where they were completely put to rout.

The campaign of Aratus and his ten thousand seems to presuppose that the isthmus was in friendly hands. So large an
army, as Beloch and De Sanctis have observed, could not have
been transported by sea. But if Antigonus was once more in
occupation of Corinth, as Tarn maintains, both land and sea routes
were subject to his control; and it cannot be thought that he
would have remained inactive while the Achaeans marched north
to attack his friends the Aetolians. Neither would Aratus, after
what had passed between him and the Macedonian king, have
dared to denude the country of its man-power, thus giving
Antigonus the chance to bar with his fleet the return of the

---

[23] *Arat.* 16, 1, *note.*   [24] Polyb. 20, 4.

Achaean expeditionary force, or to swoop down with his army upon the unprotected Achaean cities. Hence we must assume that Corinth at this time was held by Alexander, who was (as Droysen long ago maintained) not only an ally of the Achaeans, but beyond a doubt himself a participant in the war. An independent Boeotia was indeed necessary for his own security, since the country lies between Corinth and Euboea.

It has been objected by Tarn that the institution of Antigonus' Delian festivals, " Paneia " and " Soteria," commemorated his victory over the Egyptian fleet at Andros,[25] implying the recovery of his arsenals, Chalcis and Corinth. Hence Tarn's date for Alexander's death, 247 or 246.

But one may doubt whether the victory presupposes anything more than Antigonus' possession of an efficient fleet at the time. There is no difficulty in this assumption. Some five years had now elapsed since Alexander's revolt; if Chalcis and Corinth were lost there were dockyards in *esse* or in *posse* at Demetrias, Thessalonica, Cassandreia, Amphipolis, where a new fleet might be built.[26]

Of the battle of Andros we know nothing but what has been already stated—that it was a victory for Antigonus Gonatas over an Egyptian fleet commanded by Sophron, and to be dated at earliest in the latter half of 246. We should like to know, however, what brought an Egyptian fleet into the neighbourhood of Andros.

In the absence of knowledge we are reduced to conjecture. It may well be that Antigonus, taking advantage of the Aetolo-Boeotian conflict, in which we have reason to believe that the rebel Alexander was involved, sailed down from the north with his new-built fleet in hope of recovering his Euboean arsenals. On this hypothesis, Sophron's armada might have been despatched by Euergetes in response to a call for assistance from Alexander. We might further suppose that after his victory Antigonus proceeded to reduce the Euboean cities.

About this time Alexander died. Plutarch (i.e., Phylarchus) records a rumour that he was poisoned by Antigonus. This

[25] See Sect. 2, *Addendum* B. Festivals founded 245 B.C.

[26] In another connection Tarn himself writes (p. 344): ''The large coast towns of the Chalcidice possessed ample facilities for building, and he (Antigonus) had plenty of timber.''

suggests that he had been suffering from no disease familiar to the physicians of the day. It is conceivable that despairing of his fortunes he committed suicide, and that his widow Nicaea spread abroad the story of the poisoning, in order to keep up the courage of her mercenaries.

The chronological problem of Chapter 15. Antigonus, we are told by Plutarch, showed Aratus many kindnesses after his return from Egypt, and in particular, when sacrificing at Corinth, sent portions of the victims to Sicyon. During the banquet that followed, the king made a speech in which he not only eulogised "the young Sicyonian," as liberal and patriotic, but commended his sound judgment in high politics.

> "Formerly, it is true, he looked with hopeful eyes across the sea, ignoring us and admiring the wealth of Egypt, as he heard talk of elephants and fleets and palaces; but now that he has peeped behind the curtain and seen that all the grandeur there is only stage-illusion and painted show, he has come over whole-heartedly to our side. I welcome the young man myself, and am resolved to make every possible use of him, and I desire you (the guests) to treat him as a friend."

Mischief-makers reported Antigonus' words to Ptolemy, who, naturally enough, sent a messenger to complain to Aratus of his apparent treachery.

There is no reason to doubt the genuineness of this story, or that it comes from Aratus' memoirs. The presents from Antigonus and the reproaches from Ptolemy were matters within Aratus' immediate knowledge, and the speech, as given in Plutarch, may be taken as representing the report which Ptolemy had received of what Antigonus had said.

The date of the speech is a difficulty for those who begin Alexander's revolt in 253–2. If, with Tarn, they dispose of Alexander in 247, they provide, it is true, an appropriate date for the speech, but can give no satisfactory account of Aratus' march to Boeotia. If, with Beloch, they make 245 the date of the restoration of Antigonus to Corinth (which came almost immediately after Alexander's death), the speech appears "out of focus" for two reasons: —

> (1) The Achaeans had for some years past been allies of Antigonus' bitterest foe, Alexander. Aratus, as strategos,

had some months previously engaged in war with the Aetolians, Antigonus' friends. Four or five years had elapsed since the voyage to Egypt. Yet Antigonus coolly explains Aratus' alleged conversion to the Macedonian side as the result of what he had seen " behind the curtain " at Alexandria, and magnanimously offers a job in his diplomatic service to the strategos of the Achaean League!

(2) Philadelphus, who had contributed the money required to settle the troubles at Sicyon, died at the beginning of 246; it would have been his son Euergetes that sent Aratus the reproachful message. But Plutarch's narrative, naturally understood, implies that the remittances and remonstrances came from the same person.

And if the speech was made " immediately after the battle of Andros," [27] it would be pointless to praise Aratus' political insight. The issue had then been decided. The only place where the speech is in its proper setting is where Plutarch has placed it—shortly after Aratus' return from Egypt.

We have now examined the evidence available for the chronology of Alexander's reign at Corinth. We have seen the difficulties which arise if we date the reign either from 253–2 to 245; or from 253–2 to 247. The hypothesis that the secession began after Aratus' return from Egypt and continued till after his Boeotian campaign (i.e., from 250 to 245), which in essentials is that proposed by De Sanctis, avoids these difficulties and creates no new ones.

CHRONOLOGICAL SUMMARY.

(Dates derived from ancient sources, literary or epigraphic, or immediately deducible therefrom, are indicated by an asterisk.)

*271.   Aratus' birth.
*264.   Cleinias murdered; Aratus in exile at Argos.

---

[27] Cary writes (p. 402): "The most likely occasion for Gonatas to celebrate a festival at Corinth and to make disparaging remarks about the hollowness of Ptolemy's (i.e., Euergetes') might was immediately after the battle of Andros." Ferguson, however, J.H.S., xxx (1910), p. 207, thinks these "disparaging remarks" were "a jibe at Philadelphus notorious aversion to campaigning." Cf. Plut. Mor. 183 (Apophthegms of kings and generals).

*255.   Peace between Macedon and Egypt.
*253.   Institution of Delian *Antigoneia.*
  252 (May). Liberation of Sicyon.
         (Summer). Aristodemus of Megalopolis murdered.
         (later). Spartans defeated at Mantinea by Arcadians,
             Achaeans, and Sicyonians under Aratus.
*251–0 (prob. May, 251). Sicyon joins Achaean League.
  251 (Autumn). Aratus' voyage to Egypt.
  250 (Spring). Return of Aratus: Antigonus at Corinth.
         (later). Revolt of Alexander.
*249.   Institution of the " *Second Ptolemaieia.*"
  249.   Aristomachus of Argos in alliance with Athens against
             Alexander.
  249 or 248. Abortive attempt of Sicyonians under Aratus upon
             Acrocorinthus; alliance between Alexander and
             the Achaeans.
*245.   Aratus' first strategia: Boeotian defeat at Chaeronea.
  245.   Antigonus' defeat of Egyptian fleet off Andros.
         Antigonus' recovery of Euboea: death of Alexander:
             Antigonus' recovery of Corinth.
*245.   Institution of *Paneia* and *Soteria.*
*243 (Summer). Acrocorinth captured by Aratus.

[The battle of Andros may belong to 246, and similarly Antigonus'
    recovery of Euboea, if we suppose the two events to be closely
    connected.]

SECTION IV.—*Aratus and the Extrusion of Macedon.*

The capture of Acrocorinthus in 243, while it made the
Achaean League vastly stronger—for with Corinth came in
Megara, Troezen, and Epidaurus (*Ar.* 24)—brought down upon
it the assured enmity of Antigonus, whose grievance was the more
bitter because Aratus had snatched the fortress from him in time
of peace. This is admitted by Polybius, who speaks of the
injustice done to the royal house of Macedon.[1]

  [1] Polyb. 2, 50, 9. Aratus' achievement is in fact comparable to
that of Garibaldi in 1860 when he wrested Sicily from the Neapolitan
Government.

The Achaeans had now two enemies beyond the isthmus, for the Aetolians had not forgotten the raiding expedition of 245; but, for the moment, the initiative remained with Aratus. His policy of expelling the Macedonians "bag and baggage" from Greece was indicated by the decree appointing Ptolemy Euergetes to the titular "hegemony of the League by land and sea" (*Arat.* 24).

Pursuing this policy, he invaded Attica and raided Salamis; but released his prisoners without ransom, in evidence that the object of his hostility was not Athens, but Antigonus (*Ar.* 24). About the same time, he organised a conspiracy against Aristomachus, the tyrant of Argos (*Ar.* 25). The Attic campaign belongs to the autumn of 243 or the spring of 242; the conspiracy may have been timed to break out when his period of office was over. It proved a failure; the leaders quarrelled, and one of them turned informer.

But such schemes were brought to a halt by the invasion of the Aetolians in 241, in reprisal for the Achaean violation of their territory four years before. During the interval, they had been occupied in extending their influence in West Peloponnesus.

Incidental references in Polybius and Pausanias suggest that soon after 245 Aetolia took up the cause of the Eleans, who had a traditional claim upon the Arcadian district of Tryphylia.[2] Unable to stand up to the Aetolians, the Arcadian League broke in pieces. We find Lydiades tyrant at Megalopolis, Nearchus at Orchomenus, Mantinea an independent community, Phigalea actually in "isopolity" with the Aetolians, with whom the neutral state of Messenia also allied itself.

Had it not been for this extension of Aetolian influence in the west during the years 245–1, by which the states were enabled to maintain their traditional policy of "particularism" against the Achaean ideal of a united Peloponnesus, Aratus might have been able in course of time to bring into the League all Peloponnesus

---

[2] For the Triphylian war see Beloch 4, 1, p. 619. Lydiades' seizure of the *tyrannis* cannot be precisely dated, but it must come after the battle of Mantinea, where his command was shared with a colleague, Lacydes. As tyrant he came to terms with Elis, ceding to the Eleans the fort of Alipheira (Polyb. 4, 77). For Orchomenos see Syll.³ 490. As evidence of an independent Mantinea we find in the Delian proxeny list of 236 B.C. the "ethnikon," Μαντινεύς [H. von Gaertringen, IG. v, 2, p. xxiii]. Phigalea in isopolity with Aetolia, Polyb. 4, 3, 6; Messenia, 4, 6, 11.

except Sparta, and Cleomenes might have found it expedient to come to an accommodation with a power too strong to be overthrown by force of arms. But, as it was, the Achaean ideal had been frustrated in advance.

The Aetolian Invasion of 241. The attack made upon the Achaeans was the result of an understanding between the Aetolians and Antigonus, who contracted to partition the territory of the League between them.[3] They might readily have attained their object if they had mobilised all their resources. The Aetolians could have called upon their West-Peloponnesian allies, and Macedon upon the tyrants of Argos, Phlius, Hermione, Megalopolis and Orchomenos, to assail the Achaeans within Peloponnesus; a combined army of Macedonians and Aetolians might have forced the isthmus, while a Macedonian fleet was operating in the Corinthian Gulf. But nothing of the kind occurred. The tyrants remained inactive; Elis and Messenia did not stir; Antigonus himself was content to be a sleeping partner in the enterprise.

Aratus, who evidently had ample notice of the danger, immediately called on Sparta for assistance. His alliance with the Spartans is generally held to date from the revolution which began at Sparta in 243. But no Spartan government, however constituted, could be indifferent to the return of Antigonus to Corinth, for Macedon had always been the enemy of Sparta and friend of Megalopolis.

Accordingly, King Agis marched to the isthmus at the head of an army. It was towards midsummer; the crops had almost all been gathered in, and in Peloponnesus the harvest—except in upland districts—comes about the end of May. The reference in Plutarch to the harvest fixes the date, for between the capture of Corinth and the death of Antigonus the only year when Aratus was holding office in June was 241.

No sooner had the allies met at the isthmus when a difference arose between them. Agis was all for fighting, but Aratus would not risk a battle, and preferred "as the harvest was already secured" to let the invaders pass into Peloponnesus. Agis was commended and dismissed (*Agis* 15, *Arat.* 31).

---

[3] Polyb. 2; 43: 9; 34. The allusion must be to the affair of 241. Polybius does not say that Antigonus had undertaken to support the Aetolians in the war.

How is Aratus' conduct to be explained? It seems as though he had originally expected to be faced with a combined Macedonian and Aetolian invasion. In that event he could not have avoided battle, and would have needed all the forces he could get together. It is possible that the Aetolians themselves expected to be joined at the isthmus by a Macedonian contingent, for otherwise they might more conveniently have crossed by sea to Elis and mustered their army there.

But Aratus never fought a battle if he could avoid it. He knew he was but a mediocre general, and, to make things worse, he was liable on the eve of battle to attacks of· neurasthenia (*Ar.* 29), which never troubled him when leading a forlorn hope.

So, finding no Macedonians at the isthmus but merely a moderate force of Aetolians, he felt he could deal with the situation by methods of his own, as in fact he did.

Beloch's notion,[4] that he declined battle in order to save his army from contamination of Spartan "communism," is inconsistent with the fact that he had himself summoned the "communists" to the isthmus.

Nor is there much basis for the theory that he used the city of Pellene as a bait to lure the Aetolians to their destruction. We cannot suppose that "when they suddenly seized the town," it was because Aratus had sent agents in advance to arrange that it should be left unguarded. He was blamed for not fighting at the isthmus, but there is no evidence that he was held responsible for the sack of Pellene.[5]

The rout of the Aetolians, while still engaged in plundering, is characterised by both Polybius and Plutarch as a brilliant achievement, worthy to be compared with the liberation of Sicyon and Corinth (Pol. IV. 8; *Ar.* 31, 32).

When the Boeotians in 245 lost a thousand men at Chaeronea they were so demoralised that they gave up the struggle with Aetolia and sued for peace. It is not surprising, therefore, that

4, 1, p. 626. All that Plutarch says or implies (Ag. 14) is that the wealthier Achaeans feared the influence of the Spartan example on their own lower classes (δῆμοι).

[5] Tarn, C.A.H. vii, p. 735, supposes that the revolt of Pellene to Cleomenes in 225 was due to what happened in 241. But on the same occasion Cleomenes almost succeeded in capturing Sicyon by the help of traitors within the walls, though the Sicyonians had no such grievance against Aratus as Tarn attributes to the Pellenians.

the Aetolians now, having lost seven hundred, were only concerned about returning home. It is characteristic of Aratus that he did nothing to stop them.

The Interval of Peace, 241–238. Very soon after their victory the Achaeans came to terms with Aetolia and Macedon, and Macedon's client states, Athens and Argos. It is again characteristic of Aratus that he broke the peace, as soon as he found it convenient, by renewing his attacks on Athens and Argos. At some time during the year 241–40 the Argive tyrant Aristomachus was murdered by slaves, and Aratus saw his chance to intervene. But the Argives refused to rise against the new tyrant Aristippus. The tyrant in turn (*Ar.* 25) "with Antigonus' aid" planned Aratus' assassination, while at the same time he arraigned the Achaeans before an arbitration tribunal for breach of the peace. When the case came on Aratus did not appear, being presumably out of office, which suggests that the suit was heard during the year 240–239.

The second breach of the peace was the attempt made by Aratus' agent Erginus to surprise Piraeus, which occurred at the end of Antigonus' or the beginning of Demetrius' reign. The " Demetrian war" was regarded by the Athenians as beginning in 238.[6]

The behaviour which Plutarch attributes to the Achaeans is noteworthy, and true to human nature, then and now. If an enterprise proves successful (like Aratus' attack on Corinth), popular morality justifies the means adopted; censure is reserved for the law-breaker who fails, as Aratus did at Argos and Piraeus.

Yet we may well wonder why the Achaeans consented to go before an arbitration tribunal at the suit of a tyrant, who was held by the Greeks to be outside all law; nor can we understand on what basis the arbitrators assessed plaintiff's damages at something over a hundred pounds (*Arat.* 25, 5 note).

The Achaean League in the " Demetrian War" (238–230). After the death of Antigonus, the Achaeans and Aetolians, who had been fighting one another not nine months before, actually became allies; while the Aetolians did not renew with Demetrius the alliance which they had made with his father. On the

---

[6] IG.[2] ii. 1, 1299: cf. Ferguson, p. 44. Demetrius had succeeded his father, Antigonus Gonatas, in the spring of 240: see Dinsmoor, p. 109.

contrary, the new king soon went to war with them on behalf of the Epirots.

It appears that some time after the death of Pyrrhus an arrangement had been made with his son Alexander by the Aetolians to partition the territory of Acarnania, the northern half to be annexed to Epirus. But now the Aetolians demanded the whole.

They were well aware what they were doing. The house of Pyrrhus was represented at this time by a boy and a number of women. The Queen-mother Olympias appealed for aid to Demetrius, to whom, as he happened to be without a wife at the moment, she offered her daughter Phthia.[7] The match took place about 239, for their son was born in 238.

Details of the conflict on the Acarnanian front are wanting, but it is clear that the Aetolians failed to secure Northern Acarnania.

The Achaean alliance, however, enabled a war of attrition to be carried on against the Macedonian interest in Argolis and Attica, simultaneously with the conflict in Acarnania.

The Athenians, as already stated, recognised the war as beginning in the year when Lysias was archon, which Ferguson equates with 238–7 B.C. In that year, as an inscription records, their general, Aristophanes of Leuconoe, "placed neither his personal safety nor anything else before the interests of the country." Next year, when Cimon was archon, the same Aristophanes was occupied with measures of defence. In Ecphantus' year, 236–5, the harvest was brought in under military protection.[8] In 232, if that is the year of Diomedon, a special appeal was made to provide money for the country's protection.[9] Finally, we have a decree passed after the conclusion of the war, when Athens had regained her freedom. This decree honoured Eurycleides, who had been mainly responsible for the administration of the state, because, "when the land was lying untilled and unsown during the war," he provided the funds which enabled it to be tilled and sown.[10]

In Plutarch we read that Aratus "attacked Piraeus not twice or thrice but many times." Of these "many times" two only

---

[7] Justin 27; 1, 1–2. Philip was actually a son of Demetrius and Phthia (not of Chryseis) as Tarn has shown from contemporary inscriptions [C.Q., 1924, p. 17].

[8] IG.[2] ii, 1, 1299.   [9] IG.[2] ii, 791.   [10] IG.[2] ii, 1, 834.

are mentioned—the occasion of unknown date when he broke his thigh, fleeing over the Thriasian plain, and his demonstration in force after his defeat at Phylacia (Phylace), which most probably occurred in 233.

Similarly, Plutarch tells of many attacks, open or secret, made by Aratus upon Aristippus, tyrant of Argos. He describes (*Ar.* 27. 28. 29) certain of these operations: (1) a night assault on the city followed by some eighteen hours of fighting within the walls; (2) after the abandonment of this method, a battle at the river Chares (Charadrus[11]), in which Aratus threw away a certain victory, but recovered his reputation by capturing Cleonae, where he celebrated the Nemean games[12]; (3) the battle outside the town of Cleonae, at which Aristippus was killed.

" Immediately" after this, Aratus turned upon Lydiades of Megalopolis, who abdicated his tyranny and joined the city to the League. Lydiades' abdication must be placed in 235–4,[13] and consequently the battle outside Cleonae in the same year. As this battle comes "a little while after" the battle at the Charadrus, we may (with Beloch) regard the year 235–4 as the date of all these events.

When the first Aristomachus of Argos was killed in 241, Aratus' attempt to surprise the city was foiled by the promptitude of Aristippus. Now Aristippus (235) was dead, but Aratus was again disappointed, for " Agias and the younger Aristomachus burst into the city with royal (Macedonian) troops, and seized the government" (*Arat.* 29. 6). The new tyrant was beyond a doubt a younger brother of his predecessor.[14]

To this Aristomachus there is a reference in Polybius which has occasioned some perplexity to modern historians. Polybius (2. 59) states that on a certain occasion when Aratus entered Argos, but was forced to retire for want of Argive support, Aristomachus put eighty of the leading men to death with torture as adherents of the Achaeans. Freeman (p. 312) remarks that this agrees with nothing elsewhere mentioned of the reign of Aristomachus, and asks if it is to be placed at the beginning of his tyrannis.

The objection to this arrangement, as he has noticed himself, is that, according to Plutarch (*Ar.* 27), Aratus' fight within the

---

[11] See note on ch. 28.　　　　[12] They fell in the uneven years B.C.
[13] Lydiades was strategos in 234–3, 232–1, and 230–229.
[14] See note on *Arat.* 25. 4.

walls of Argos and retirement for want of Argive support occurred
in the reign of Aristippus—either in 237–6, or (as Beloch places
it) early in 235. Such an incident is not likely to have occurred
twice. It is possible, however, to reconcile Plutarch and Polybius
if we assume that the massacre of the eighty citizens belongs to
the reign of Aristippus, but was carried out by Aristomachus,
acting on his brother's behalf. A close co-operation between
brothers in the conduct of affairs is just what we might expect.
A familiar instance is that of Hippias and Hipparchus, the sons
of Pisistratus, at Athens. Polybius was concerned to saddle
Aristomachus with the massacre; he was not concerned with the
question whether it happened before or after he succeeded
Aristippus as tyrant.

The presence of Agias and his Macedonian mercenaries in
Argos evidently induced Aratus to leave Aristomachus alone and
turn to Megalopolis. Lydiades, however, realised that he could
hold out no longer. Already he had felt the pressure of the
League. It was probably in the previous year (236–5) that the
Achaean strategos Dioetas took the town of Heraea[15] from him.
He accordingly abandoned the tyranny, and Megalopolis entered
the League, to be followed by Orchomenos and Mantinea.[16]

Thus the Aetolian campaigns between 245 and 241, which had
as their immediate result the aggrandisement of Aetolia herself
and her Elean allies, had led indirectly to the absorption of
nearly all Arcadia in the Achaean confederacy. But Megalopolis
brought with her that *damnosa hereditas*, her perpetual feud with
Sparta, while Orchomenos and Mantinea remained Spartan in
sympathy. Towards the end of the 'thirties these cities, apparently
with the consent of the Achaeans, transferred their allegiance to
the Aetolian[17] League.

The year 235–4 had, on the whole, been a successful one for
the Achaeans, but the Macedonian interest in Peloponnesus was
not yet crushed. A Macedonian general Bithys appeared with
an army in Arcadia,[18] and at Phylacia[19] gave Aratus so sound a
drubbing that the Achaeans were scattered abroad, and Aratus

---

[15] Polyaen. 2, 36: Beloch 4, 1, p. 632.
[16] The commonly accepted date *c.* 234 for the entrance of Mantinea
is conjectural. It assumes that when Megalopolis (and her satellite
townships) came in Mantinea found abstention no longer feasible.
[17] Polyb. 2, 57, 1: 46, 2.   [18] *Arat.* 34.
[19] Phylacia = Phylace in Arcadia (Beloch): see note on *Arat.* 34, 2.

himself was thought to be either slain or taken prisoner. The presence of Bithys in Peloponnesus is best explained, if with Ferrabino[20] we connect it with the submission of Boeotia to Demetrius, mentioned incidentally by Polybius[21] From Boeotia his army presumably was sent by sea to Argolis.

What precisely Bithys intended to do in Arcadia was never revealed. His victory was not followed up. The successes of Macedon in Acarnania, where, in Cary's words, "they fought the Aetolians to a standstill," in Boeotia, and in Arcadia had been rendered futile by the appearance of a new and formidable enemy. The barbarous Dardanians had assailed Macedon's northern frontier. From 232 Greece saw Demetrius no more. His garrisons in Piraeus and Argos were left in the air.

The commanders were prepared to disband their forces if the mercenaries could be paid off. Fifty talents were required for the garrison at Argos and one hundred and fifty for that of Piraeus. In raising the money for this purpose Aratus co-operated generously.

The Argive settlement, indeed, was delayed for some months by jealousy between Aratus and Lydiades, but by May 228 not only had Diogenes, the Macedonian governor of Piraeus, handed over the fortress to Athens, but Aristomachus the tyrant of Argos was strategos of the Achaean League.

Aratus' satisfaction, however, was not complete, for he could not persuade Athens to abandon her newly won independence. Instead of joining the Achaeans, she preferred a policy of general neutrality, remaining during the last quarter of the third century "the calm centre of a whirlpool."

Results of the war. The war had begun in a contest between Aetolia and Epirus for the northern half of Acarnania. When Demetrius was no longer able to help Epirus he delegated the task to Agron, king of Illyria, but the Illyrians quickly reduced both Epirus and Acarnania to a condition of vassalage under themselves. Had it not been for Agron's sudden death and his widow Teuta's quarrel with Rome in 229 B.C., Aetolia itself might have suffered at their hands.

As things turned out, Aetolia gained the adhesion of Ambracia,[22] and after Demetrius' death in 230 seized the southern half of

---

[20] P. 292.

[21] Polyb. 20, 5, 3: since the defeat of 245 at Chaeronea Boeotia had been an ally of Aetolia.   [22] It was Aetolian in 219, Polyb. 4, 61.

Thessaly, taking advantage of a Thessalian revolt against Macedon.[23]

The Achaeans in turn had abolished the Peloponnesian tyrants and secured an independent and neutral Athens. Within Peloponnesus the League now included every state that was willing to be included. Outside the League were the Spartans, who remained independent, and Messenia, which, together with the Arcadian cities, Tegea, Mantinea, Orchomenos and Phigalea, was attached to the Aetolian League by the comparatively loose association known as "isopolity."

The two Leagues were still allies, but the causes which had brought about the alliance were no longer in operation.

CHRONOLOGICAL SUMMARY.

245. Aratus' first strategia: Aetolians defeat Boeotians at Chaeronea.

245–1. Arcadian League dissolved in consequence of assistance of Elis by Aetolia in Triphylian war: Lydiades, tyrant of Megalopolis, Nearchus of Orchomenos: Mantinea becomes independent.

243. Aratus ii: Corinth, Megara, Troezen enter Achaean League.
Achaean raids on Attica and Salamis.

241. Aratus iii: Aetolians defeated at Pellene.
Murder of Aristomachus, tyrant of Argos, who is succeeded by Aristippus.

240. Aristippus awarded damages by Mantinean arbitrators against the Achaeans for attacks on Argos during peace.
Erginus' attempt on Piraeus.
(Spring). Death of Antigonus Gonatas and succession of his son Demetrius (Dinsmoor, p. 109).

239. Aratus iv.
Dispute between Aetolia and Epirus over northern Acarnania. Alliance between Aetolians and Achaeans.

[23] *Prol. Trog.* 28, Justin 28, 14. The conquest of this part of Thessaly by the Aetolians is inferred by Beloch, 4, 2, p. 413, from the position in 184 B.C. That by 228 peace had been made between Aetolia and Macedon appears from Polyb. 2, 45, 2.

238 (Summer). Archonship of Lysias at Athens (Ferguson), in whose year the "Demetrian war began."

237. Aratus v.

236. Dioetas, Achaean strategos : Heraea taken from Lydiades.

235. Aratus vi : nocturnal attempt on Argos : battle at R. Charadrus : capture of Cleonae by Achaeans : Aristippus slain in battle near Mycenae : abdication of Lydiades; Megalopolis enters the League, followed by Orchomenos and Mantinea.

234. Lydiades' first Achaean strategia.

233. Aratus vii : Battle of Phylace.

232. Lydiades ii : withdrawal of Demetrius from Greece.

231. Aratus viii.

230. Lydiades iii : negotiations for cession of Piraeus begun.

229. Aratus ix : Argos, Hermione, Phlius join the League. Death of King Demetrius.

228. Aristomachus Achaean strategos : Athens regains Piraeus. Aegina enters the League : Antigonus makes peace with Aetolia and becomes king of Macedon.

ADDENDUM : *Aratus at Cynaetha.* Polybius (9, 17) tells how Aratus, ὁ τῶν Ἀχαιῶν στρατηγός, attempted on some occasion unspecified to capture Cynaetha by treachery, but came to grief through mistaking the movements of a man attending to his private concerns for the signal which he had arranged upon with the conspirators inside the town. In consequence, Aratus " not only failed in his attack but involved his partisans in the greatest calamities . . . What shall we say was the cause of the catastrophe ? το ποιήσασθαι τὸν στραγηγὸν ἁπλοῦν τὸ σύνθημα νέον ἀκμὴν ὄντα καὶ τῆς τῶν διπλῶν συνθημάτων ἀκριβείας ἄπειρον."

Cynaetha is a town in the N.-W. of Arcadia, quite near the Achaean border. When and in what circumstances was Aratus likely to have attacked it ?

This problem has been carefully examined by Walbank, J.H.S., lvi (1936), p. 64. He rightly maintains that the use of the term στρατηγός implies that Aratus was at the time *Strategos of the League*; also the words νέον ἀκμὴν ὄντα suggest that he was not more than thirty years of age. On these grounds his fiasco at Cynaetha must have occurred in one of his strategiai,

245–4, 243–2, 241–0.   But, as we have seen, the first two of these were otherwise occupied.

Walbank reconstructs the situation on the hypothesis that after the collapse of the Arcadian League in the Triphylian War (c. 244) Cynaetha passed into the hands of the Eleans, behind whom stood the far more formidable Aetolians.   The situation of the town made it under such conditions a menace to Achaea. Hence Aratus' eagerness to get hold of it.   His abortive attempt was made at the beginning of his strategia, 241–0, and precipitated the Aetolian invasion, which ended in the rout of Pellene.   Between this event and the Aetolo-Achaean alliance of 239, Cynaetha was secured by the Achaeans in a second but unrecorded campaign.

SECTION V.—*The Ambition of Cleomenes.*

The Social Problem in Sparta and elsewhere in Peloponnesus.

Reference has already been made to the Spartan revolution[1] of 243 B.C, and the execution of Agis two years later.   Power was now in the hands of the conservatives led by the reactionary king, Leonidas; but their position was not an enviable one.   The perioeci and the unprivileged Spartans had acquired an ideal and a programme; it was unlikely that they could be kept in subjection indefinitely.   The state was also assailed from outside.   A number of Spartans, implicated in Agis' revolution, had taken refuge with the Aetolians, who presently[2] took up their cause and invaded Laconia.   The city of Sparta they failed to capture; but they ravaged the countryside, penetrating as far as Taenarum, where they sacked the temple of Poseidon.   No less than fifty thousand helots or perioeci—if we can accept the almost incredible figures of Plutarch (Phylarchus)—were carried into captivity. The Spartan government—so low had Sparta fallen—consoled themselves with the thought that the invasion had at least diminished the number of their domestic enemies (Plut. *Cleom.* 18 : Pol. 4, 34; 9, 34).   It was enough for King Leonidas if the existing system could be made to last his time.

[1] On the antecedents of Agis' revolution, see my article in *Hermathena,* 1935.

[2] In 240 (Beloch) or 236 (Pozzi).

The decline of Sparta had in fact been going on so long that
it might almost seem part of the order of nature. It had begun
even before the Boeotian war of 371 B.C., when at Leuctra, as
Aristotle puts it, " the city sank under a single defeat." The
loss of Messenia had followed immediately; and as the larger part
of the Spartans lived on the produce of Messenian allotments
tilled for them by Messenian helots, the economic system of
Sparta was at once thrown out of gear. During the war, the
state might find occupation and some sort of subsistence for the
expropriated lot-holders, but after the battle of Mantinea (362)
it became obvious that Messenia was not likely to be reconquered.
Spartans who had no economic basis at home must earn their
livelihood as mercenary soldiers abroad. Emigration, formerly a
capital offence, now became a common practice, and the law for-
bidding alienation of allotments was modified, presumably with
the object of making emigration easier.

The free circulation of money in Sparta must have begun by
the end of the fourth century, for, in the first half of the third,
King Areus actually issued a currency stamped with his own name.
Evidently, by the time of Agis, the " Lycurgan " system was but
a memory.[3] More and more the poorer Spartans allowed themselves to be bought out by their wealthier neighbours; estates
increased in size as they diminished in number.

Thus it had come about that, whereas in 370 there may have
been between two and three thousand Spartan citizens, the number
had been reduced by 243 to seven hundred, of whom " perhaps
one hundred " still held allotments or landed property (Plut.
Agis 5): "The mass of the (Spartan) population (i.e., the
remaining six hundred) sat idle in the city without means and
without political rights, feebly and spiritlessly warding off
hostilities from without and always watching for some crisis to
bring about a change in their present circumstances."

Agis had declined to use force against his opponents, but
Cleomenes approached the problem with no such scruples. However, his revolution of 227 B.C. cost only fifteen lives. The
constitution became something very like a dictatorship, or, as the
Greeks said, a tyranny, which enabled Cleomenes to put in

[3] How the regulations respecting the syssitia were evaded in the
days of Areus and Acrotatus is described by Phylarchus, cited in
Athenaeus [F.H.G. i, p. 346].

operation the essential part, if not the whole, of Agis' proposals.[4] By promotion from the perioeci and naturalisation of foreigners he raised the citizen body to four thousand, debts being cancelled and private ownership of land abolished.   Thus the two major parts of the programme which appears among the Greeks as the pale counterpart of modern communism were actually carried out.[5]

Yet Cleomenes was more like a Fascist than a communist. He was not concerned to organize a model community of prosperous citizens.   Sparta must have an adequate population, because she was to resume her ascendancy in Peloponnesus.   Her citizens, like their ancestors, must live by the state because, like their ancestors, they were to be full-time servants of the state; and the state was to employ them in war and government alone. The restoration of the " Lycurgan " discipline could mean nothing else.   Under the new *régime* the Spartans, as Plutarch says, " gave a great display of courage and discipline in their effort to win back the hegemony of Hellas for Lacedaemon and to recover Peloponnesus " (*Cleom.* 18).   But Cleomenes knew no argument but force.

By introducing new blood into the body politic and at the same time awakening the old Spartan ideals, he saved an exhausted aristocracy (for the Spartans were nothing else) from the ruin that awaited it.

But at this time distress was prevalent in other cities than Sparta.   In cities where men bought and sold, paid wages and drew them, the free labourer and artisan were stricken by an economic disease which the patience and discernment of some modern scholars have revealed to us.[6]

From a study of the temple accounts of Delos between the years 314 and 250 in comparison with various fourth-century accounts, especially those of Eleusis in 329, Tarn has reached the conclusion that

> " the position of the working man in the third century at
> Delos was a very bad one; the unskilled easily fall below

[4] Plutarch does not say whether he adopted Agis' scheme (*Ag.* 8) of redistributing the territories of the perioeci into 15,000 lots.

[5] The others were confiscation of personal property by the state and the liberation of slaves to ensure the success of the revolution.   In Sparta, however, nothing was done for the helots.

[6] See *The Hellenistic Age* (p. 108): The Social Question in the Third Century.   In this article Tarn acknowledges obligations to Glotz.

the bare level of subsistence, and the skilled are very hard
put to it to bring up even one or two children . . . so far
as the island world can inform us the third century on the
social side was getting into a very unhealthy state; the
poor were getting poorer and the gap between rich and
poor was widening . . .   From 400 to 329 wages rose
with the rise of prices; after Alexander's time wages seem
to lose all relation with prices and fall while prices still
rise."

Tarn refers to no less than four disturbances in the islands—at
Naxos, Amorgos, Ceos, Syros—arising from economic causes, in
all of which the suzerain power, Egypt or Macedon, was compelled to intervene.   We have some evidence that similar conditions prevailed in Peloponnesus.

Among the most influential citizens of Megalopolis was the poet
Cercidas.   At some crisis in the city's history, perhaps in 235,
when Lydiades resigned the tyranny, perhaps in 217, when civil
dissension broke out over the rebuilding of the city (which
Cleomenes destroyed in 223), he was called in as lawgiver.   At
the battle of Sellasia he commanded a contingent.   In politics he
was a close adherent of Aratus; in morals he ranked as a supporter
of the Cynic school.   Among recently discovered fragments of his
poems[7] is one that speaks of the unjust distribution of wealth
among mankind.   The poet inveighs against misers and spend-
thrifts; what hinders Providence, he asks, from emptying such
men of their swinish wealth to bestow it on the poor for their
little outgoings?   How can we adore as gods beings who neither
hear nor regard us?   Since it is vain to look for redress to
Heaven, be the task our own to heal sickness and relieve poverty.
At the conclusion of the poem the papyrus is damaged, but enough
is legible to make it pretty certain that the closing lines contained
a warning of what would happen " if the wind changed "; then
would the rich perforce disgorge the gifts of fortune.

    This might seem commonplace enough were it not for the
poet's political record, and the fact, attested by Tarn, that prior
to Cercidas " there is only one doubtful reference in Greek
literature to poverty as a matter for compassion."

    Cercidas, however, is not alone in testifying to the unrest of

---

[7] Powell, *Collectanea Alexandrina* (1925), p. 203 [frg. 4].   See also
Powell and Barber, *New Chapters in Greek Literature* (first series).

the time. In Teles' diatribe, *On Exile*, which shortly after Agis' death he delivered in Megara (at the time a member of the Achaean League), we find the Spartan scheme of social reconstruction referred to in terms which show how much interest it had aroused beyond the bounds of Sparta.[8] Teles' reference confirms what Plutarch tells us of the impression which Agis produced when he marched his army through the territory of Achaea (*Ag.* 14) to join Aratus at the isthmus : —

> " The rich Achaeans indeed did not like his revolutionary proceedings, fearing they might become an incitement and example to the populace everywhere."

These fears were realised fifteen years later when, under Cleomenes, Sparta was no longer their ally but their enemy.

> " Unrest had fallen on the Achaeans and the cities resolved to revolt, the populace in the various places having conceived the hope of division of lands and abolition of debts." [9]

Just as in the islands the worst sufferers from the economic depression were the urban artisans, so in Peloponnesus it is in the cities, Corinth, Argos, Pellene, Sicyon, that we find evidence of discontent. In the country districts the strain was probably less severe. If the Peloponnesian farmers still cultivated their own lands as in the fifth century, when Thucydides (1. 101) described them as αὐτουργοί (and there is no reason to assume any change in the tenure of land during the interval), they would naturally be less affected than townsfolk by fall in wages or rise in prices.

The urban masses were distressed and discontented, and political thinkers had drawn up a programme of social reform, but there was no organised movement, revolutionary or constitutional, among the people to get changes carried out. While in the fourth century there was certainly something of the social-revolutionary leader in Euphron of Sicyon (368 B.C.), the third-century tyrants in Peloponnesus from Iseas of Cerynea to

---

[8] τὸ δὲ μέτοικον εἶναι ὄνειδος ἡγούμεθα. Λακεδαιμόνιοι οὐδὲν τῶν τοιούτων ὄνειδος ἡγοῦνται ἀλλὰ τὸν μὲν μετασχόντα τῆς ἀγωγῆς καὶ ἐμμείναντα κἂν ξένος κἂν ἐξ εἵλωτος ὁμοίως τοῖς ἀρίστοις τιμῶσι: *Teletis Reliquiae*, ed. Hense, p. 20. As the speech was delivered *after* Agis' death, Teles must have ignored the counter-revolution at Sparta.

[9] *Cleom.* 17, 5.

Lydiades of Megalopolis were a quite different sort of people. Again, in the constituent cities of the Achaean League, the democratic forms of the constitution might have been used to enact a system of social reform, but there is no trace of any attempt so to use them. The Achaeans had always been content with the middle-class "liberalism" of which Aratus was the typical representative.

It cannot be said that the poor in the Achaean cities became class-conscious until repeated disaster on the field of battle had broken the spell of the national idea. It was only then that they began to hope that in their enemy the King of Sparta they might find a deliverer out of their distresses.

Cleomenes' Attitude to the Social Problem outside Laconia. It is recorded by Plutarch, here evidently echoing Phylarchus, that Cleomenes promised the Achaeans that "he would do many good things to the cities" (*Arat.* 38). This phraseology is familiar to us from inscriptions.[10] It is a piece of common form which may mean anything or nothing. In the mouth of Cleomenes it meant nothing for the cause of the poor. Neither in Argos nor in Corinth did he make the slightest effort to bring on the social revolution. In Argos, this proved disastrous for himself. The populace was easily persuaded to break away from the Spartan cause, while the issue between Cleomenes and the king of Macedon was still undecided. They were displeased, Plutarch tells us, "because he had not brought about the expected abolition of debts" (*Cleom.* 20). Yet he had held Argos for more than nine months. But, in fact, there is no evidence that Cleomenes, any more than Aratus, either had or professed to have any social policy for Peloponnesus[11]: and because nothing was done in the third century to ameliorate the lot of the poor, the problem became

---

[10] Thus in IG. 7, 506, Ptolemy I is πολλῶν καὶ μεγάλων ἀγαθῶν αἴτιος τοῖς τε νησιώταις καὶ τοῖς ἄλλοις Ἕλλησι. In Rehm, *Milet.* iii 3, No. 138, he is πολλῶν ἀγαθῶν παραίτιος: cf. also IG. xii, 1291.

[11] In *Cleom.* 16, 7 the most serious charge brought by Aratus (in his *Memoirs* doubtless) against Cleomenes is said to have been ἀναίρεσις πλούτου καὶ πενίας ἐπανόρθωσις. This, however, refers to what Cleomenes effected *at Sparta*. Aratus no doubt impressed upon his supporters that what Cleomenes had done at home he might repeat elsewhere, but that is no proof that Cleomenes contemplated anything of the sort.

more desperate in the second, and is to be ranked among the causes of the loss of Greek independence.

The Antecedents of the Cleomenic War. When Leonidas died (235 B.C.)[12] his son Cleomenes, still little more than a boy, became sole king of Sparta. Agis' brother, Archidamus, who should have been his colleague, was in exile. Sparta was ruled by the ephors, and as their policy was purely passive Spartan history remains a blank till 229.

The Cleomenic war was of Cleomenes' own making. The ephors had no more desire for war than Aratus. They were, however, men of no great foresight or capacity, and were played upon by the king, who aimed at goading the Achaeans into a declaration of war.

Lydiades, it is true, was just as eager for war as the Spartan king. As early as 234, when appointed strategos for the first time, he "wanted to invade Laconia forthwith," i.e., to declare war on Sparta. But though Lydiades was in office, Aratus was in power, and there was no declaration of war either in 234 or in 232, when Lydiades was elected a second time in spite of Aratus' opposition, or in 230, when he held the strategia for the third and last time.[13]

During this year indeed the strength of Aratus' position even when out of office was made manifest. A quarrel arose between the two leaders over the admission of Argos into the League. Aratus before leaving office had almost completed preliminary arrangements with the tyrant Aristomachus; but when Lydiades became strategos he induced Aristomachus to apply for admission through himself, alleging that Aratus was "ill-disposed and irreconcilable always towards tyrants." Eager to reap where Aratus had sown, he did not shrink from misrepresentation to gain some personal credit. Aratus countered him by inducing the synodos to refuse the Argive petition, which next year was unanimously granted on his own proposal (*Arat.* 35).

[12] Or 237 acc. to Tarn C.A.H. vii, p. 753.
[13] *Arat.* 30, 8, στρατειὰν παρήγγελλεν (conative impf.). It may be observed that in *Cleom.* 3 Plut. has reproduced a passage of Phylarchus in which it is insinuated that the real aggressor was not Cleomenes but Aratus.

In 229 Cleomenes managed to take the first step towards war. We have seen that the Arcadian towns of Orchomenos and Mantinea, which were members of the Achaean League for a few years after 235, had been allowed to transfer themselves to the Aetolian. In 229, the Leagues were allies in name, but friends no longer. The Aetolians, having made a separate peace with Antigonus Doson, the new ruler of Macedon,[14] now gave the Spartans to understand that Orchomenos and Mantinea, as well as Tegea and Caphyae,[15] were theirs for the taking. The ephors could not resist such a temptation. The territory of the four towns, Tegea, Mantinea, Orchomenos, Caphyae, formed a corridor stretching northwards from the Laconian border half-way to the Gulf of Corinth, and separating Megalopolis from Argos. Their acquisition would immensely improve Sparta's chances in a war with the Achaeans.

According to Polybius, the Aetolians allowed Cleomenes to seize these cities because they regarded with jealousy the progress of the Achaean League. The new transfer—for such it was in fact—was obviously made with the approval of the majority in the cities concerned. What they hoped to gain by thus changing their allegiance is obscure; they were imbued with the particularist spirit which kept cities at enmity with their immediate neighbours, and cherished the memory of ancient feuds.

Confronted with this new danger, Aratus and his colleagues defined their policy: "to begin war on none but to resist the attacks of the Lacedaemonians" (Pol. 2. 46).

Emboldened by success, these now advanced a stage further. Cleomenes persuaded the ephors to allow him to fortify the temple of Athena in the district of Belbina, which lay on the border between Laconia and Megalopolis, and was claimed by both Spartans and Achaeans.[16] At this time it was held by Megalopolis in virtue of a decision given by an arbitration court in the time of Philip II of Macedon.[17]

Aratus retorted by an attempt upon Orchomenos and Mantinea which failed because his friends within the walls were afraid to

---

[14] Pol. 2, 45: Αἰτωλοὶ . . . ἀπετόλμησαν Ἀντιγόνῳ τε . . . καὶ Κλεομένει . . . κοινωνεῖν καὶ συμπλέκειν ἀμφοτέροις ἅμα τὰς χεῖρας. But in fact with Antigonus they merely concluded peace.   [15] Pol. 2, 46 : Caphyae, *Cleom.* 4.

[16] Cleomenes' seizure of Belbina came after the acquisition of the corridor towns : κατὰ τοὺς ἑξῆς χρόνους (Polyb. 2, 46). In *C.A.H.* vii, p. 753, Tarn reverses the order.   [17] Livy 38, 34.

play their part. The behaviour of the ephors at this point showed a strange instability of purpose. They recalled Cleomenes, but when Aratus shortly afterwards captured Caphyae they sent him out again. He thereupon seized Methydrium, a place a little to the west of Mantinea, and then, turning eastwards, raided Argolis.[18] It is clear that the ephors' control over the king was becoming weaker and weaker. His last activities were intended to provoke the Argives and Megalopolitans into forcing the hand of the League. This object was soon attained.

In May, 228, Aristomachus of Argos became strategos, and, it appears, summoned a syncletos, which declared war on Sparta.[19] One might have expected Aristomachus in concert with Lydiades to seize the opportunity, and get the campaign started before Aratus, who was away in Athens, could return and hamper their policy. On the contrary, it was Aratus whom Aristomachus consulted, and, although he protested by letter against the strategos' proposal, the latter summoned him home. Aratus accordingly returned and took part in the campaign. Aristomachus' insistence on his presence was a tribute to his dominating influence; he felt that without him he could do nothing. He was soon to find that with him he could do nothing either. It seems that at Aratus' instance the campaign had been diverted from an invasion of Laconia to an attack on the cities of the corridor,[20] but when on the way twenty thousand Achaeans found themselves confronted at Pallantium by Cleomenes with a force of five thousand, Aristomachus under Aratus' tutelage threw away a unique chance of finishing the war before it was properly begun.

There were naturally loud protests from the " young bloods " of the army (*Cleom.* 4, 9), and Lydiades raised the matter at the autumn synodos. Some months later (January, 227) Aratus and

---

[18] *Cleom.* 4.

[19] Pol. 2, 46: οἱ προεστῶτες (= δημιουργοί) συναθροίσαντες τοὺς Ἀχαιοὺς ἔκριναν μετὰ τῆς βουλῆς ἀναλαμβάνειν φανερῶς τὴν πρὸς τοὺς Λακεδαιμονίους ἀπεχθείαν. If Beloch is correct in postulating a stated meeting of the synodos about the end of May, it was to this meeting that the proposed war with Sparta was submitted. Those who admit only two regular meetings must assume that Aristomachus had a special meeting called. The synodos (βουλή) having approved the declaration of war, two courses were open, (1) the synodos might leave it to the army to ratify or reject the declaration of war, or (2) a syncletos might be summoned for that purpose (see Sect. 7).

[20] See note on *Arat.* 35, 7. The suggestion is due to Walbank.

Lydiades met at the polls. The question at stake was one of divergent methods, but "personalities" as usual played their part. One might infer that the passage in the *Aratus* in which Lydiades is compared to a cuckoo which had been a hawk and might become a hawk again, was a purple patch from an election speech, which Aratus afterwards inserted in his memoirs.[21] Aratus won the election, becoming strategos for the tenth time[22]; Lydiades received the command of the cavalry.

Aratus could now put in practice his policy of caution. He started with a reasonable chance of success. If the Achaean generals had possessed the ability to prevent Cleomenes from forcing their hand, and the Achaean people the endurance needed for a war of attrition, the Spartans might in the course of a few campaigns have grown weary of the struggle; notoriously ineffective in besieging cities, they could gain a decision only by victory in the field. But Lydiades was responsible for one disaster by refusing to adhere loyally to Aratus' policy, and neither Aratus himself nor his successor Hyperbatas (226–5) was a match for Cleomenes in generalship. He could make them fight when they did not want to fight, and then defeat them. Finally, the tidings of the social revolution at Sparta (227 B.C.) were not without effect in weakening the power of the Achaeans to resist.

The Campaigns of 227–6. Aratus began by an invasion of Elis,[23] capturing Lasion (*Cleom.* 14, 5); but on his way home Cleomenes met him near Mount Lycaeum, forced him to fight, and defeated him.

At Lycaeum, as at Phylace six years previously, Aratus was "missing, believed killed," and the trick—for trick it surely was—succeeded once again. It enabled him to swoop down suddenly upon Mantinea and capture the town, which, after an Achaean garrison had been installed, and a reasonable number of well-disposed persons placed on the roll of citizens, was duly re-admitted into the League.[24] The Mantineans had been considerately treated, but the Spartan faction in the town, as the event showed, refused to be reconciled.

---

[21] *Arat.* 30.

[22] δωδέκατον in *Arat.* 35, 7, is an error. (See note.)

[23] *Cleom.* 5, 1. As Walbank (p. 81) points out, "Elis is the natural base for an Aetolian attack in the Peloponnesus and affords *via* Messenia means of communication with Sparta."

[24] *Arat.* 36 (where see note), *Cleom.* 5, Pol. 2, 58.

So far, Cleomenes had made no real headway. He had gained, it is true, one substantial victory, but the precious corridor in Arcadia was closing up. The loss of Caphyae and Mantinea left Orchomenos isolated, with Achaean territory all around her. At home the ephors began to be critical, and Cleomenes " thinking that the authority of their office would be weakened if the King-ship became balanced and complete," recalled Agis' brother Archidamus from his exile in Messenia. It was, however, of no avail, for the unfortunate man was murdered on his return by the same faction that had compassed the death of his brother[25]; while people who did not like Cleomenes gave out that the whole thing was his doing.[26]

It was only by bribery that Cleomenes gained permission from the ephors to resume the campaign. This time he captured Leuctra, a fortress near Megalopolis. The Achaeans hurried to the spot, and Aratus, engaging the enemy at Ladoceia, drove them back to their camp, but refused to advance further. Lydiades now, in defiance of Aratus' orders, led his cavalry into action. The locality should have been familiar to him, but he had lost his judgment as well as his temper. When his troopers had become entangled in a place " full of vines, trenches, and walls," Cleomenes launched his mercenaries upon the disordered Achaeans. The battle which had begun with a victory ended in a rout, for the survivors of the cavalry fled back to the main body and threw it into confusion. Lydiades himself had fallen. Aratus' unwillingness to support him produced the disagreeable impression that he had purposely abandoned a political opponent.[27] At the next meeting of the synodos (autumn, 227) the anger of the people showed itself in a resolution to withhold further supplies (Ar. 37 n.). This was unreasonable, for Lydiades had perished by adding rashness to insubordination; and Aratus' Fabian policy had been endorsed by the people at the last election.

Aratus' resentment at this " vote of censure," though at first it made him inclined to resign office, quickly cooled. He finished his year with a small success. Still operating in the corridor Caphyae–Tegea, he captured Cleomenes' step-father Megistonous

[25] *Cleom.* 5.

[26] So Polyb. 5; 37. I have followed Cary (p. 404) in accepting the *Cleomenes* version (Phylarchus), rejecting that of Polybius, which probably comes from Aratus' memoirs.

[27] *Arat.* 35; *Cleom.* 6.

in a fight near Orchomenos, in which three hundred perished on
the Spartan side.[28]   The probable date is February, 226.

Cleomenes, however, shortly after his victory at Ladoceia went
home to make the revolution (*Cleom.* 7).   Henceforth there was
but one party and one policy at Sparta.

Events of 226–5.   Fortune now turned decisively against the
Achaeans.   At Mantinea the Spartan faction rose against the
garrison and called in their friends (Plut. *Ar.* 39; *Cleom.* 14;
Pol. 2. 58. 4).   From Mantinea, Cleomenes, marching northwards, invaded the territory of old Achaea, intending either to
force a decision or to bring Aratus' policy into discredit.
According to Plutarch (*Cleom.* 14), he found the Achaean army
under Hyperbatas encamped near Hecatombaeum, a fortress south
of the city of Dyme, and actually took up a position between the
army and the town, whence he turned upon the Achaeans and dealt
them a crushing blow.[29]   He then recovered Lasion and handed
it back to the Eleans (autumn, 226).   There was no further
fighting, for the Achaeans knew themselves beaten; negotiations
for peace were opened without delay.

A conference was called to meet at Argos,[30] and the Spartan
terms were enunciated: Cleomenes to receive the hegemony of
the League for life; land and prisoners to be restored to the
Achaeans.   What the hegemony implied in the mouth of
Cleomenes is not immediately obvious, but Tarn (C.A.H. vii,
p. 756) is probably correct in explaining: —

> "He meant to be General for life, as Antigonus was of
> Thessaly, and to make the League the kernel of his new
> confederacy with Sparta playing Macedonia's part."

The conference failed to meet at the appointed time, for
Cleomenes had fallen ill, but the truce continued, and the
Spartan proposals were favourably considered by the Achaeans
at the meeting, which Cleomenes should have attended (probably
in spring of 225).   Aratus opposed them, " but the people refused
to listen to him, being intimidated by the boldness of Cleomenes;

---

[28] *Arat.* 38; 1 n.   At this point the *Aratus* completely abandons the
chronological order.

[29] Walbank thinks that Hyperbatas trapped Cleomenes between Dyme
and his own army; but the king preferred to fight rather than retreat
by the coast road.

[30] εἰς Λέρναν, *Cleom.* 15, is an error; cf. *Arat.* 39, and note thereon.

they even justified the claim of the Lacedaemonians in seeking to organise Peloponnesus according to its traditional form" (*Cleom.* 16). Two years before the Achaeans had voted war with Sparta, but their military disasters or the glamour of Spartan "communism" had taught them to see the issues in a new light. This abortive conference is ignored altogether in the *Aratus*.

Before the date fixed for the resumption of the conference with Cleomenes came round Aratus, strange to say, had regained sufficient influence to raise the question whether Cleomenes was to bring his army into Argos or to leave it outside the city. Aratus proposed that he should enter Argos with three hundred men; if he distrusted the Achaeans they would give him hostages.[31]

The peace party could hardly insist that Cleomenes was entitled to bring into the city whatever forces he liked; but Cleomenes, whether influenced by pride or policy, professed himself insulted, and abandoned the whole negotiation. From Lerna, where he had halted on his way to the conference, he sent a declaration of war, not to Argos but to the more distant Aegium, and following on the heels of his herald invaded Achaea a second time, when he took Pellene with the complicity of the citizens.[32] Caphyae was also lost to the Achaeans about the same time.[33] The result of the capture of Pellene was to "carry the Arcadian corridor to the Corinthian Gulf, splitting the League in two."[34] Then he turned east, and during the Nemean truce of 225 took Argos by surprise, aided by the treachery of the ex-tyrant Aristomachus.[35]

The Achaean strategos at this time was Timoxenus, who had been chosen in January, 225, when Aratus, though it was "his turn," refused office.[36] Aratus was accused of abandoning his country in her distress, but in fact he was preparing to call in Macedon to redress the balance in Peloponnesus.

The Appeal to Antigonus Doson. In condemning Aratus for recalling the Macedonians to Peloponnesus (*Arat.* 38; cf. *Cleom.* 16) Plutarch adds:—

> "And yet he leaves no word unspoken in explaining the necessity for so doing."

---

[31] *Arat.* 39. This account is preferable to that of *Cleom.* 17. See note *ad loc.*

[32] *Arat.* 39; *Cleom.* 17.　　[33] Pol. 2; 52, 2.　　[34] Walbank, p. 96.

[35] Cf. Pol. 2; 60, 6.　　　　　[36] *Cleom.* 15: cf. *Arat.* 38, 1.

The explanation, however, he omits to record, and justifies the omission by remarking—

> "Polybius says that a long time previously and before the necessity arose . . . Aratus had private conversations with Antigonus, and put forward the Megalopolitans to ask the Achaeans to call Antigonus in . . . A similar account of the transaction is given by Phylarchus, in whom, without Polybius' testimony, it would not be right to place absolute confidence."

There was evidently some discrepancy between what Plutarch read in Aratus and in Polybius.[37] The latter actually tells us that

> "Aratus was often forced to speak and act towards the public in contradiction to his true sentiments . . . and consequently there are some particulars which he did not commit even to his commentaries."

Polybius, as a member of the governing class at Megalopolis, would naturally have access to unpublished information about the negotiations with Antigonus. The design, he informs us, of calling in the Macedonians first occurred to Aratus

> " after the war had lasted some time and Cleomenes had revolutionised the constitution of the country and was conducting the war with extraordinary skill and boldness,"

i.e., in the late summer of 227, when the Achaeans had been defeated at Ladoceia (Megalopolis), the battle where Lydiades was slain.

In the circumstances, as Aratus had the wit to see, any such suggestion coming from him would be likely to produce a bad impression. Hence he left the introduction of the proposal to his Megalopolitan friends, Cercidas the poet and Nicophanes, who carried a resolution in the local assembly to send a deputation to the League (presumably at the next synodos, autumn, 227), with the object of obtaining permission to open conversations with Antigonus. Permission was granted, and the king received the two Megalopolitans in audience.

[37] Pol. 2; 47.

They stated their case thus (2. 49): There is a danger that Aetolia may become the active ally of Sparta; this would result in the subjugation of the Achaeans; and the next step might be a combination of Spartans, Aetolians, Achaeans, and Boeotians against Macedon.   In reply, Antigonus wrote to the people of Megalopolis offering them his assistance if the Achaeans agreed. This offer was considered by the League—perhaps at the spring synodos of 226—and after a discussion Aratus rose and urged that they should continue to carry on the war by their own efforts and have recourse to their friends only when they had tried their own resources to the uttermost.   This policy was accepted (2. 50). In the next chapter Polybius continues—

> "But when Ptolemy began to furnish Cleomenes with supplies . . . and when the Achaeans had suffered three defeats at Lycaeum, at Ladoceia, and a third time decisively at a place called Hecatombaeum, where their whole forces had been engaged, no further delay was possible, and they were compelled to appeal unanimously to Antigonus."

So, according to Polybius, the private negotiations with Antigonus began after the battle of Ladoceia (late summer of 227), and the public decision to ask for his intervention was taken some time after the battle of Hecatombaeum (late summer, 226).

Ferrabino,[38] however, is convinced that Polybius, in seeking to combine what he had heard at Megalopolis with what he had read in Aratus' commentaries, got the story wrong.   It was not in 227, when the Achaeans had already twice suffered defeat, but in 229, after Cleomenes had taken over from Aetolia the towns in the Arcadian corridor, that the first negotiations with Antigonus began. Ferrabino argues that the Achaean fear of Aetolian intervention had passed away by 227.

But we must remember that the statements attributed to Cercidas and his colleague were an *ad hominem* argument addressed to the king of Macedon.   If it be granted that the motive of the Aetolians in their benevolent neutrality towards Sparta was the humiliation of the Achaean League, it might fairly be argued that the danger of their active intervention was not yet over, for after Ladoceia in 227 the Achaeans were not yet humiliated. Suppose that the tide of Spartan success were checked, and that

[38] P. 260.

Cleomenes proved unable by himself to subdue the Achaeans, it was still quite likely that the Aetolians would enter the lists themselves in support of Sparta.

But the most effective argument against Ferrabino's hypothesis of an appeal to Doson in 229 lies in the condition of the Macedonian kingdom in that year. There would have been little use then in appealing for Macedonian aid, since in 229–8, as Cary remarks,

> "Doson was struggling, like Philip II in 359, against Balkan invaders and domestic strife; it required several years before he was strong enough to assist the Achaean League,[39]

while another critic has pointed out the inconsistency between the alleged appeal to Antigonus in 229 and the liberation of Piraeus from Antigonus, in which Aratus was engaged that very same year. Ferrabino has convinced himself that Aratus cunningly contrived to have it both ways[40]; but can it be doubted that if Antigonus had been prepared to act at all in Greece in 229 it would have been to secure his fortresses in Attica? Polybius' chronology is not to be discarded in favour of an hypothesis itself involving a paradox.

On the other hand, Polybius' statement that, after the Achaean disaster at Hecatombaeum, " delay in settling with Antigonus was no longer possible," must be taken in a qualified sense; for from Plutarch we know that the first thing the Achaeans did after the disaster was to ask the Spartan king to negotiate with them (*Cleom.* 15; *Arat.* 39); and that the armistice continued until Cleomenes, offended at the preliminary conditions proposed for the second conference (c. June, 225), renewed the war some nine or ten months after Hecatombaeum.

Only when relations with Cleomenes were broken off could the Achaeans publicly approve an alliance with Macedon—what-

[39] *C.R.* xlviii (1934), p. 37.
[40] "E poiche la liberazione di Atene ci riusci datata nel giugno 228, concluderemo che alla liberazione di Atene dal re Macedone, cui Arato contribui, son parallele le trattative, fra il re Macedone e i Megalopolitani, che Arato suggeri: conclusione importantissima nel rispetto politico." Ferrabino, p. 262.

ever Aratus may have been doing unofficially to prep.ire the way. But now, when they had virtually rejected peace with Sparta on Cleomenes' terms, there was nothing left but alliance with Macedon on Antigonus' terms. One may suppose that, having driven Cleomenes to break up the conference, Aratus came forward straight away with proposals for a Macedonian alliance, and that, as no one had anything else to suggest, the decree was carried "unanimously," dissentients remaining silent, or having withdrawn from the syncletos.

Aratus now sent his son to Antigonus " to confirm the agreement." The question whether he was acting officially or not depends upon the time when the younger Aratus was sent; before the end of July his father had become " strategos autocrator."

But the difficulty still remained that Antigonus demanded Acrocorinth, and the Achaeans, so long as Corinth continued in the League, could not concede the demand. Things were now at a standstill or, in the official language of Polybius (2; 57), the determination of the matter was postponed to investigate the question of securities to be given to the king. Meanwhile Cleomenes was making an unopposed progress through the cities. Timoxenus (elected strategos in January, 225) was helpless. During the Nemean truce Cleomenes captured Argos, and almost immediately afterwards (early August) Corinth seceded. Aratus and Antigonus could now come to terms.

But it is impossible to sketch the course of the Cleomenic war in its later developments until we have first considered the question, When did it end ? What is the date of Sellasia ? and with the Sellasia problem is bound up the question of the Achaean strategos-list.

The Date of Sellasia. Writing in 1863, Freeman recommended the Sellasia problem " to the attention of professed chronologers." The chronologers, however, could come to no agreement, and for nearly sixty years the issue between the dates 222 and 221 remained undecided, until at last an accumulation of evidence from Egyptian sources rendered the later date untenable.

After the battle, we are told, Cleomenes took refuge with Ptolemy Euergetes, hoping that Egyptian intervention might some day restore him to his throne. At Alexandria he gradually made such a favourable impression on the king that he promised his help, and meantime began to pay him (ἐδίδου) a yearly pension, most of which went in charity (*Cleom.* 32). Euergetes, then, must have lived for an appreciable time after Cleomenes' arrival in Egypt. But as it is now ascertained from Egyptian sources that he died not later than July, 221, and as Sellasia was fought in summer—Polybius (2. 65) records that Antigonus began his final campaign θέρους ἐνισταμένου — it follows that it was not fought in 221.[41]

On the other hand, if the battle was fought in 222, how did it come about that Antigonus Doson, a week or ten days after his victory, went to Argos for the Nemean Games (Polyb. 2, 70)? It is well known that these games were held in the *uneven* years B.C. This consideration has led Ferrabino[42] to conclude that the true date of Sellasia is July, 223; and he shows that, by assuming Antigonus to have conducted a winter campaign, January to March, 224, followed by two ordinary campaigns in 224 and 223, it is possible to work in the facts known to us from Polybius and Plutarch.

Ferrabino's argument would be difficult to controvert—for winter campaigns were not unknown in the third century—were it not that Polybius (4, 35), writing of the early spring of 219, affirms that the Spartans had been without a king " for almost three years," whereas if Sellasia belongs to the summer of 223 the period is three years and eight months.

Either, then, Polybius made a mistake in his calculation or else the Nemean festival of 223 was not held till July, 222.

While there is no reason to think that any of the Panhellenic festivals had been omitted hitherto, we know that the Nemean games were put off for some months in B.C. 195.[43] Nor should we disregard the statement of Polybius (5. 106), that after the peace of Naupactus (217) "the Achaeans, as soon as they had put an end to the (social) war (τὸν πόλεμον),returning to their customs and regular habits . . . restored the traditional sacrifices, games (πανηγύρεις), and other religious observances established in the several states. For in most of them these practices had almost passed into oblivion by reason of the continuance of the late wars (τῶν προγεγονότων πολέμων)."

In the latter sentence Polybius appears to include the Cleomenic as well as the social war; in any case the passage shows that between 220 and 217 many festivals had been omitted.

---

[41] Cf. Dinsmoor, pp. 108, 487, 508.　　　　[42] P. 268.

[43] Livy, 34, 41. The Panathenaea were omitted altogether in 278.

Hence there is nothing surprising in the hypothesis that the Nemean games were postponed in 223, and indeed there were adequate grounds for the postponement. In 225 Cleomenes had captured Argos during the Nemean truce. When, some months later, the city revolted against the Spartans, its new government would naturally feel disinclined to take any risk till Cleomenes was finally disposed of; and the reasonableness of such an attitude becomes still more apparent when we remember that in the winter preceding Sellasia the Spartans captured Megalopolis by surprise.

Next summer, however, the situation was completely changed. The long war had ended in victory; peace was restored; Cleomenes had fled from Peloponnesus. The festival which it was too dangerous to celebrate last year could now be held under the happiest conditions in the presence of the king whom all Achaea delighted to honour.

An assumption of this kind presents less difficulties than the assumption that Polybius made a mistake about the date of Sellasia.

The Strategos-list. Given Sellasia in 222, we have two alternative arrangements (proposed by Beloch and Tarn respectively) for the strategos-list during the years 226–5, 225–4, and 224–3.

The facts to be accounted for are : —

1. Hyperbatas (strategos for 226–5) was succeeded by Timoxenus (*vice* the unwilling Aratus)[44];

2. On the occasion of the secession of Corinth (*Arat.* 40) the Corinthians commanded Ἀράτῳ τῷ στρατηγοῦντι καὶ τοῖς Ἀχαιοῖς to withdraw from the city (Pol. 2. 52).

3. When Argos revolted from Cleomenes (an event which, given Sellasia in 222, must be assigned to 224), the Achaeans marched to the help of the Argives " with Timoxenus the strategos" (Pol. 2, 53).

It would seem that if the strategoi succeeded one another in the regular manner we have four strategoi, Hyperbatas, Timoxenus, Aratus, and Timoxenus again, for the three years, 226–5, 225–4, and 224–3.

[44] *Arat.* 38: *Cleom.* 15.

This was the difficulty Beloch had to face when he became convinced that Sellasia was fought in the summer of 222.

His solution is to assume that Hyperbatas, if he was not killed at Hecatombaeum, resigned his office after that disaster, whereupon Timoxenus was appointed in his stead for the remainder of the year. Timoxenus was succeeded by Aratus in May, 225, and during Aratus' strategia Corinth seceded. In May, 224, Timoxenus entered office once more, and about July marched with the Achaeans to Argos.

Among the objections which might be urged against this scheme, the fatal one is that we have no warrant for dividing the year 226–5 between Hyperbatas and Timoxenus. It is true that if a strategos died or resigned when in office, his strategia by law devolved upon his predecessor. It is true that Hyperbatas' predecessor was Aratus. It is true that on one occasion, the date of which Plutarch has not precisely defined, Aratus declined to be elected strategos. But Plutarch's language clearly suggests that what Aratus refused was not the latter half of Hyperbatas' strategia, but the "turn" ($\tau\acute{\alpha}\xi\iota\varsigma$) which for twenty years past had fallen to him every second year.

Hence Tarn's arrangement (C.A.H. vii, p. 863) is to be preferred. Unlike Beloch he has not based his scheme on an unproved and improbable hypothesis, but relies on Aratus' election as strategos autocrator (*Arat.* 41), which for Beloch is devoid of any special significance. In Tarn's view Aratus was strategos autocrator not only for part of 225–4, but likewise for 224–3, 223–2, and 222–1, the rule requiring the lapse of a year before re-election being obviously inapplicable to this extraordinary office.

Date of Aratus' Appointment as Strategos Autocrator. He received the office about the middle of July, 225—a fact which emerges from a comparison of *Arat.* 40, *Cleom.* 19, and Polybius 2. 52.

Aratus, having arrested and executed Sicyonians involved in treasonable activities, proceeded to Corinth to deal with traitors there in the same way (*Arat.* 40), and on his arrival received news of the loss of Argos (*Cleom.* 19). He quickly found that the hostile attitude of the Corinthian population made it impossible to carry out his intention. Instead, " the Corinthians " (i.e., the mob) summoned him to a meeting in the temple of Apollo.

Recognising that their object was to arrest or kill him as the preliminary to secession (πρὸ τῆς ἀποστάσεως), he led his horse to the door of the temple, but before the meeting was properly constituted quietly withdrew. Crossing the Agora, he climbed Acrocorinthus to exhort the Achaean commander to hold the fortress at all hazards, and then rode away to Sicyon (*Arat.* 40, *n.*).

In the light of this account, what are we to make of Polybius' statement (2; 52) that the Corinthians commanded "τῷ Ἀράτῳ τῷ στρατηγοῦντι καὶ τοῖς Ἀχαιοῖς" to withdraw from the city?

It is plain that the command was not conveyed by word of mouth to Aratus when in Corinth, but subsequently, through a herald sent to Sicyon; that by "the Achaeans" is meant the garrison in the citadel; and that the words τῷ στρατηγοῦντι indicate that Aratus was strategos of the League at the time. But as the Corinthian revolt occurred during Timoxenus' year, the inference is that Aratus when he went to Corinth was already strategos autocrator. Hence the bestowal of ἐξουσία ἀνυπεύθυνος with which Aratus is endowed in *Arat.* 40, and his appointment as strategos autocrator (ch. 41) were one and the same; the ecclesia which appointed him was doubtless summoned when the cavalry and mercenaries were recalled from Argos to Sicyon in order to prevent a revolutionary outbreak; whose withdrawal, we are told, gave Cleomenes the opportunity to enter Argos during the Nemean truce.[45]

The grounds for holding (with Tarn) that Aratus' office of strategos autocrator lasted to May, 221, are:—

1. that an emergency appointment might reasonably be expected to continue till the emergency was over—though it is quite possible that Aratus went through the form of re-election in January, 223 and 222;

---

[45] *Cleom.* 17, 7: Ferrabino (p. 264) without entering into the details of the problem comes to a similar conclusion. Tarn (*loc. cit.*) follows Plutarch in putting Aratus' appointment as strategos autocrator *after* his visit to Corinth, and hence has to explain Polybius' words τῷ στρατηγοῦντι as referring merely to a *de facto* command. By the gratuitous assumption that Aratus' appointment involved Timoxenus' retirement, he has to refer the words μετὰ Τιμοξένου τοῦ στρατηγοῦ to a *de facto* command also; but despite Polybius' inaccurate terminology in other respects, Tarn can adduce no evidence for his use of the word στρατηγός for any other Achaean commander except the στρατηγός of the League. There is no reason to suppose that Timoxenus did not retain office till the end of his term (May, 224).

2. that Aratus was censured for the execution of Aristomachus in 224, as well as for the treatment of Mantinea in 223, which suggests that he was in office at any rate during 224–222 (*Arat.* 45);

3. that on the hypothesis of three consecutive extraordinary strategiai from 224–221 the seventeen strategiai which Plutarch assigns to Aratus are accounted for.

We may, therefore, tabulate the strategos-list from 227 to 221 as follows : —

227–6. Aratus (tenth strategia).	224–3. Aratus xi ⎫
226–5. Hyperbatas.	223–2. Aratus xii ⎬ *Autocrator.*
225–4. Timoxenus (first).	222–1. Aratus xiii ⎭

(Aratus' appointment as strategos autocrator dates from July, 225.)

The strategos-list to 227. The earlier years, as Beloch has observed, cause no difficulty. A passage in Polybius[46] fixes the liberation of Corinth (which occurred in Aratus' second strategia) at mid-summer, 243. From several passages in Plutarch (*Arat.* 24. 38; *Cleom.* 15) we learn that Aratus was accustomed to hold office every second year. The first occasion on which this practice was abandoned was when he refused election in January, 225, and Timoxenus was appointed in his place. Within the period 245–227 inclusive we have ten uneven years, in each of which we conclude that Aratus entered upon a strategia.

The year 227–6 saw Aratus' capture of Mantinea, for Polybius (2, 57) puts it four years before the advent (παρουσία) of Antigonus. Since Antigonus arrived in Peloponnesus in 224, Polybius is evidently reckoning inclusively, for otherwise the capture of Mantinea would be in 228–227, when Aratus was not in office. Aratus' strategia was preceded by Aristomachus'. He in turn was preceded by Aratus, who this year (229–8) negotiated the entry of Argos into the League. Immediately before this came the last of Lydiades' three strategiai, the first being 234–3. Before Lydiades, only one even year B.C. can be filled; Beloch assigns 236–5 to Dioetas.

---

[46] See note on *Arat.* 18.

The years after Sellasia.   Neither is there any controversy about these years, which were filled as follows : —

Pol. 4. 7	...	221–220—Timoxenus ii.
4. 7	...	220–219—Aratus xiv.
4. 37	...	219–218—Aratus the Younger.
4. 82	...	218–217—Eperatus.
5. 91	...	217–216—Aratus xv.
5. 106	...	216–215—Timoxenus iii.
⎰ Plut. *Arat.* 48	...	215–214—Aratus xvi.
⎱ Pol. 7. 14	...	214–213—Strategos unknown.
Arat. 53	...	213–212—Aratus xvii.

Events from the secession of Corinth to the arrival of Antigonus in Peloponnesus.   Cleomenes had gained Corinth, but he realised that the path was thereby smoothed for alliance between the Achaeans and Macedon.   In his memoirs (cited in *Cleom.* 19) Aratus remarked that Cleomenes' joy at receiving the offer of Corinth was tempered not a little with mortification at his own escape.   He goes on to state that Cleomenes sent Megistonous to offer him a large sum of money for the surrender of Acrocorinthus, to which he replied with a *non possumus*.

Cleomenes then left Argos and secured the adherence of Troezen, Epidaurus, and Hermione before he entered Corinth (*Cleom.* 19, with which cf. *Arat.* 40 *ad fin.*).   He was unable to expel the Achaean garrison from the citadel, but constructed some fortifications to prevent them from raiding the city.

After a delay of some months, he sent another ambassador, Tritymallus the Messenian (the Tripylus of *Arat.* 41), to propose a joint occupation of Acrocorinth and a pension for Aratus of twelve talents per annum.   Rather than throw away the chances of a settlement, he was prepared to abate his claims and increase his bribe.   But Aratus was indifferent to money, and had no mind to concede the hegemony.

One might have supposed that after the secession of Corinth Aratus would have forthwith called a syncletos and carried through the arrangement with Macedon.   He did nothing of the kind.   He seems to have calculated that Cleomenes would be able to effect little during the winter, and that the Achaean masses, in whose hands the decision lay, needed further time in order to realise that their only hope of salvation was in the King of

Macedon. If there was to be no winter campaign there was nothing to gain by precipitating the inevitable decision.

When Tritymallus returned empty-handed after his interview with Aratus, it became apparent to Cleomenes that there was no further hope of compromise. He accordingly began a blockade of Sicyon, evidently with the object of securing Aratus' person. By this time (mid-January, 224: see ch. 41, 7, note) the League embraced only the old Achaean cities (Pellene excepted), Megalopolis, Stymphalus (Pol. 2. 55), and Sicyon. For three months the blockade continued. But the Spartans were so ineffective that Aratus at length, without any particular difficulty, made his way down to the shore (a couple of miles off), and thence by sea to Aegium. There the Achaeans were assembled for the April meeting of 224 B.C., and this meeting, expanded into a syncletos for the purpose, finally completed the settlement with Antigonus.

Cleomenes, then, having come to know (ἐπιγνοὺς) that the Achaeans were making a compact with the Macedonian king (συντιθεμένους τὰ πρὸς τὸν Ἀντίγονον, Pol. 2. 52) evacuated Sicyonian territory in order to block the approaches to Peloponnesus.[47]

Cleomenes' loss of Corinth and Argos. When Aratus crossed from Aegium to meet Antigonus he found him in Pegae (*Ar.* 44), the Megarian port on the Gulf of Corinth, now included in the Boeotian League. As the Aetolians refused him passage by land he had been forced to take the sea-route by Euboea (Pol. 2. 53). Of the events that followed there is a comparatively full account in *Cleom.* 20–21, with shorter notices in *Arat.* 44 and Polybius 2. 53. The accounts are consistent; that found in the *Cleomenes* is evidently drawn from Phylarchus. Aratus' memoirs, it may be supposed, did little more than record the part played by Aratus himself, which was but a small one.

Cleomenes decided not to defend the isthmus, but to prevent Antigonus from advancing into Peloponnesus by either of the two feasible routes—the coast road leading to Sicyon or the pass east of Acrocorinth. Antigonus began to fear he would have to convey his troops by sea to Sicyon, a troublesome business, as his fleet was on the wrong side of the isthmus. Hampered by a shortage of supplies, he tried to steal through Lechaeum, the western port

---

[47] For the chronological confusion in *Cleom.* 19, 4, see note on *Arat.* 42, 1–2.

of Corinth, but was thrust out of the town (*Cleom.* 20; cf. *Arat.* 44, " there were conflicts about the city "). But that same evening a message came by sea to Aratus from Aristoteles of Argos, who promised to organise a revolt against the Spartans if Aratus would come to his aid. Aratus accordingly sailed for Epidaurus from the isthmus with 1,500 men (*Arat.*), but the Argives revolted independently, and attacked the Spartans in the citadel (*Arat.* and *Cleom.*). They were encouraged by the arrival of the Achaean forces from Sicyon under Timoxenus (*Cleom.* and Polybius), who had, presumably, like Aratus received information of the intended revolt. Towards midnight (περὶ δευτέραν φυλακήν, *Cleom.*) the news of the rising reached Corinth, and Cleomenes sent Megistonous, his stepfather, with two thousand men to Argos. Megistonous made his way into the city, but was killed in the fighting, and, after many messages had been sent to Cleomenes from the garrison, he became alarmed lest the enemy might secure Argos, and so pass into Laconia. He accordingly evacuated Corinth, hurried to Argos in person, and, having managed to enter the citadel (*Cleom.*), was winning back the city (*Cleom.*, Polyb., *Arat.*), when Aratus came up (*Arat.*), and shortly afterwards Antigonus (*Arat.* and *Cleom.*); whereupon he withdrew to Mantinea (*Arat.* and *Cleom.*).

Aristomachus, formerly tyrant and later Achaean strategos, was foolish enough to remain in Argos after Cleomenes' departure and was executed for treason. Polybius (2. 59–60) rebukes Phylarchus for his highly coloured account of the cruelties inflicted upon Aristomachus, but at the beginning of 2, 60 himself admits the torturing, though at the end of the chapter he denies that Aristomachus suffered anything worse than death by drowning.[48] Aratus, who was now both Argive strategos as well as strategos autocrator of the League, was blamed (by Phylarchus) for having suffered such cruelties to be perpetrated (*Arat.* 44; the subject is not touched in *Cleom.*).

Only one more event in the campaign of 224 is recorded—the reduction by Antigonus of the frontier forts of Belbina and Aegys, which he handed over to Megalopolis.

[48] οὐδ' Ἀντιγόνῳ προσαπτέον οὐδ' Ἀράτῳ παρανομίαν ὅτι λαβόντες κατὰ πόλεμον ὑποχείριον τύραννον στρεβλώσαντες ἀπέκτειναν, ὅν γε καὶ κατὰ τὴν εἰρήνην τοῖς ἀνελοῦσι καὶ τιμωρησαμένοις ἔπαινος καὶ τιμὴ συνεξηκολούθει παρὰ τοῖς ὀρθῶς λογιζομένοις. The use of ὅτι indicates that the *killing* and *racking* are mentioned as facts. But at the end of the chapter Polybius writes : ἀλλ' ὅμως ... οὐδενὸς ἔτυχε δεινοῦ πλὴν τοῦ καταποντισθῆναι.

Antigonus' Campaign of 223. Of this a summary account is found in Pol. 2. 54. The campaign began with an investment of Tegea, in which the Achaeans co-operated. Antigonus then marched into Laconia, hoping to gain a decision, but was recalled by the news that the garrison of Orchomenos had started to join Cleomenes. Turning back, Antigonus carried the town by assault, terrified Mantinea into unconditional surrender, received the submission of Heraea and Telphusa, and returned to Aegium, where he attended the autumn session of the Achaean synodos.

The treatment of Mantinea (cf. Polyb. 2; 57, 58) was described in the most vivid colours by Phylarchus, on whose narrative is based the reference in *Arat.* 45. Plutarch there says that

> " the Achaeans put to death the chief and most noted citizens, and of the rest sold some as slaves, while others they sent in chains to Macedon, enslaved their wives and children, and confiscated their property."

Polybius says that

> " nothing worse befell them than enslavement and confiscation."

If Polybius means to convey that there were no executions, his statement evidently falls short of the truth. His special pleading in regard to Aristomachus and Mantinea is the work of a man whose conscience is not altogether at ease. Although half a century had passed when these chapters were composed, he writes with the vehemence of a party pamphleteer.

The imperialists of fifth-century Athens had, on one memorable occasion, declined to visit a whole community with vengeance for the treason of a dominant faction. Two centuries had passed since then; the standard of public opinion was higher than in the time of the Peloponnesian war. The revival of the principle of vicarious punishment, and in particular its revival by Aratus and the Achaeans who disclaimed imperialistic ambitions, had evidently shocked the conscience of contemporaries; Polybius' outburst against Phylarchus betrays a consciousness that his fellow-countrymen and his hero Aratus had acted, as Plutarch puts it, οὐχ Ἑλληνικῶς.

The name of the city was changed by the Achaeans to Antigoneia, and this shocked Plutarch more than the treatment meted out to the inhabitants. " It was neither necessary nor honourable and cannot be excused."

In the autumn of 223 Antigonus sent his Macedonians home for the winter. He himself was at Aegium in conference with the synodos, when news was brought of an event which Plutarch in the *Aratus* has not even mentioned—Cleomenes' surprise and capture of Megalopolis. The account in *Cleom.* 23 (derived from Phylarchus; cf. Polybius 2. 63) describes how Aratus wept as he broke the news to the assembly, which immediately dissolved. Megalopolis was plundered and destroyed, as the citizens from their asylum in Messenia refused the king's offer to give them back their city and property if they would come over to his side.

Antigonus now took up residence in Argos, where, helpless in the absence of his Macedonians, he was forced to watch the devastation of the countryside by the Spartans (*Cleom.* 25).[49]

The Victory of Antigonus. Next year, when the Macedonian forces had returned, Antigonus marched to the Spartan frontier. The battle of Sellasia followed, in which the Spartans were finally defeated (July, 222). Whether Aratus played any part in the battle is unknown.

Cleomenes sailed to Egypt, where he was treated with consideration, but the king's sincerity in promising to restore him was never put to the test, for Euergetes died about July, 221. His libertine son Philopator, taking offence at a free-spoken criticism, imprisoned Cleomenes. After a time he managed to escape, and tried to raise a revolution in Alexandria, but meeting with no support committed suicide in despair.

Antigonus Doson was the first conqueror to enter Sparta (Pol. 2. 70; 4, 24, 59; *Cleom.* 30).[50] The territory known as Denthaliatis, west of Taÿgetus, was retroceded to Messenia (Tac. *Ann.* 4. 43). The kingship was abolished and the ephorate restored. As the ephors were elected by the people, and the people meant the holders of land, the question arises whether the land settlement of Cleomenes was abolished or retained.

At Sellasia the Spartan losses had been heavy. Plutarch (*Cleom.* 28) writes: "They say that all the Lacedaemonians perished except two hundred, being six thousand in number." In the six thousand are included helots and perioeci, but a large proportion of the slain were Spartans of Cleomenes' creation.

---

[49] As Beloch has pointed out, *Cleom.* 26 is dittography: there was but one invasion of the Argolid.

[50] See J. H. S. (1934), p. 34n., for Tarn's explanation of the origin of Eusebius' error in asserting that Gonatas captured Sparta.

Many lots must have remained unfilled. In 218 one Chilon attempted a revolution, believing that "if he took the same course as Cleomenes and gave the common people hopes of land allotments and re-division of property, the masses would quickly follow him" (Pol. 4. 81). One would like to know what exactly Polybius meant in this passage by the "common people."

At any rate it is clear that the peace-terms which Polybius and Plutarch praise for their moderation and magnanimity were no settlement at all. Power was placed in hands too weak to retain it. Sparta remained a nuisance or a danger to the Achaean League to the end of Greek independence. It is interesting to speculate on what would have happened if the conquerors, instead of seeking credit for moderation and magnanimity, had made the cities of the perioeci independent, and by emancipating the helots created a new Laconia, for which the day of Sellasia would have been the dawn of freedom.

But such a conception was outside the range of either Antigonus or Aratus.

CHRONOLOGICAL TABLE.

243–241. Agis and the Social Reformers in power at Sparta.
    241. Fall of Agis.
    240. Aetolian raid on Laconia (Beloch).
235–4. Accession of Cleomenes to the Spartan throne; Lydiades retires from the tyranny at Megalopolis.
234–3. Lydiades strategos of the Achaean League.
233–2. Aratus vii.
232–1. Lydiades ii.
231–0. Aratus viii.
230–229. Lydiades iii: death of Demetrius of Macedon: he is succeeded by Antigonus Doson.
229–228. Aratus ix: Cleomenes acquires the cities of Tegea, Mantinea, Orchomenos and Caphyae. Argos enters the Achaean League.
    228. Cleomenes fortifies the Athenaeum in Belbina, captures Methydrium and raids Argolis. Declaration of war against Sparta secured by Aristomachus the strategos. Achaeans refuse battle at Pallantium.
227–6. Aratus x. (Lydiades appointed Hipparch.) Achaeans capture Lasion but are defeated at Mt. Lycaeum.

Aratus captures Mantinea. Battle of Ladoceia; Lydiàdes killed. Cleomenes at Sparta inaugurates the social revolution. Megalopolitan envoys meet Antigonus Doson.

226–5. Aratus' victory at Orchomenos (February). Hyperbatas Achaean strategos. Battle of Hecatombaeum; Achaeans sue for peace.

225 (probably early spring) First (abortive) conference with Cleomenes; Timoxenus I (May). Second conference with Cleomenes broken off (c. June). Cleomenes renews the war; Achaean negotiations with Antigonus. Cleomenes captures Pellene and other places. A syncletos at Sicyon appoints Aratus strategos autocrator. During the Nemean games Cleomenes captures Argos (July). He allies himself with Ptolemy Euergetes. Aratus' punitive visit to Corinth, which secedes from the League and joins Cleomenes (August). Cleomenes sends Megistonous as his envoy to Aratus.

225 (July)–221. Aratus, strategos autocrator.

224. Cleomenes sends Tritymallus to Aratus, who rejects his proposals. Cleomenes' siege of Sicyon (January). Aratus escapes to Aegium (April), where a syncletos comes to terms with Antigonus. Aratus and Antigonus in the Megarid. Revolt of Argos: insurgents aided by Aratus, Antigonus and Timoxenus the Achaean strategos of 225–4. Cleomenes abandons Argos (early May). Corinth surrenders to Antigonus. Athenaeum in Belbina recovered by Antigonus.

223 (summer). Antigonus' Arcadian campaign; his capture of Mantinea: execution of Aristomachus for treason. Cleomenes captures Megalopolis (autumn).

222. Euergetes abandons Cleomenes: Cleomenes raids Argolis (spring). Battle of Sellasia (July). Antigonus captures Sparta after Cleomenes' flight to Egypt. Antigonus' victory over the Illyrians.

SECTION VI.—*Aratus and the Symmachy.*

During the first year of his campaigns in Peloponnesus Antigonus Doson, aided no doubt by Aratus, drew up the constitution of a new League, to embrace Macedon and her allies, independent or subject. The constitution having been approved by the various powers concerned, the " Symmachy" came into being, and it was the Symmachy, in name at least, that vanquished Cleomenes at Sellasia. The Symmachy was a League of Leagues. Macedon itself became τὸ κοινὸν τῶν Μακεδόνων ; subject to the Macedonian king were the Leagues of Thessaly and Euboea, and along with these were the independent Leagues of Achaea, Boeotia, Phocis, Epirus, and Acarnania (Polyb. 4; 9, 4; 15; 1, 1; 11; 5, 4).

The constitution of the Symmachy contained the remarkable provision that federal decrees, to be effective, had to be ratified by the several states, and that individual states were free to contract out of federal wars. The hegemony, of course, was in the hands of the Macedonian king.

From the Achaean point of view the new arrangement involved the disadvantages that Corinth, Orchomenos, and Heraea were retained by Macedon, and that the League could no longer conduct an independent foreign policy, but the opportunities for Macedonian aggression were considerably less than under either the constitution imposed by Philip the Second or that of Demetrius the Besieger. After Sellasia the Spartans were enrolled in the Symmachy (Pol. 4, 24, 5–6), which thus included all Greece except Elis, Messenia, Athens, and Aetolia.

Shortly before Sellasia Antigonus received news that the Illyrians were invading Macedon and fresh from his victory he turned to meet the new enemy. Both Polybius (2, 70) and Plutarch (*Cleom.* 27) comment on the fact that Cleomenes, if he had postponed the battle for a few days, might have saved his crown.

Antigonus defeated the Illyrians, but, being by hereditary tendency consumptive, was seized with a hæmorrhage during the excitement of battle, and from the illness thus contracted never recovered. He died in 221 B.C.

Every reference alike in the *Aratus* and in Polybius suggests that the king's relations with Aratus had been consistently cordial.

Polybius, indeed (2; 71), observes: " His death meant a great loss to the Greeks, whom he had inspired with good hopes not only by his support in the field, but still more by his character and good principles." But in *Cleom.* 16 Plutarch after blaming Aratus "for inviting Antigonus into Greece and filling Peloponnesus with Macedonians whom he had himself in his youth expelled from the peninsula when he freed Acrocorinthus," adds the remark, "and that too though in his *Memoirs* he had said all manner of evil against this very Antigonus." One is driven to the conclusion that Plutarch composed this sentence in haste, writing of Doson but thinking of Gonatas.

After Sellasia, Plutarch loses his two main sources, Aratus' *Memoirs* and Phylarchus' history. He betrays a certain eagerness to bring his biography to an end. His account of events henceforth is little more than a summary of certain passages of Polybius; as an historical source it has no independent value. To the " Social War," which with its preliminaries occupied three years, he allots precisely two pages.

The Antecedents of the Social War (220 B.C.). The Aetolians, still nominally in alliance with the Achaeans, were displeased at the establishment of the Symmachy, which hemmed them in on every side. The weakness of the Achaeans, exhausted by the Cleomenic war, and the death of Antigonus, whose successor Philip was still a youth, led them to believe that a policy of aggression was likely to prove more profitable than dangerous. The war, however, was actually brought on by the misconduct of one Dorimachus, who had been put in charge of Phigalea, the Arcadian city lying to the north of Messenia, which like Messenia itself had entered into relations of "isopolity" with Aetolia. According to Polybius (4; 3, 4), Dorimachus actually allowed some pirates, clients of his own, to plunder freely in Messenia. At last, however, he was forced by the complaints of the Messenians to return to Aetolia. He collected a private army there, and shipped his troops to Achaea, whence they made their way, plundering as they went, to Phigalea. From this base they pillaged Messenia, as if it were enemy territory. The war party in Aetolia now began to commit unofficial acts of hostility against Achaea, Acarnania, Epirus, and Macedon simultaneously.

The Messenians, hitherto free from foreign complications, now applied to the Achaeans for leave to enter the Symmachy (not the League). Their request was referred to the Symmachy as a whole (Pol. 4; 12, 9), but in the meantime the Achaeans made a separate alliance with Messenia. Aratus, who had induced Timoxenus, the strategos for 221–0, to hand over his seal to him as his successor five days before the legal date, assembled the Achaean citizen-levy on the Messenian border and ordered Dorimachus to leave Messenia, and in withdrawing not to enter Achaean territory.

Dorimachus made a show of obeying this order, and Aratus dismissed the greater part of his army, but on learning that the retreating Aetolians were actually traversing Achaean territory he attacked them near Caphyae, under unfavourable conditions, and was severely defeated (early summer, 220).

As this was the last battle in which we read of Aratus commanding an army we may appropriately recall Polybius' judgment of his qualities as a general: "Whenever he attempted a campaign in the field he was slow in conception, timid in execution, and without personal gallantry in the presence of danger. Peloponnesus was filled with trophies marking his defeats, and in this particular kind of warfare he was always easily defeated." The Aetolians now boldly marched through the peninsula, attacked Pellene, ravaged Sicyonian territory, and returned home by way of the isthmus.

Not long after this reverse there was a meeting of the Achaean synodos. A lenient view was taken of Aratus' mismanagement, and a new force was mobilised to protect Messenia. The Spartans, who, it appears, were not only members of the Symmachy but also allies of the Achaean League, were instructed to co-operate with the Messenians. The members of the Symmachy were requested to admit Messenia, and to declare war on Aetolia.

The official Aetolian attitude was shown in the decision of the Assembly at Thermum (spring, 220)—to maintain peace with Sparta and Messenia, and even with the Achaeans, provided they abandoned their alliance with Messenia (Pol. 4; 15), i.e., provided they accepted the *status quo*.

Philip and the Epirots replied to the Achaeans, accepting Messenia as a member of the Symmachy, but refusing to declare war on Aetolia (Pol. 4; 16).

The Aetolian war party invaded Achaean territory with a body of volunteers aided by Illyrian pirates. The Aetolians captured the Arcadian Cynaetha by help of traitors, massacred the inhabitants, and burned the town (Polyb. 4, 15). The raiders escaped, for Aratus was unwilling to risk a second Caphyae, while all the time the Aetolian strategos Ariston insisted that Aetolia was not at war with any member of the Symmachy.

It was not till the autumn of 220 that war was formally declared against Aetolia by the Symmachy, under the presidency of Philip at Corinth. But so long as Phigalea remained in Aetolian hands, Messenia refused to co-operate, while Sparta[1] soon ranged herself definitely with Aetolia and Elis. But the Social War, destructive as it was of life and property, was marked by futile activities on both sides, and ended in an anticlimax.

Events of 219–18. In Peloponnesus the territories of the Achaeans were ravaged at various points by the Spartans, Aetolians, and Eleans. The most serious of these activities was the Elean raid on Old Achaea. So weak was the Achaean defence that the Eleans actually captured a fort near Dyme. So incompetent was the strategos for this year, the younger Aratus, that the cities of Dyme, Pharae, and Tritaea resolved to pay no more federal taxes but, instead, to hire a private army. To this federation within the state Freeman (p. 417) gave the appropriate name of Sonderbund.

Outside Peloponnesus the most remarkable events of the summer of 219 were the destructive attacks of the Aetolians on the Macedonian Dium (Polyb. 4, 62) and the Epirotic Dodona (4, 67). Philip was hampered by a new Dardanian invasion.

Not till the autumn did he intervene in Peloponnesus; but his intervention when it came was effective. Elis was raided, Triphylia—that ancient source of quarrel between Elis and her neighbours—captured and retained by Philip, as well as Phigalea; Aetolian raiders would trouble Messenia no more (Polyb. 4, 81).

But the spirit of goodwill shown by Philip to Aratus was not shared by the Macedonian chiefs, who wished to reduce the Achaeans to the subject position of the Thessalians. Their leader Apelles (chosen by Antigonus as one of Philip's guardians) began the work by interfering with the Achaean army, and then, when the king at Aratus' instance forced him to desist (Polyb. 4, 76), turned to the field of politics.

The Achaean elections for 218–217 were now at hand. Apelles

---

[1] Polyb. 4, 35–37. Early in 219 there was a revolution in Sparta and two kings were appointed, Cleomenes' nephew, Agesipolis, still a child, and one Lycurgus, unconnected with either of the royal houses.

found a candidate to oppose Aratus in a certain Eperatus of Pharae, one of the three cities of Old Achaea which had formed the "Sonderbund" in the previous year. Aratus was too politic to face the opposition which Apelles "by mingled threats and entreaties" had organised; he put up Timoxenus in his stead. But Apelles still counted for much with Philip; he persuaded him to visit Aegium at the time of the election and there use his influence on Eperatus' behalf. Timoxenus was defeated (Polyb. 4, 82).

Philip now (early spring, 218) launched another blow at Elis on behalf of the old Achaean towns. In this raid the Elean strategos Amphidamus was taken prisoner, but at his own suggestion sent back to Elis with Philip's terms of settlement, which were generous in the extreme. None the less, they were rejected by the Eleans, and Amphidamus had to flee for his life.

In this incident Apelles saw a chance of discrediting Aratus. He accused him of engaging in a disloyal intrigue with Amphidamus against his Macedonian allies. But Aratus found means to produce the Elean strategos, and confronted by his evidence Apelles' case collapsed.

Events of 218–17. Eperatus had been elected, but proved unable to "manage Congress," particularly in the matter of finance (Polyb. 5, 1). Philip accordingly persuaded the demiourgoi to summon a special synodos—it was not a matter for a syncletos—at Sicyon (*c.* June, 218). This was the prelude to his complete reconciliation with Aratus, and a satisfactory financial settlement was obtained. Philip now improvised a fleet of transports, by means of which he carried out a highly successful raid upon Aetolia itself.

But the success was gained in spite of the disloyalty of the Macedonian chiefs. Before the expedition set out Apelles, unable to retain his influence over Philip and unwilling to submit to its loss, conspired with Leontius and Megaleas; the two last were to remain with the king, and to damage his service by neglecting it; while Apelles betook himself to Chalcis in order to divert supplies from the royal army (Polyb. 5, 2).

Leontius and Megaleas, however, played their part poorly. Their too obvious incompetence was bound to arouse suspicion, and they made the position worse for themselves by insulting Aratus in a drunken brawl which followed a banquet given by Philip before leaving Aetolia. Megaleas was fined twenty talents for disorderly conduct, Leontius insolently offering bail on his behalf. Later there was a regular investigation, and Megaleas' fine was confirmed (Polyb. 5, 15–16). On returning to Peloponnesus, Philip engaged in a whirlwind campaign in the Eurotas valley. There was much plunder, but no sign of surrender from the Spartans or their Elean and Aetolian allies.

Leontius now went a stage further in his treasonable activities. At Corinth the peltasts mutinied; all Philip could do was to assemble the troops in the theatre and smooth the matter over by tactful talk.

When Apelles returned from Chalcis he was mortified by a cool reception from Philip; and soon afterwards Leontius was arrested and executed.

"Just then Philip received certain letters from Phocis which Megaleas had written to the Aetolians urging them to continue the war, as Philip was exhausted through lack of supplies." The king now arrested Apelles, and sent a confidential officer to seize Megaleas, who had fled to Thebes. Both Apelles and Megaleas committed suicide (Polyb. 5, 28–29).

It was the news of these events which, according to Polybius, determined the Aetolians not to appear at a conference which had been arranged to meet at Rhium. So the war dragged on; but Philip cared little, "for he was confident of success and had no intention of coming to terms." Towards winter (218) he returned to Macedon.

In Peloponnesus Eperatus proved no more competent than the younger Aratus the year before; the Eleans renewed their raids on Old Achaea; the cities refused to pay their assessments; the mercenaries were getting no wages, and began to disband. With the return of Aratus to power, however, a reorganisation was effected, and the position showed signs of improvement.

The Peace of Naupactus (*Summer*, 217). Realising that the war could not be ended by the methods hitherto adopted Philip collected a vast siege-train during the winter of 218–217. After testing it on the northern frontier-post of Bylazora held by the Dardanians, he turned south and stormed the Aetolian fortress of Phthiotic Thebes near the Gulf of Pagasae. This new departure, together with the tidings from Italy, where Hannibal had just defeated the Romans at Lake Trasimene, induced the Aetolians to accept a fresh offer of mediation by Rhodes, Chios and Egypt. A conference met at Naupactus and a general settlement followed,

h

by which each side kept what it had acquired. The honours and most of the profits of the war went to Philip.

The Messenian incident. This mysterious affair is thus explained by Holleaux in C.A.H. viii, p. 120 : —

" Hardly had Philip (spring, 215) allied himself with Hannibal than his relations with the Achaeans became strained . . . Neither Rome nor Carthage meant anything to them; moreover, they were unwilling to strengthen Philip by contributing to his military successes. The king came into the Peloponnesus and found Aratus hostile to his designs.

" Then, to set them further at variance, occurred the obscure affair of Messene . . . Called in as arbitrator, Philip is said to have secretly incited the populace, who massacred the magistrates and 200 optimates. The victors were willing it seems for him to occupy Ithome. During his possible absence in Italy . . . might not the Aetolians invade the Peloponnese? . . . By occupying Ithome he would hold in check Elis and Sparta . . . and thereby paralyse Aetolia itself. Meanwhile Aratus and his son had hastened to Messene on the heels of Philip, intending to counter the democratic victory . . . To see Philip intriguing, playing the demagogue, apparently seeking to establish himself in Messene, filled them with anger . . . Having gone to offer sacrifice with Aratus and Demetrius . . . Philip put . . . the question : Was he to keep the fortress? Demetrius encouraged him . . . Aratus countered with a vehement homily—Philip yielded, but henceforth the two men hated one another. Sulky and peevish, Aratus left the king, and next year refused point-blank to accompany him into Illyria."

Let us now turn to the ancient sources for the incident, Polyb. 7, 11–13[2] and *Arat.* 49, 3–50. The latter may be thus analysed :

(1) A class war having broken out at Messene, (2) Philip arrives [from Triphylia] and sets the factions at each other's throats; the "authorities" and almost two hundred of the upper class are slain. (3) Next day Aratus and his son appear at

---

[2] Polyb. 7, 10 (Hultsch) is a fragment relating to what happened at Messene *after* democracy had been established there. Hence it must be later in time than the events recorded in *Arat.* 49–50 and Polyb. 7, 11–13.

Messene. (4) The younger Aratus upbraids Philip severely; the king listens with surprising patience. (5) In company with the elder Aratus and Demetrius of Pharos Philip climbs Ithome, and after sacrifice at the temple on the summit asks his companions to advise whether he should take possession of the citadel. Demetrius' counsel to seize it by all means is opposed by Aratus, who for the time being prevails with the king.

The matters comprised under (1), (2), and (3) are mentioned in Polybius 7, 13; that under (5) is found with slight divergences in Polyb. 7, 11. If no parallel to (4) occurs in the extant parts of Polybius, we are justified in assuming that the material comes from a part of the history now lost.

Comparing the statements enumerated above with the account cited from Holleaux, we find that the modern historian has taken some liberties with Polybius. Firstly, there is no reason to suppose that Philip was called in as arbitrator by the Messenians, except that he was hegemon of the symmachy—which, of course, claimed no control of the domestic affairs of constituent states. Secondly, Holleaux has no authority for picturing Aratus as an unauthorised interloper hurrying to the scene "on Philip's heels." Thirdly, the hypothesis that the victors in the civil strife "were willing for Philip to occupy the citadel" is an unjustified assumption. If Philip had come to an understanding with the "socialistic" party, how are we to account for his violent attacks on Messene a year later, in one of which Demetrius of Pharos lost his life? Fourthly, there is no basis for the notion that Philip wished to garrison Ithome in order to protect Peloponnesus from further Aetolian attacks. He was already in occupation of the strongholds of Orchomenos and Heraea and of the whole district of Triphylia.

It seems clear enough that Philip's object in proposing to seize Ithome was simply what Demetrius (according to Polybius) said it ought to be—namely, to dominate Peloponnesus; but that the king was disconcerted by the sudden arrival of Aratus, who in this matter, he began to realise, stood for a public opinion which Philip was not yet ready to defy. Not long afterwards Aratus discovered that Philip had seduced his son's wife, Polycrateia. This outrage, combined with considerations of public policy, made him averse from any further co-operation with Philip (Arat. 51).

During the next strategia (213–12) Aratus died, convinced that he had been poisoned at Philip's instigation, but in reality, it would seem, the victim of pulmonary consumption.

Aratus' significance in Greek history is that he developed
the small league of the Achaean townships into a large state
with an area of 4,500 square miles and a population of half a
million—a work which, had he not lived, would never have been
accomplished at all.   Apart from Aratus, there were in Peloponnesus during the latter half of the third century only three
men of marked ability—Cleomenes, Lydiades, and Philopoemen.
But neither the Spartan nor the Megalopolitans could have
abolished the Macedonian interest in the peninsula, which was
the first step to its unification in any form.

Aratus did what he did by reason of his unique ability as a
guerrilla leader, a party chief, and a diplomatist, but his work was
marred and his glory tarnished by serious faults, intellectual
and moral.   He failed to see that it was impossible to defend a
large federation by petty warfare or diplomatic manœuvring; he
failed to grasp the necessity of an effective military organisation;
till his last days he failed to realise his own complete incompetence
as a general on the field of battle; finally, the long years during
which he had guided the policy of the state in sole reliance on
his own judgment had left him unwilling to foster new talent and
incapable of co-operating with men of independent character.

Aratus may have thought that when the last tyrant disappeared
from Peloponnesus a new era of peace would begin.   Unaware
alike of the ambitions and ability of Cleomenes, he could not
foresee that the League was entering upon a struggle for its very
existence.

Cleomenes, if he at all resembled the portrait which Phylarchus
painted and Plutarch reproduced, was an extraordinarily attractive
character, and it is not surprising that he has been a favourite
among the more sentimental of modern historians.   Thus
Schömann has written, and Blass has endorsed the verdict : —
"Aratus was a man worthy of the Greece of his own day, but
Cleomenes was far greater than his time, and fit to be compared
with the earlier heroes of Greece"; Tarn has extolled Cleomenes
as "an infinitely greater and nobler man" than Aratus; and
Freeman has called Sellasia "one of the saddest names in Greek
history."

But if after these flights we descend to the region of prosaic
fact, we cannot escape from the conclusion that, whatever were
the virtues of Cleomenes, he was guilty of wanton aggression in

his relations with the Achaeans. Without any sort of justification or excuse he invaded their territory, and having asserted his superiority with the sword proposed to them to tear up their constitution and to substitute a new instrument, which would have left the Federation without any obvious function save to provide troops and money for the wars in which the king of Sparta as its "hegemon" should see fit to involve it.

On the other hand, Aratus, whatever his failings, had spent his whole life and wealth in asserting and maintaining liberty and popular government.[3] If such a thing as a moral issue is to be admitted in international relations it is plain that the Achaeans were in the right and Cleomenes in the wrong.

After the rout of Hecatombaeum the only choice for the Achaeans lay between the acceptance of Cleomenes' hegemony with—let us remember—all that it implied, and Antigonus' hegemony, involving little more than the sacrifice of Corinth, which had already seceded from the League.

If we are willing to grant that a state which cannot maintain its independence against external aggressors by its own efforts is justified in choosing from two humiliating alternatives that which involves the less sacrifice of independence, then it cannot be denied that the Achaeans chose wisely under Aratus' guidance.

But the Macedonian alliance, though it made possible the continued existence of the Achaean federation, brought no lasting peace; and the new war forced upon the League by the brigand state of Aetolia revealed the continuance among the Achaeans of the same military incompetence as had marked the war with Cleomenes. For this the responsibility lies at the door of Aratus; and it imparts to his career an element of tragedy.

CHRONOLOGICAL TABLE.

224. Establishment of the Symmachy.

221 (May). Achaean strategos : Timoxenus iii.
    Death of Antigonus Doson.
    Death of Ptolemy Euergetes (about July).
    The Aetolian Dorimachus in Messenia.

220 (early spring). Aetolian raid on Messenia.
    (May). Aratus xiv.

---

[3] So far, that is, as these can be predicated of a slave-owning community.

Battle at Caphyae: Aratus defeated.

(late summer). Philip's visit to Corinth: Symmachy declare war on Aetolia.

219 (early spring). Cleomenes' death in Egypt.

Lycurgus and Agesipolis chosen kings of Sparta, which allies herself with Aetolia.

Sparta declares war on the Achaean League.

(May). Aratus the Younger enters office.

Aetolian raid on Old Achaea.

Dyme, Pharae and Tritaea form a Sonderbund.

Aetolians raid Dium (Macedon) and Dodona.

Philip in Peloponnesus: Apelles' first intrigue.

218. Subjugation of Triphylia by Philip and Achaeans.

Apelles gets Eperatus elected Achaean strategos.

Philip and Achaeans invade N. Elis.

The incident of Aratus and Amphidamus.

(May). Eperatus enters office.

The Achaean synodos transferred from Aegium to Sicyon.

Apelles retires to Chalcis.

Philip's Aetolian expedition.

Megaleas condemned.

Philip's expedition against Laconia.

Philip's return to Corinth: Apelles' return and rebuff.

(Autumn). Execution of the Macedonian malcontents.

Military weakness in Achaea.

217 (May). Aratus xvi.

Aratus attempts a military re-organisation.

Philip captures Bylazora and Phthiotic Thebes.

The Peace of Naupactus, ending the Social War.

216 (May). Timoxenus iv.

215 „ Aratus xvi.

The Messenian affair.

214. Strategos unknown.

Philip retreats from Romans in Illyria.

Demetrius of Pharos killed before Messene.

213 (May). Aratus xvii.

Death of Aratus.

SECTION VII.—*Some features of the Achaean constitution.*[1]

The Achaean assemblies. These were officially known as Synodos and Syncletos respectively, but Polybius often departs from official usage, and refers to either assembly as "the Achaeans," "the Many," or "the Ecclesia." To the Synodos he occasionally gives the name *agora*.

The Synodos was the assembly which met regularly to deal with the ordinary business of the League. The question of its composition has been much discussed. It will be more convenient to deal with it later.

The Syncletos was a mass meeting of citizens over thirty years of age, specially summoned to decide on questions of peace or war, of concluding alliances with other states, or of despatching assistance to friendly powers. In later times it was also called to hear and deal with communications from the Roman Senate. A meeting of the Syncletos could deal only with matters placed on its *agenda* by the government; as a rule this business had already been considered by the Synodos. The voting in a Syncletos appears to have been by cities.

As evidence for the nature and functions of the Syncletos the following texts are cited : —

(1) IG. vii, 411 : the Oropians (*c.* 150) send envoys to ask aid against Athens. They appear before a synodos, which resolves συναγαγεῖν σύγκλητον ἐν Ἄργει περὶ τούτων.

(2) Polyb. 29, 23 (8), 1 : Ambassadors from Egypt ask aid against King Antiochus. The synodos (τὸ πλῆθος τῶν Ἀχαιῶν) is sympathetic, but the opposition protests against a decision as *ultra vires*, ὡς οὐκ οὔσης ἐξουσίας κατὰ τοὺς νόμους ἐν ἀγορᾷ βουλεύεσθαι περὶ βοηθείας. Later, συγκλήτου συναχθείσης ἐν ᾗ συνέβαινε μὴ μόνον συμπορεύεσθαι τὴν βουλήν, ἀλλὰ πάντας ἀπὸ τριάκοντα ἐτῶν, the request was granted.

(3) Polyb. 22, 12 (16), 5 [otherwise denoted as 23, 12]. Envoys at Rome defend the Achaean government for refusing to grant audience of a syncletos to a Roman *legatus*, νόμον γὰρ εἶναι παρὰ τοῖς Ἀχαιοῖς μὴ συγκαλεῖν τοὺς πολλοὺς ἐὰν μὴ περὶ συμμαχίας

---

[1] The most recent compendious account of the Achaean constitution will be found in Busolt's *Griechische Staatskunde* revised by Swoboda (Munich, 1926).

ἢ πολέμου δέῃ γίνεσθαι διαβούλιον ἢ παρὰ τῆς Συγκλήτου (i.e., the Roman Senate) τις ἐνέγκῃ γράμματα.

Voting by cities: Livy 32, 22 and 23; *Id.* 38. 32. (The view that the number of votes possessed by each city depended on its population is based on the analogy of Aetolia, where the cities elected *councillors* in number proportional to population.)

A syncletos could meet at any time in any city of the League.

It appears from Polyb. 4, 7 that a Synodos having come to a preliminary decision concerning war, peace, or alliance might summon *a levy of the citizen militia with power to act as a syncletos* in rejecting or ratifying the preliminary decision. Thus the synodos of April, 220, was in favour of assisting the Messenians against Aetolian aggression, and accordingly resolved βοηθεῖν τοῖς M. καὶ συνάγειν τοὺς Ἀχαιοὺς ἐν ὅπλοις· ὃ δ᾽ ἂν τοῖς συνελθοῦσι βουλευομένοις δόξῃ, τοῦτ᾽ εἶναι κύριον. On such occasions men between twenty and thirty, eligible neither for syncletos nor synodos, had a voice in the final decision of national policy.

Synodos. The grand problem of Achaean constitutional history relates to the composition of the Synodos. Schweighaüser, who has been followed by Beloch, Tarn, De Sanctis, Swoboda, and others, held that the Synodos was not a primary assembly, but a council (βουλή) composed of elected representatives.[2]

The large size of the Boule strongly favours its identification with the Synodos. In Polyb. 22, 10 [23, 7], it is stated that King Eumenes in 185 B.C. offered the League a gift of 120 talents, the interest therefrom to be applied to paying the bouleutai. From this passage Tarn (C.A.H. vii, p. 737) has calculated the number of members of the Boule.

> " If we suppose three annual meetings of three days each and interest at 8 per cent., then, taking the usual indemnity at a drachma a day, the Council would number over 6,000 members; this may be too high, but it was certainly very large and quite unlike any Council known."

From the same passage De Sanctis has drawn an inference which points more directly to the identity of Synodos and Boule. The

---

[2] That the council was an elected body appears from Polyb. 2, 57, where it is stated that the Achaean cities employed the same officers and βουλευταί. On the Aetolian analogy they are held to have been elected by the cities in numbers proportional to their military strength.

acceptance of Eumenes' offer to pay the bouleutai was opposed by a speaker in the Synodos on the ground, πάντας ἅμα δωροδοκεῖσθαι, i.e., " You are all accepting a bribe."

In this connection Polyb. 29, 23 (8), 1 has to be cited again. The proposal of a synodos to give assistance to Egypt was referred to a Syncletos, ἐν ᾗ συνέβαινε μὴ μόνον συμπορεύεσθαι τὴν βουλήν, ἀλλὰ πάντας ἀπὸ τριάκοντα ἐτῶν. Such a remark would be without point unless the members of the Boule formed a numerically appreciable part of the mass meeting.

Again, *Cleom.* 25 refers to a synodos thus : (οἱ 'Αχαιοὶ) ἐτύγχανον ἐν Αἰγίῳ βουλὴν ἔχοντες.

Finally, in Polyb. 2, 50, 10 : 22, 13, 6 (cf. 11, 9, 8), the synodos is mentioned as meeting in a βουλευτήριον.

In two passages, however, Polybius calls the Synodos by the name *ecclesia.* Does the word *ecclesia* imply that the Synodos contained not only a boule but a primary assembly as well?

(1) Pol. 4, 7 : the Achaeans meet at Aegium καθηκούσης αὐτοῖς ἐκ τῶν νόμων συνόδου (April, 220 B.C.). συνελθόντες δ' εἰς τὴν ἐκκλησίαν, they vote aid to Messenia, subject to ratification of the decree by the militia when mobilised.

It is true that the term *ecclesia* ought to refer to a primary assembly, but in the present instance the proceedings of such an assembly would have been otiose, inasmuch as the proposals were referred to another primary assembly, i.e., the army, for final decision.[3]

Hence we must conclude that Polybius has referred to the boule as an " ecclesia," a terminological inexactitude natural enough if membership of the boule ran into four figures.

(2) Pol. 28, 3 : two Roman *legati* arrived in Peloponnesus intending (it was rumoured) to go before an *ecclesia* and bring accusations against certain Achaean politicians. However, συναχθείσης αὐτοῖς τῆς βουλῆς, they contented themselves by addressing some general exhortations to the bouleutai.

The most probable explanation is that here also Polybius has applied the name "ecclesia" to the Boule. We should, therefore,

---

[3] This objection seems to have escaped Cary who writes (p. 285): "The Achaean constitution provided for a spring and autumn session of a Parliament consisting of a primary assembly and a council of Deputies."

regard the Synodos as a council possessing for most purposes the powers of a sovereign assembly.[4]

The remarkable distinction between Syncletos and Synodos is not likely to have been an original feature of the Achaean constitution. One might suppose that, like the Acarnanian, Aetolian, Arcadian, Epirot, and Magnesian Leagues, the Achaeans once possessed a Parliament consisting of a Council and a primary assembly. Before Sicyon entered the League its federal business was rarely of serious importance; the periodic journeys to Aegium may have been felt a burden, with the result that attendance fell off, until finally the plan was devised of separating the really important functions of the "Parliament"—war, peace, alliances— from its comparatively routine business. The former the sovereign people kept in its own hands; the latter might safely be left to its elected representatives, who, being elected, were under an obligation to attend. When this change was effected the council may have been enlarged, and the number of stated meetings increased from two to four.

The Electoral Congress (ἀρχαιρεσίαι). Beloch (4, 2, p. 230) has shown from the time-indications in Polybius' account of Philip's movements in the winter of 219–18 (Pol. 4; 67–87) that this body met about January to elect officers, who took up their duties in the following May. Its constitution was apparently the same as that of a Syncletos. The ecclesia which elected Aratus strategos autocrator (*Arat.* 41) was evidently a syncletos anticipating the elections due in the following January.[5]

Stated meetings of the Synodos: a stated meeting (καθήκουσα ἐκ τῶν νόμων σύνοδος) in April, before the incoming officers took over their duties, is clearly indicated in Polyb. 4, 7, 1: another in September is mentioned in 4, 26, 7.

Two other stated meetings are postulated by Beloch (4, 2, p. 231), following Unger. A καθήκουσα σύνοδος (the words ἐκ τῶν νόμων being, however, omitted) is recorded in Polyb. 4, 14, 1, as meeting between the Nemean and Olympian festivals, i.e., *about the end of July*; and another at the same season in

---

[4] Strachan-Davidson's account, that they *expected* to be received by an *ecclesia* (syncletos) but were *actually* received by a *boule* (synodos) fails to explain the use of ecclesia in 4, 7.

[5] At a later time (after the Social War) the strategos-year was changed to begin in autumn with a consequent change in the date of the elections (see Beloch, *loc. cit.*).

5, 102, 5. In 4, 26, 7 we find a καθήκουσα σύνοδος mentioned as coming *about the end of May.*

One might infer that the April and September sessions were *obligatory* under the original constitution whereas the May and July sessions were merely *customary,* the custom having developed with the increase of the League's business.

It may be assumed that (1) extraordinary meetings of the Synodos were summoned when required, and (2) meetings of the Synodos were on occasion supplemented by a Syncletos; a procedure which seems to be implied in *Arat.* 42 and Polyb. 4, 26. In Aratus' time the regular meetings of the Synodos were held in Aegium, the federal capital.

The Government of the League, ἀρχή, ἄρχοντες, συναρχίαι, consisted of the strategos[6] and the ten demiourgoi elected annually.[7] They summoned the Synodos, and on occasion the Syncletos, at meetings of which the demiourgoi (without the strategos) acted as presidents (Livy 32, 22). The functions of the Government were very much those of a modern cabinet, the strategos corresponding to Prime Minister.

In military affairs the strategos was almost irresponsible. It is true that the issue of peace or war was entrusted to the Syncletos; it is also true that the strategos was subjected to the judgment of the Synodos *after the fact* [cf. *Arat.* 37]; but while war lasted he had undivided control of the army.[8]

It is generally held that the strategos "held office for a year only; he was incapable of immediate re-election, but he might be chosen again the year after."[9]

[6] Previous to the year 255–4 two strategoi were elected annually (Polyb. 2, 43).

[7] Polyb. 23, 5, 16; cf. *Arat.* 43.

[8] This enabled Aratus to use Achaean forces for his unauthorised attacks on Corinth, Argos, and Athens in time of peace.

[9] Freeman, p. 237, whose argument is however obscured by the fact that he supposed ἐπεί to be the reading of the mss. in the crucial passage *Arat.* 24, 5, which actually runs :

(Ἄρατος) οὕτω . . . ἴσχυσεν ἐν τοῖς Ἀχαιοῖς ὥστ' εἰ μὴ κατ' ἐνιαυτὸν παρ' ἐνιαυτὸν αἰνεῖσθαι στρατηγὸν αὐτόν.

Ferrabino thinks that Plut. here used εἰ because the bar to immediate re-election was not law but custom, and that in emergencies the custom could be disregarded. But on this supposition the power to decide remained in the hands of the electors, and instead of εἰ μὴ ἐξῆν Plutarch ought to have written εἰ μὴ ἐδόκει.

It seems to me that if Plut. really wrote εἰ μὴ ἐξῆν here (which I

It appears probable that no candidate could be elected strategos until he had attained the age of thirty, but this condition might be waived. [*Intro.*, Sect. III. p. xxxiv *n.*]

A strategos vacating office by death or resignation was succeeded by his predecessor until the next regular Synodos (Polyb. 39, 8), which, it may be presumed, had power to determine whether the substitute should complete the year or whether a special election should be held.

The strategos' symbol of office was a seal (*Arat.* 38).

The League and the States. The community as a whole was known as the Achaeans, while in official documents the city to which an individual belonged was appended, e.g., Ἀχαιὸς ἀπ᾽Αἰγίρας. Thus Plutarch is speaking with complete accuracy when he remarks of the Sicyonians, Δωριεῖς ὄντες ὑπέδυσαν ὄνομα . . , Ἀχαιῶν.

Outside his own city an Achaean possessed no public rights; his private rights (it would seem) were recognised throughout the League.[10]

The several cities might not mobilise armed forces without leave of the strategos; or carry on private negotiations with foreign powers unless previously authorised by a Synodos—an exception of which Aratus took advantage for the preliminary conversations with Antigonus Doson in 225 B.C.

To enable a state to enter the League a decree of the Synodos was required, which had to be ratified by a Syncletos.

Of the first stage we have an example in *Arat.* 35. For the complete procedure Swoboda refers to Polyb. 23, 15 and 24, 2. In the former passage a Synodos approves the re-admission of Messenia; in the latter the treaty with Messenia is ordered to be engraved on a tablet. The second meeting was plainly a Syncletos; we note the presence of some Spartans bearing a letter from the Roman Senate.

---

very much doubt) he did so merely to add emphasis to his assertion by a rhetorical under-statement (''if'' instead of ''because''). It is more probable, however, that Coraes was right in correcting εἰ to ἐπεί. [ἐπεὶ μὴ is not infrequent in post-classical Greek.]

Note, however, that if A. held office in alternate years only his strategia of 227–6 was his 10th, not, as stated in *Arat.* 35, his 12th.

[10] Aratus' strategia at Argos (44, 5) was probably due to a specific enactment in his favour. As to private rights: he held property at Corinth (*Arat.* 41 and 44), while his son was married to an Argive woman, Polycrateia (see note on *Arat.* 49, 2).

In addition to an undertaking to obey the federal laws and contribute assessments to the treasury, the several states on entering the League incurred special obligations contained in the treaties which they had signed. Thus, when Orchomenos, *c.* 235,[11] entered the League, a body of Achaeans was settled there to secure its fidelity. At Mantinea on its re-admission (227) the citizen body was reconstituted and an Achaean garrison installed (*Arat.* 36, Polyb. 2, 58).

A garrison was permanently maintained on Acrocorinthus (*Arat.* 34).

A state could not retire from the League at will; however, for reasons unknown to us, Orchomenos and Mantinea (*c.* 230) were allowed to join the Aetolian League, and Megara was in 224 instructed to join the Boeotian (Polyb. 20, 6, 8) because the Achaeans could no longer protect her.

---

[11] A portion of this treaty is preserved (IG. v. 2, 344 = Syll³. 490; also in Freeman, p. 647). Orchomenos left the League *c.* 330, was attached to Sparta from 229–223 and to Macedon from 223–*c.* 199 when it was re-admitted to the League. The indemnity granted to Nearchus and his sons indicates that IG. v. 2, 344 refers to its original admission. On the later occasion there was no retiring tyrant to claim protection.

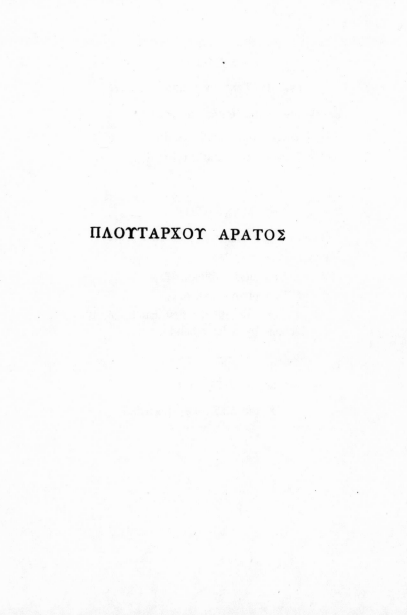

ΠΛΟΥΤΑΡΧΟΥ ΑΡΑΤΟΣ

SYMBOLS

MANUSCRIPTS.

G codex Sangermanensis (Coislinianus), 219.

P cod. Palatinus, 283.

R cod. Vaticanus Urbinas, 97.

L cod. Laurentianus, 69, 6.

(G^1, P^1, etc., denote the first hand; G^2, P^2, corrections by a later hand.)

———

Codices Parisini, 1671–1674.

(On the MSS., see Appendix.)

ΑΡΑΤΟΣ

1. Παροιμίαν τινὰ παλαιὰν ὦ Πολύκρατες, δείσας μοι δοκεῖ τὸ δύσφημον αὐτῆς, ὁ φιλόσοφος Χρύσιππος οὐχ ὃν ἔχει τρόπον ἀλλ' ὡς αὐτὸς ᾤετο βέλτιον εἶναι διατίθεται· τίς πατέρ' αἰνήσει, εἰ μὴ εὐδαίμονες υἱοί ; Διονυσόδωρος δ' ὁ Τροιζήνιος ἐλέγχων αὐτὸν ἀντεκτίθησι 2 τὴν ἀληθινὴν οὕτως ἔχουσαν·   d

τίς πατέρ' αἰνήσει,εἰ μὴ κακοδαίμονες υἱοί ; καί φησι τοὺς ἀφ' αὑτῶν οὐδενὸς ἀξίους ὄντας, ὑποδυομένους δὲ προγόνων τινῶν ἀρεταῖς καὶ πλεονάζοντας ἐν τοῖς ἐκείνων ἐπαίνοις, ὑπὸ τῆς παροιμίας ἐπιστομίζεσθαι. ἀλλ' 3 ᾧ γε φύσει "τὸ γενναῖον ἐπιπρέπει ἐκ πατέρων" κατὰ Πίνδαρον ὥσπερ σοί, πρὸς τὸ κάλλιστον ἀφομοιοῦντι τῶν οἴκοθεν παραδειγμάτων τὸν βίον, εὔδαιμον ἂν εἴη τὸ μεμνῆσθαι τῶν ἀπὸ γένους ἀρίστων, ἀκούοντας περὶ αὐτῶν ἀεί τι καὶ λέγοντας. οὐ γὰρ ἰδίων ἀπορίᾳ καλῶν 4 ἐξαρτῶσιν ἀλλοτρίων ἐπαίνων τὴν δόξαν, ἀλλὰ τοῖς ἐκείνων τὰ οἰκεῖα συνάπτοντες, ὡς καὶ τοῦ γένους καὶ τοῦ βίου καθηγεμόνας εὐφημοῦσι.

Διὸ κἀγὼ τὸν Ἀράτου τοῦ σοῦ πολίτου καὶ προπάτορος 5 βίον, ὃν οὔτε τῇ δόξῃ τῇ περὶ σεαυτὸν οὔτε τῇ δυνάμει καταισχύνεις, ἀπέσταλκά σοι συγγραψάμενος, οὐχ ὡς οὐχὶ πάντων ἀκριβέστατά σοι μεμεληκὸς ἐξ ἀρχῆς ἐπίστασθαι τὰς ἐκείνου πράξεις, ἀλλ' ὅπως οἱ παῖδές σου Πολυκράτης καὶ Πυθοκλῆς οἰκείοις παραδείγμασιν ἐντρέφωνται, τὰ μὲν ἀκούοντες τὰ δ' ἀναγινώσκοντες ἅπερ [οὖν] αὐτοὺς μιμεῖσθαι προσήκει· φιλαύτου γὰρ 6 ἀνδρός, οὐ φιλοκάλου, πάντως ἀεὶ βέλτιστον <ἑαυτὸν> ἡγεῖσθαι.

---

1. 1. διατίθεται, P : διατίθεσθαι GRL.   αἰνήσει PR αἰνέσει GL.
2. ἀρεταῖς GL ἀρετὰς PR.   3. ᾧ : οἷς Herwerden   4. συνάψαντες G.
5. καταισχύνεις G¹ καταισχυνεῖς G²PL καταισχύνεῖς R. [οὖν] Aldine. πάντως
codd. πάντων Paris. 1673.   6. <ἑαυτὸν> Xylander, Anon.

2. Ἡ Σικυωνίων πόλις ἐπεὶ τὸ πρῶτον ἐκ τῆς ἀκρά-
του καὶ Δωρικῆς ἀριστοκρατίας ὥσπερ ἁρμονίας συγχυ-
f θείσης εἰς στάσεις ἐνέπεσε καὶ φιλοτιμίας δημαγωγῶν,
οὐκ ἐπαύσατο νοσοῦσα καὶ ταραττομένη καὶ τύραννον
ἐκ τυράννου μεταβάλλουσα, μέχρι οὗ Κλέωνος ἀναιρεθέντος εἵλοντο Τιμοκλείδαν ἄρχοντα καὶ Κλεινίαν, ἄνδρας ἐνδόξους τὰ μάλιστα καὶ ἐν δυνάμει τῶν πολιτῶν
2 ὄντας. ἤδη δέ τινα τῆς πολιτείας κατάστασιν ἔχειν δο-
1028 κούσης, Τιμοκλείδας μὲν ἀπέθανεν, Ἀβαντίδας δ᾽ ὁ Πα-
σέου τυραννίδα πράττων ἑαυτῷ τὸν Κλεινίαν ἀπέκτεινε,
καὶ τῶν φίλων καὶ οἰκείων τοὺς μὲν ἐξέβαλε τοὺς δ᾽ ἀν-
εῖλεν· ἐζήτει δὲ καὶ τὸν υἱὸν *αὐτὸν ἀνελεῖν Ἄρατον,
3 ἑπταετῆ καταλελειμμένον. ἐν δὲ τῇ περὶ τὴν οἰκίαν
ταραχῇ συνεκπεσὼν τοῖς φεύγουσιν ὁ παῖς καὶ πλανώμε-
νος ἐν τῇ πόλει περίφοβος καὶ ἀβοήθητος, κατὰ τύχην
ἔλαθεν εἰς οἰκίαν παρελθὼν γυναικός, ἀδελφῆς μὲν
Ἀβαντίδου Προφάντῳ δὲ τῷ Κλεινίου ἀδελφῷ γεγαμη-
4 μένης, ὄνομα Σωσοῦς. αὕτη δὲ καὶ τὸ ἦθος οὖσα γεν-
b ναία, καὶ σὺν θεῷ τινι τὸ παιδίον οἰομένη καταπεφευγέναι
πρὸς αὐτήν, ἀπέκρυψεν ἔνδον εἶτα νυκτὸς εἰς Ἄργος ὑπεξέ-
πεμψεν. **3.** οὕτω δ᾽ ἐκκλαπέντι τῷ Ἀράτῳ καὶ διαφυ-
γόντι τὸν κίνδυνον, εὐθὺς μὲν ἐνεφύετο καὶ συνηύξετο
τὸ σφοδρὸν καὶ διάπυρον μῖσος ἐπὶ τοὺς τυράννους·
τρεφόμενος δὲ παρὰ τοῖς ἐν Ἄργει ξένοις καὶ φίλοις
πατρῴοις ἐλευθερίως, καὶ τὸ σῶμα βλαστάνον ὁρῶν εἰς
εὐεξίαν καὶ μέγεθος, ἐπέδωκεν ἑαυτὸν ἀσκήσει τῇ περὶ
παλαίστραν, ὥστε καὶ πένταθλον ἀγωνίσασθαι καὶ στε-
2 φάνων τυχεῖν. ἐπιφαίνεται δ᾽ ἀμέλει καὶ ταῖς εἰκόσιν
ἀθλητική τις ἰδέα, καὶ τὸ συνετὸν τοῦ προσώπου καὶ
c βασιλικὸν οὐ παντάπασιν ἀρνεῖται τὴν ἀδηφαγίαν καὶ τὸ
3 *σκαφεῖον. ὅθεν ἐνδεέστερον ἴσως ἢ πολιτικῷ προσῆκον
ἦν ἀνδρὶ περὶ τὸν λόγον ἐσπούδασε· καίτοι γεγονέναι
κομψότερο<ν εἰκὸ>ς εἰπεῖν ἢ δοκεῖ τισιν ἐκ τῶν ὑπομνημάτων κρίνουσιν, ἃ παρέργως καὶ ὑπὸ χεῖρα διὰ τῶν ἐπιτυ-
4 χόντων ὀνομάτων ἁμιλλησάμενος κατέλιπε. χρόνῳ δ᾽

---

2. 2. αὐτὸν Ed; αὐτοῦ.   3. 2. σκαφεῖον Sintenis : σκάφιον GPL σκαφίον R.
3. κομψότερο<ν εἰκὸ>s εἰπεῖν Henry. κομψότερος εἰπεῖν. δοκεῖ G δοκεῖν PRL.

ὕστερον Ἀβαντίδαν μὲν οἱ περὶ Δεινίαν καὶ Ἀριστοτέλη 4
τὸν διαλεκτικόν, εἰωθότα τοῖς λόγοις αὐτῶν κατ' ἀγορὰν
σχολαζόντων ἑκάστοτε παρεῖναι καὶ συμφιλονικεῖν,
ἐμβαλόντες εἰς τοιαύτην διατριβὴν καὶ κατασκευάσαντες
ἐπιβουλὴν ἀνεῖλον, Πασέαν δὲ τὸν Ἀβαντίδου πατέρα
τὴν ἀρχὴν ὑπολαβόντα Νικοκλῆς δολοφονήσας ἑαυτὸν d
ἀνέδειξε τύραννον. τοῦτον ἐμφερέστατον λέγουσι τὴν 5
ὄψιν Περιάνδρῳ τῷ Κυψέλου γενέσθαι, καθάπερ
Ἀλκμαίωνι μὲν τῷ Ἀμφιάρεω τὸν Πέρσην Ὀρόντην,
Ἕκτορι δὲ τὸν Λακεδαιμόνιον νεανίσκον, ὃν ἱστορεῖ
Μυρσίλος ὑπὸ πλήθους τῶν θεωμένων ὡς τοῦτ' ἔγνωσαν
καταπατηθῆναι.

4. Τοῦ δὲ Νικοκλέους τέσσαρας μῆνας τυραννοῦντος,
ἐν οἷς πολλὰ κακὰ τὴν πόλιν ἐργασάμενος ἐκινδύνευεν
ὑπ' Αἰτωλῶν ἐπιβουλευομένην αὐτὴν ἀποβαλεῖν, ἤδη
μειράκιον ὁ Ἄρατος ὢν ἀξίωμα λαμπρὸν εἶχε δι'
εὐγένειαν καὶ φρόνημα, ὃ διέφαινεν οὐ μικρὸν οὐδ'
ἀργόν, ἐμβριθὲς δὲ καὶ παρ' ἡλικίαν ἀσφαλεστέρᾳ e
γνώμῃ κεκραμένον. ὅθεν οἵ τε φυγάδες μάλιστα τὸν 2
νοῦν ἐκείνῳ προσεῖχον, ὅ τε Νικοκλῆς οὐκ ἠμέλει τῶν
πραττομένων, ἀλλ' ἀδήλως ἀπεθεώρει καὶ παρεφύλαττεν
αὐτοῦ τὴν ὁρμήν, τόλμημα μὲν οὐδὲν τηλικοῦτον δεδιὼς
οὐδ' ἔργον οὐδὲν οὕτω παρακεκινδυνευμένον, ὑποπτεύων
δὲ τοῖς βασιλεῦσιν αὐτὸν διαλέγεσθαι φίλοις οὖσι καὶ
ξένοις πατρῴοις.

Καὶ γὰρ ἀληθῶς ὁ Ἄρατος ἐπεχείρησε τὴν ὁδὸν 3
ἐκείνην βαδίζειν. ὡς δ' Ἀντίγονος μὲν ὑπισχνούμενος
ἠμέλει καὶ παρῆγε τὸν χρόνον, αἱ δ' ἀπ' Αἰγύπτου καὶ
παρὰ Πτολεμαίου μακρὰν ἦσαν ἐλπίδες, ἔγνω δι' αὐτοῦ
καταλύειν τὸν τύραννον. 5. πρώτοις δὲ κοινοῦται τὴν f
γνώμην Ἀριστομάχῳ καὶ Ἐκδήλῳ. τούτων ὁ μὲν ἐκ
Σικυῶνος ἦν φυγάς, ὁ δ' Ἔκδηλος Ἀρκὰς ἐκ Μεγάλης
πόλεως, ἀνὴρ φιλόσοφος καὶ πρακτικός, Ἀρκεσιλάου
τοῦ *Ἀκαδημιακοῦ γεγονὼς ἐν ἄστει συνήθης. δεξαμένων 2

---

4. ἐκβαλόντες G.   5. Μυρσίλος] μυρσίλος PR μυρτίλος GL² μυρτίλος L¹.
4. 2. ἀπεθεώρει PL παρεθεώρει G.   3. παρῆγε G παρῆκε PRL.   5. 1. Ἀκαδημιακοῦ Sintenis : ἀκαδημαϊκοῦ.

δὲ τούτων προθύμως, διελέγετο τοῖς ἄλλοις φυγάσιν,
1029 ὧν ὀλίγοι μὲν αἰσχυνθέντες ἐγκαταλιπεῖν τὴν ἐλπίδα
μετεῖχον τῶν πραττομένων, οἱ δὲ πολλοὶ καὶ τὸν
Ἄρατον ἐπειρῶντο κατακωλύειν ὡς ἀπειρίᾳ πραγμάτων
3 θρασυνόμενον. βουλευομένου δ' αὐτοῦ χωρίον τι τῆς
Σικυωνίας καταλαβεῖν, ὅθεν ὡρμημένος διαπολεμήσει
πρὸς τὸν τύραννον, ἧκεν εἰς Ἄργος ἀνὴρ Σικυώνιος ἐκ
τῆς εἰρκτῆς ἀποδεδρακώς· ἦν δὲ τῶν φυγάδων ἑνὸς
Ξενοκλέους ἀδελφός· καὶ τῷ Ἀράτῳ προσαχθεὶς ὑπὸ
τοῦ Ξενοκλέους, ἔλεγε τοῦ τείχους, καθ' ὃν ὑπερβὰς
αὐτὸς ἐσώθη τόπον, ἐντὸς μὲν ὀλίγου δεῖν ἐπίπεδον εἶναι,
b προσπεφυκότα χωρίοις πετρώδεσι καὶ ὑψηλοῖς, τὸ δ' ἔξω-
4 θεν ὕψος ὑπὸ κλιμάκων οὐ πάνυ *δυσέφικτον. ὡς δὲ ταῦτ'
ἤκουσεν ὁ Ἄρατος, ἐκπέμπει μετὰ τοῦ Ξενοκλέους οἰκέτας
ἰδίους δύο Σεύθαν τε καὶ Τέχνωνα κατασκεψομένους τὸ
τεῖχος, ἐγνωκὼς εἰ δύναιτο κρύφα καὶ πρὸς ἕνα κίνδυνον
ὀξέως τὸ πᾶν ἀναρρῖψαι μᾶλλον, ἢ μακρῷ πολέμῳ καὶ
φανεροῖς ἀγῶσιν ἰδιώτης ἀντικαθίστασθαι πρὸς τύραννον.
5 ὡς δ' ἐπανῆλθον οἱ περὶ τὸν Ξενοκλέα, τοῦ μὲν τείχους
εἰληφότες μέτρα καὶ τοῦ τόπου τὴν φύσιν ἀπαγγέλλοντες
οὐκ ἄπορον οὐδὲ χαλεπήν, τὸ δὲ λαθεῖν προσελθόντας
ἐργῶδες εἶναι φάσκοντες ὑπὸ κηπουροῦ τινος κυναρίων,
c μικρῶν μὲν ἐκτόπως δὲ μαχίμων καὶ ἀπαρηγορήτων,
εὐθὺς ἐνίστατο τὴν πρᾶξιν.

6. Ἡ μὲν οὖν τῶν ὅπλων παρασκευὴ συνήθης ἦν,
πάντων ὡς ἔπος εἰπεῖν τότε κλωπείαις χρωμένων καὶ
καταδρομαῖς ἐπ' ἀλλήλους· τὰς δὲ κλίμακας Εὐφράνωρ
ὁ μηχανοποιὸς ἀναφανδὸν ἐπήξατο, τῆς τέχνης αὐτῷ τὸ
ἀνύποπτον διδούσης, ἐπεὶ καὶ αὐτὸς ἦν τῶν φυγάδων.
2 ἄνδρας δ' αὐτῷ τῶν μὲν ἐν Ἄργει φίλων ἕκαστος [ἐξ
ὀλίγων] δέκα παρέσχεν, αὐτὸς δὲ τῶν ἰδίων οἰκετῶν
τριάκοντα καθώπλισεν. ἐμισθώσατο δὲ καὶ διὰ Ξενοφίλου
*πρώτου τῶν ἀρχικλώπων οὐ πολλοὺς στρατιώτας, οἷς
d διεδόθη λόγος ὡς ἐπὶ τὰς ἵππους τὰς βασιλικὰς εἰς τὴν

---

4. δυσέφικτον Sintenis, to heal the hiatus: ἀνέφικτον.   5. ἄπορον GL
ἄβατον PR.   6. 2. [ἐξ ὀλίγων] Ziegler. Ξενοφίλου πρώτου Anon: πρώτου
Ξενοφίλου.

Σικυωνίαν ἔξοδος ἔσοιτο. καὶ προεπέμφθησαν οἱ πολλοὶ
σποράδες ἐπὶ τὸν Πολυγνώτου πύργον, ἐκεῖ κελευσθέντες
περιμεῖναι. προεπέμφθη δὲ καὶ Καφισίας ὑπ' αὐτοῦ 3
μετὰ τεσσάρων ἄλλων εὔζωνος οὓς ἔδει πρὸς τὸν
κηπουρὸν ἀφικέσθαι σκοταίους, φάσκοντας ὁδοιπόρους
εἶναι καὶ καταυλισαμένους αὐτόν τε συγκλεῖσαι καὶ τοὺς
κύνας· οὐ γὰρ ἦν ἄλλῃ παρελθεῖν. τὰς δὲ κλίμακας
διαλυτὰς οὔσας ἐμβαλόντες εἰς ἀχάνας καὶ κατακαλύψαν-
τες ἐφ' ἁμαξῶν προαπέστειλαν. ἐν τούτῳ δὲ κατασκόπων 4
τινῶν ἐν Ἄργει τοῦ Νικοκλέους φανέντων καὶ περιιέναι e
λεγομένων ἀδήλως καὶ παραφυλάττειν τὸν Ἄρατον, ἅμ'
ἡμέρᾳ προ[σ]ελθὼν καὶ φανερὸς ὢν ἐν ἀγορᾷ διέτριβε
μετὰ τῶν φίλων· εἶτ' ἀλειψάμενος ἐν τῷ γυμνασίῳ καὶ
παραλαβών τινας ἐκ τῆς παλαίστρας τῶν εἰωθότων πίνειν
καὶ ῥᾳθυμεῖν μετ' αὐτοῦ νεανίσκων *ἀπῆγεν οἴκαδε·
καὶ μετὰ μικρὸν ἑωρᾶτο τῶν οἰκετῶν αὐτοῦ δι' ἀγορᾶς ὁ
μὲν στεφάνους φέρων, ὁ δὲ λαμπάδας ὠνούμενος, ὁ δὲ
τοῖς εἰθισμένοις παρὰ πότον ψάλλειν καὶ αὐλεῖν γυναίοις
διαλεγόμενος. ταῦτα δ' οἱ κατάσκοποι πάνθ' ὁρῶντες
ἐξηπάτηντο καὶ πρὸς ἀλλήλους ἀναγελῶντες ἔλεγον· "οὐ- 5
δὲν ἦν ἄρα τυράννου δειλότερον, εἰ καὶ Νικοκλῆς f
τηλικαύτην πόλιν ἔχων καὶ τοσαύτην δύναμιν ὀρρωδεῖ
μειράκιον εἰς ἡδονὰς καὶ πότους μεθημερινοὺς τὰ τῆς
φυγῆς ἐφόδια καταχρώμενον." 7. οἱ μὲν οὖν οὕτω
παραλογισθέντες ἀπηλλάγησαν.

Ὁ δ' Ἄρατος εὐθὺς μετ' ἄριστον ἐξελθὼν καὶ συνάψας
πρὸς τὸν Πολυγνώτου πύργον τοῖς στρατιώταις εἰς Νεμέαν
προ[σ]ῆγεν ὅπου τὴν πρᾶξιν ἐξέφηνε τοῖς πολλοῖς *τότε
πρῶτον, ὑποσχέσεις τε καὶ παρακλήσεις ἐποιήσατο. καὶ 2
σύνθημα παραδοὺς Ἀπόλλωνα ὑπερδέξιον προῆγεν ἐπὶ 1030
τὴν πόλιν, συμμέτρως τῇ περιφορᾷ τῆς σελήνης ἐπιταχ-
ύνων καὶ πάλιν ἀνιεὶς τὴν πορείαν, ὥστε τῷ μὲν φωτὶ
χρῆσθαι καθ' ὁδόν, ἤδη δὲ δυομένης περὶ τὸν κῆπον εἶναι
πλησίον τοῦ τείχους. ἐνταῦθα Καφισίας ἀπήντησεν 3
αὐτῷ, τῶν μὲν κυναρίων οὐ κρατήσας — ἔφθη γὰρ

---

6. 4. προ[σ]ελθὼν Solanus. ἀπῆγεν Sintenis: ἀπῆρεν.   7. 1. προ[σ]ῆγεν
Juntine. τότε Schaefer: τὸ δὲ. προῆγεν G προσῆγεν PRL.

ἀποπηδήσαντα—, τὸν δὲ κηπουρὸν ἐγκεκλεικώς. ἀθύ-
μους δὲ τοὺς πλείστους γενομένους καὶ κελεύοντας
ἀπαλλάττεσθαι παρεθάρρυνεν ὁ Ἄρατος, ὡς ἀπάξων ἂν
4 οἱ κύνες ἄγαν ἐνοχλῶσιν αὐτοῖς. ἅμα δὲ τοὺς τὰς
b κλίμακας φέροντας προπέμψας, ὧν Ἔκδηλος ἡγεῖτο καὶ
Μνασίθεος, αὐτὸς ἐπηκολούθει σχολαίως, ἤδη τῶν
κυναρίων εὐτόνως ὑλακτούντων καὶ συμπαρατρεχόντων
τοῖς περὶ τὸν Ἔκδηλον. οὐ μὴν ἀλλὰ προσέμειξάν τε
τῷ τείχει καὶ προσήρεισαν τὰς κλίμακας ἀσφαλῶς.
5 ἀναβαινόντων δὲ τῶν πρώτων, ὁ τὴν ἑωθινὴν φυλακὴν
παραδιδοὺς ἐφώδευε κώδωνι, καὶ φῶτα πολλὰ καὶ
θόρυβος ἦν τῶν *ἀποπορευομένων. οἱ δ' ὥσπερ εἶχον
αὐτοῦ πτήξαντες ἐπὶ τῶν κλιμάκων, τούτους μὲν οὐ
χαλεπῶς ἔλαθον, ἄλλης δὲ φυλακῆς ἐναντίας ταύτῃ
6 προσερχομένης εἰς τὸν ἔσχατον κίνδυνον ἦλθον. ὡς δὲ
c κἀκείνην διέφυγον παρελθοῦσαν, εὐθὺς ἀνέβαινον οἱ
πρῶτοι Μνασίθεος καὶ Ἔκδηλος, καὶ τὰς ἑκατέρωθεν
ὁδοὺς τοῦ τείχους διαλαβόντες, ἀπέστελλον Τέχνωνα
πρὸς Ἄρατον ἐπείγεσθαι κελεύοντες. 8. ἦν δ' οὐ πολὺ
διάστημα ἀπὸ τοῦ κήπου πρὸς τὸ τεῖχος καὶ τὸν πύργον,
ἐν ᾧ κύων μέγας ἐφρούρει θηρατικός. αὐτὸς μὲν οὖν
οὐκ ᾔσθετο τὴν ἔφοδον, εἴτε φύσει νωθὴς ὢν εἴτε μεθ'
ἡμέραν κατάκοπος γεγονώς. τῶν δὲ τοῦ κηπουροῦ
κυναρίων κάτωθεν ἐκκαλουμένων αὐτόν, ὑπεφθέγγετο τυ-
φλὸν καὶ ἄσημον τὸ πρῶτον, εἶτα μᾶλλον ἐπέτεινε παρερ-
2 χομένων· καὶ κατεῖχεν ἤδη πολὺς ὑλαγμὸς τὸ χωρίον,
d ὥστε τὸν πέραν φύλακα κραυγῇ μεγάλῃ πυνθάνεσθαι τοῦ
κυνηγοῦ, πρὸς τίνα τραχέως οὕτως ὁ κύων ὑλακτεῖ, καὶ
3 μή τι γίνεται καινότερον. ὁ δ' ἀπὸ τοῦ πύργου <πρὸς>
αὐτὸν ἀντεφώνησε μηδὲν εἶναι δεινόν, ἀλλὰ τὸν κύνα
πρὸς τὸ φῶς τῶν τειχοφυλάκων καὶ τὸν ψόφον τοῦ
κώδωνος παρωξύνθαι. τοῦτο μάλιστα τοὺς Ἀράτου στρατιώτας ἐπέρρωσεν, οἰομένους τὸν κυνηγὸν ἐπικρύπτειν
κοινωνοῦντα τῇ πράξει, εἶναι δὲ πολλοὺς καὶ ἄλλους ἐν

3. ἀθύμως G.   4. εὐτόνως GL ἐντόνως PR.   5. ἀποπορευομένων
Henry : ἐπιπορευομένων   8. 2. γένηται G¹.   3. <πρὸς> αὐτὸν Anon,
Stephanus. αὐτὸν PR αὐτῷ GL. τοῦ κώδωνος G²PRL τῶν κωδώνων G¹ (erased).
παρωξύνθαι G παρωξύνεσθαι R₁ παροξύνεσθαι R²PL.

τῇ πόλει τοὺς συνεργοῦντας. οὐ μήν ἀλλὰ τῷ τείχει 4
προσβαλόντων, χαλεπὸς ἦν ὁ κίνδυνος καὶ μῆκος
ἐλάμβανε, τῶν κλιμάκων κραδαινομένων εἰ μὴ καθ᾽ ἕνα
καὶ σχολαίως ἀναβαίνοιεν· ἡ δ᾽ ὥρα κατήπειγεν, ἤδη
φθεγγομένων ἀλεκτρυόνων καὶ ὅσον οὔπω τῶν ἐξ ἀγροῦ e
τι φέρειν εἰωθότων πρὸς ἀγορὰν ἐπερχομένων. διὸ καὶ 5
σπεύδων ὁ Ἄρατος ἀνέβαινε, τεσσαράκοντα τῶν πάντων
ἀναβεβηκότων πρὸ αὐτοῦ· καὶ προσδεξάμενος ἔτι τῶν
κάτωθεν ὀλίγους, ἐπὶ τὴν οἰκίαν τοῦ τυράννου καὶ τὸ
στρατήγιον ἐπῆλθεν· ἐνταῦθα γὰρ οἱ μισθοφόροι παρε-
νυκτέρευον. ἄφνω δ᾽ ἐπιπεσὼν αὐτοῖς καὶ συλλαβὼν
ἅπαντας, οὐδένα δ᾽ ἀποκτείνας, εὐθὺς διεπέμπετο πρὸς
τοὺς φίλους ἀνακαλούμενος ἕκαστον ἀπ᾽ οἰκίας. καὶ 6
συνδραμόντων πανταχόθεν, ἡμέρα μὲν ὑπέλαμπεν ἤδη
καὶ τὸ θέατρον ἦν ὄχλου μεστόν, ἔτι πρὸς τὴν ἄδηλον f
αἰωρουμένων φήμην καὶ σαφὲς οὐδὲν εἰδότων ὑπὲρ τῶν
πραττομένων, πρίν γε δὴ προελθὼν ὁ κῆρυξ εἶπεν, ὡς
Ἄρατος ὁ Κλεινίου παρακαλεῖ τοὺς πολίτας ἐπὶ τὴν
ἐλευθερίαν. 9. τότε δὲ πιστεύσαντες ἥκειν ἃ πάλαι
προσεδόκων, ὥρμησαν ἀθρόοι πρὸς τὰς θύρας τοῦ
τυράννου πῦρ ἐπιφέροντες. ἤρθη δὲ φλὸξ μεγάλη καὶ
καταφανὴς μέχρι Κορίνθου τῆς οἰκίας ἀναφθείσης, ὥστε
θαυμάσαντας τοὺς ἐν Κορίνθῳ παρὰ μικρὸν ὁρμῆσαι 1031
πρὸς τὴν βοήθειαν. ὁ μὲν οὖν Νικοκλῆς ἔλαθε διά τινων 2
ὑπονόμων ὑπεκδὺς καὶ ἀποδρὰς ἐκ τῆς πόλεως, οἱ δὲ
στρατιῶται καταπαύσαντες μετὰ τῶν Σικυωνίων τὸ πῦρ
διήρπαζον τὴν οἰκίαν. καὶ* οὔτε ταῦτ᾽ ἐκώλυσεν ὁ
Ἄρατος, τά τε λοιπὰ χρήματα τῶν τυράννων εἰς μέσον
ἔθηκε τοῖς πολίταις. ἀπέθανε δ᾽ οὐδεὶς οὐδ᾽ ἐτρώθη 3
τοπαράπαν τῶν ἐπελθόντων οὐδὲ τῶν πολεμίων, ἀλλὰ
καθαρὰν καὶ ἄθικτον αἵματος ἐμφυλίου τὴν πρᾶξιν ἡ
τύχη διεφύλαξε.

Κατήγαγε δὲ φυγάδας τοὺς μὲν ὑπὸ Νικοκλέους ἐκ- 4
πεπτωκότας ὀγδοήκοντα, τοὺς δ᾽ ἐπὶ τῶν ἔμπροσθεν τυ- b
ράννων οὐκ ἐλάττους πεντακοσίων, οἷς μακρὰ μὲν ἡ

---

5. ἐπῆλθεν PRG¹L² ἐπανῆλθεν L¹G² ἀνῆλθεν Coraes.   6. εἰδότων (erased)
R² : εἰδότος R¹PGL.   9. 2. ὑπεκδὺς LG² ὑπ^{εισ}δὺς PR ὑπεισδὺς erased G¹
(apparently). ἀνήρπαζον G¹. οὔτε Coraes : οὐδὲ.

5 πλάνη καὶ ὁμοῦ τι πεντηκονταετὴς ἐγεγόνει. κατελθόν-
τες δ᾽ οἱ πλεῖστοι πένητες, ὧν κύριοι πρότερον ἦσαν ἐπε-
λαμβάνοντο, καὶ βαδίζοντες ἐπὶ τὰ χωρία καὶ τὰς οἰκίας
δεινὴν ἀπορίαν τῷ Ἀράτῳ παρεῖχον, ἐπιβουλευομένην
μὲν ἔξωθεν καὶ φθονουμένην ὑπ᾽ Ἀντιγόνου τὴν πόλιν
ὁρῶντι διὰ τὴν ἐλευθερίαν, ταραττομένην δ᾽ ὑφ᾽ αὑτῆς
καὶ στασιάζουσαν.

6 Ὅθεν ἐκ τῶν παρόντων ἄριστα κρίνας προσέμειξεν
αὐτὴν φέρων τοῖς Ἀχαιοῖς· καὶ Δωριεῖς ὄντες ὑπέδυσαν
c ἑκουσίως ὄνομα καὶ πολιτείαν τὴν Ἀχαιῶν, οὔτ᾽ ἀξίωμα
λαμπρὸν οὔτε μεγάλην ἰσχὺν ἐχόντων τότε. μικροπολῖται
γὰρ ἦσαν οἱ πολλοί, καὶ γῆν οὔτε χρηστὴν οὔτ᾽ ἄφθονον
ἐκέκτηντο, καὶ θαλάττῃ προσῴκουν ἀλιμένῳ, τὰ πολλὰ
7 κατὰ ῥαχίας ἐκφερομένῃ πρὸς τὴν ἤπειρον. ἀλλὰ μάλιστα δὴ διέδειξαν οὗτοι τὴν Ἑλληνικὴν ἀλκὴν ἀπρόσ-
μαχον οὖσαν, ὁσάκις τύχοι κόσμου καὶ συντάξεως
ὁμοφρονούσης καὶ νοῦν ἔχοντος ἡγεμόνος, οἳ τῆς μὲν
πάλαι τῶν Ἑλλήνων ἀκμῆς οὐδὲν ὡς εἰπεῖν μέρος ὄντες,
ἐν δὲ τῷ τότε μιᾶς ἀξιολόγου πόλεως σύμπαντες ὁμοῦ
δύναμιν οὐκ ἔχοντες, εὐβουλίᾳ καὶ ὁμονοίᾳ, καὶ ὅτι τῷ
d πρώτῳ κατ᾽ ἀρετὴν ἐδύναντο μὴ φθονεῖν ἀλλὰ πείθεσθαι
καὶ ἀκολουθεῖν, οὐ μόνον αὑτοὺς ἐν μέσῳ πόλεων καὶ
δυνάμεων τηλικούτων καὶ τυραννίδων διεφύλαξαν ἐλευθέρους, ἀλλὰ καὶ τῶν ἄλλων Ἑλλήνων ὡς πλείστους
ἐλευθεροῦντες καὶ σῴζοντες διετέλουν.

10. Ἦν δ᾽ Ἄρατος τῷ τρόπῳ πολιτικός, μεγαλόφρων,
ἀκριβέστερος εἰς τὰ κοινὰ μᾶλλον τῶν ἰδίων, πικρῶς
μισοτύραννος, ἔχθρας ὅρῳ καὶ φιλίας ἀεὶ τῷ κοινῷ
2 συμφέροντι χρώμενος. ὅθεν οὐχ οὕτως δοκεῖ γεγονέναι
φίλος ἀκριβής, ὡς ἐχθρὸς εὐγνώμων καὶ πρᾶος, ὑπὸ τῆς
πολιτείας ἐπ᾽ ἀμφότερα τῷ καιρῷ μεταβαλλόμενος,
e ὁμονοίας ἐθνῶν καὶ κοινωνίας πόλεων καὶ συνεδρίου καὶ
θεάτρου μίαν φωνὴν ἀφιέντος ὡς οὐδενὸς ἄλλου τῶν καλῶν
ἐραστής, πολέμῳ καὶ ἀγῶνι χρήσασθαι φανερῶς ἀθαρ-
σὴς καὶ δύσελπις, κλέψαι δὲ πράγματα καὶ συσκευά-

σασθαι κρύφα πόλεις καὶ τυράννους ἐπηβολώτατος, διὸ 3 καὶ πολλὰ τῶν ἀνελπίστων κατορθώσας ἐν οἷς ἐτόλμησεν, οὐκ ἐλάττονα δοκεῖ τῶν δυνατῶν ἐγκαταλιπεῖν δι᾿ εὐλά-βειαν. οὐ γὰρ μόνον ὡς ἔοικε θηρίων τινῶν ὄψεις, 4 ἐνεργοὶ διὰ σκότους οὖσαι, μεθ᾿ ἡμέραν ἀποτυφλοῦνται ξηρότητι καὶ λεπτότητι τῆς περὶ τὸν ὀφθαλμὸν ὑγρότητος, μὴ φερούσης τὴν πρὸς τὸ φῶς σύγκρασιν, ἀλλὰ καὶ δει- f νότης τίς ἐστιν ἀνθρώπου καὶ σύνεσις ἐν τοῖς ὑπαίθροις καὶ διακεκηρυγμένοις εὐτάρακτος φύσει, πρὸς δὲ τὰς ἐπικρύφους καὶ λαθραίους ἀναθαρσοῦσα πράξεις. τὴν 5 δὲ τοιαύτην ἀνωμαλίαν ἔνδεια λόγου φιλοσόφου περὶ τὰς εὐφυΐας ἀπεργάζεται, τὴν ἀρετὴν ὥσπερ καρπὸν αὐτοφυῆ καὶ ἀγεώργητον ἐκφερούσα<ς> δίχα τῆς ἐπιστήμης. ταῦτα 1032 μὲν οὖν ἐξεταζέσθω τοῖς παραδείγμασιν.

11. Ὁ δ᾿ Ἄρατος ἐπεὶ κατέμειξε τοῖς Ἀχαιοῖς ἑαυτὸν καὶ τὴν πόλιν, ἐν τοῖς ἱππεῦσι στρατευόμενος ἠγαπᾶτο δι᾿ εὐπείθειαν ὑπὸ τῶν ἀρχόντων, ὅτι καίπερ συμβολὰς τῷ κοινῷ μεγάλας δεδωκὼς τὴν ἑαυτοῦ δόξαν καὶ τὴν τῆς πατρίδος δύναμιν, ὡς ἑνὶ τῶν ἐπιτυχόντων χρῆσθαι παρεῖχεν *αὑτὸν τῷ ἀεὶ στρατηγοῦντι τῶν Ἀχαιῶν, εἴτε Δυμαῖος εἴτε Τριταιεὺς εἴτε μικροτέρας τινὸς ὢν τύχοι πόλεως.

Ἧκε δ᾿ αὐτῷ καὶ χρημάτων δωρεὰ παρὰ τοῦ βασιλέως 2 πέντε καὶ εἴκοσι τάλαντα. ταῦτ᾿ ἔλαβε μὲν ὁ Ἄρατος, λαβὼν δὲ τοῖς ἑαυτοῦ πολίταις ἐπέδωκεν, ἀπορουμένοις εἴς τε τἆλλα καὶ λύτρωσιν αἰχμαλώτων. **12.** Ἐπεὶ δ᾿ οἱ b φυγάδες ἦσαν ἀπαρηγόρητοι τοῖς ἔχουσι τὰς κτήσεις ἐνοχλοῦντες, ἥ τε πόλις ἐκινδύνευεν ἀνάστατος γενέσθαι, μίαν ὁρῶν ἐλπίδα τὴν Πτολεμαίου φιλανθρωπίαν, ὥρμη-σεν ἐκπλεῦσαι καὶ δεηθῆναι τοῦ βασιλέως, ὅπως αὐτῷ χρήματα συμβάληται πρὸς τὰς διαλύσεις. ἀνήχθη μὲν οὖν ἀπὸ Μοθώνης ὑπὲρ Μαλέας, ὡς τῷ διὰ πόρου δρόμῳ χρησόμενος. πρὸς δὲ μέγα πνεῦμα καὶ πολλὴν θάλασ- 2 σαν ἐκ πελάγους κατιοῦσαν ἐνδόντος τοῦ κυβερνήτου,

---

4. ὑπαίθροις GL ὑπαιθρίοις PR.   5. ἐκφερούσα<ς> Emperius. συμβούλας P.
11. 1. αὑτὸν τῷ ἀεὶ στρατηγοῦντι Sintenis : αὐτῷ τὸν ἀεὶ στρατηγοῦντα. τριταιεὺς G² : τριτεεὺς G¹ and R before erasure, τριτεὺς PL and after erasure R.
2. μὲν ἔλαβεν G.

παραφερόμενος μόλις ἤψατο τῆς Ἀ<ν>δρίας πολεμίας
3 c οὔσης· ἐκρατεῖτο γὰρ ὑπ' Ἀντιγόνου καὶ φυλακὴν εἶχεν·
ἣν φθάσας ἀπέβη, καὶ τὴν ναῦν καταλιπὼν ἀπεχώρησε
μακρὰν ἀπὸ θαλάσσης, ἔχων ἕνα τῶν φίλων σὺν αὐτῷ
Τιμάνθη. καὶ καταβαλόντες ἑαυτοὺς εἴς τινα τόπον ὕλης
4 γέμοντα χαλεπῶς ἐνυκτέρευον. ὀλίγῳ δ' ὕστερον ὁ φρού-
ραρχος ἐπελθὼν καὶ ζητῶν τὸν Ἄρατον ὑπὸ τῶν θερα-
πόντων ἐξηπατήθη τῶν ἐκείνου, δεδιδαγμένων λέγειν
ὡς εὐθὺς ἀποδρὰς εἰς Εὔβοιαν ἐξέπλευσε. τὰ μέντοι
κομιζόμενα καὶ τὴν ναῦν καὶ τοὺς θεράποντας ἀπέφηνε
5 d πολέμια καὶ κατέσχε. μετὰ δ' ἡμέρας οὐ πολλὰς ἐν
ἀπόροις ὄντι τῷ Ἀράτῳ γίνεταί τις εὐτυχία, Ῥωμαϊκῆς
νεὼς παραβαλούσης κατὰ τὸν τόπον, ἐν ᾧ τὰ μὲν ἐπὶ
σκοπὴν ἀνιὼν τὰ δὲ κρυπτόμενος διῆγεν. ἔπλει μὲν οὖν
ἡ ναῦς εἰς Συρίαν, ἐπέβη δὲ πείσας τὸν ναύκληρον ἄχρι
Καρίας διακομισθῆναι· καὶ διεκομίσθη κινδύνοις αὖθις
6 οὐκ ἐλάττοσι χρησάμενος κατὰ θάλατταν. ἐκ δὲ Καρίας
χρόνῳ πολλῷ περαιωθεὶς εἰς Αἴγυπτον, αὐτόθεν τε τῷ
βασιλεῖ διακειμένῳ πρὸς αὐτὸν οἰκείως ἐνέτυχε καὶ
τεθεραπευμένῳ γραφαῖς καὶ πίναξιν ἀπὸ τῆς Ἑλλάδος,
ἐν οἷς κρίσιν ἔχων οὐκ ἄμουσον ὁ Ἄρατος ἀεί τι τῶν
e τεχνικῶν καὶ περιττῶν, μάλιστα δὲ Παμφίλου καὶ Μελάν-
θου, συνάγων καὶ κτώμενος ἀπέστελλεν. 13. ἤνθει
γὰρ ἔτι δόξα τῆς Σικυωνίας μούσης καὶ χρηστογραφίας,
ὡς μόνης ἀδιάφθορον ἐχούσης τὸ καλόν, ὥστε καὶ Ἀπελλῆν
ἐκεῖνον ἤδη θαυμαζόμενον ἀφικέσθαι καὶ συγγενέσθαι
τοῖς ἀνδράσιν ἐπὶ ταλάντῳ, τῆς δόξης μᾶλλον ἢ τῆς
2 τέχνης δεόμενον μεταλαβεῖν. διὸ τὰς μὲν ἄλλας εἰκόνας
τῶν τυράννων ἀνεῖλεν εὐθὺς ὁ Ἄρατος ὅτε τὴν πόλιν
ἠλευθέρωσε, περὶ δὲ τῆς Ἀριστράτου τοῦ κατὰ Φίλιππον
ἀκμάσαντος ἐβουλεύσατο πολὺν χρόνον. ἐγράφη μὲν
γὰρ ὑπὸ πάντων τῶν περὶ τὸν Μέλανθον ἅρματι
νικηφόρῳ παρεστὼς ὁ Ἀρίστρατος, Ἀπελλοῦ συνεφα-
f ψαμένου τῆς γραφῆς, ὡς Πολέμων ὁ περιηγητὴς

---

12. 2. Ἀ<ν>δρίας Palmerius : Ὑδρίας or Ὑδρείας Bergk.   3. τιμάνθη GPRL
τιμάνθην R². 	5. ἐπὶ σκοπὴν PRL ἐπισκοπεῖν G. τεθεραπευμένῳ G θεραπευο-
μένῳ PRL. 	13. 1. μόνην G¹. 	2. ἐλευθέρωσε G. τοῦ G : omitted, PRL.
τῶν omitted, G. ὁ ἀρίστρατος G¹PRL² ὁ ἄρατος L¹G² (margin).

ἱστόρηκεν. ἦν δὲ τὸ ἔργον ἀξιοθέατον, ὥστε γνάμπτεσ- 3
θαι τὸν Ἄρατον ὑπὸ τῆς τέχνης, αὖθίς τε μίσει τῷ πρὸς
τοὺς τυράννους ἐξαγόμενον κελεύειν καθαιρεῖν. τὸν οὖν 4
ζωγράφον Νεάλκη φίλον ὄντα τοῦ Ἀράτου παραιτεῖσθαί
φασι καὶ δακρύειν, ὡς δ' οὐκ ἔπειθεν, εἰπεῖν ὅτι τοῖς
τυράννοις πολεμητέον, οὐ τοῖς τῶν τυράννων· " ἐάσωμεν
οὖν τὸ ἅρμα καὶ τὴν Νίκην, αὐτὸν δέ σοι παρέξω
τὸν Ἀρίστρατον ἐγὼ παραχωροῦντα τοῦ πίνακος." 1033
ἐπιτρέψαντος οὖν τοῦ Ἀράτου, *διήλειψεν ὁ Νεάλκης τὸν 5
Ἀρίστρατον, εἰς δὲ τὴν χώραν φοίνικα μόνον ἐνέγραψεν,
ἄλλο δ' οὐδὲν ἐτόλμησε *παρεμβαλεῖν· τοὺς δὲ πόδας
ἐξαλειφομένου τοῦ Ἀριστράτου διαλαθεῖν ὑπὸ τὸ ἅρμα
λέγουσιν.

Ἔκ τε δὴ τούτων ὁ Ἄρατος ἠγαπᾶτο, καὶ <γνώμης> 6
διδοὺς πεῖραν ἔτι μᾶλλον ἥψατο τοῦ βασιλέως, καὶ
δωρεὰν ἔλαβε τῇ πόλει πεντήκοντα καὶ ἑκατὸν τάλαντα.
καὶ τούτων τεσσαράκοντα μὲν εὐθὺς μεθ' ἑαυτοῦ κομίζων
εἰς Πελοπόννησον κατῆρε, τὰ δὲ λοιπὰ διελὼν εἰς δόσεις
ὁ βασιλεὺς ὕστερον κατὰ μέρος ἀπέστειλεν.

14. Ἦν μὲν οὖν μέγα καὶ τὸ χρήματα τοσαῦτα b
πορίσαι τοῖς πολίταις, ὅσων μικρὸν μέρος ἄλλοι
στρατηγοὶ καὶ δημαγωγοὶ λαμβάνοντες παρὰ βασιλέων
ἠδίκουν καὶ κατεδουλοῦντο καὶ προέπινον αὐτοῖς τὰς
πατρίδας, μεῖζον δ' ἡ διὰ τῶν χρημάτων τούτων
κατασκευασθεῖσα τοῖς μὲν ἀπόροις πρὸς τοὺς πλουσίους
διάλυσις καὶ ὁμόνοια, τῷ δὲ δήμῳ παντὶ σωτηρία καὶ
ἀσφάλεια, θαυμαστὴ δ' ἡ τοῦ ἀνδρὸς ἐν δυνάμει τοσαύτῃ
μετριότης. ἀποδειχθεὶς γὰρ αὐτοκράτωρ διαλλακτὴς 2
καὶ κύριος ὅλως ἐπὶ τὰς φυγαδικὰς οἰκονομίας, μόνος οὐχ
ὑπέμεινεν, ἀλλὰ πεντεκαίδεκα τῶν πολιτῶν προσκατέλεξεν
ἑαυτῷ, μεθ' ὧν πόνῳ πολλῷ καὶ μεγάλαις πραγματείαις c
κατειργάσατο καὶ συνήρμοσε φιλίαν καὶ εἰρήνην τοῖς
πολίταις. ἐφ' οἷς οὐ μόνον κοινῇ σύμπαντες οἱ πολῖται 3

---

13. 3. γνάμπτεσθαι GR¹L γνάπτεσθαι P κάμπτεσθαι R². κελεύει G¹.
4. φησι PR. 5. διήλειψεν Anon : διελήφεν. παρεμβαλεῖν Ed. : παραβαλεῖν.
6. <γνώμης> Ziegler. καὶ omitted in P before ἑκατόν. εἰς δ' (= τέσσαρας) δόσεις
Mahaffy. 14. 1. ὅσων PR ὅσον GL μικρὸν L σμικρὸν GPR : μεῖζον Paris.
1672 (Reiske): μείζων. τοῖς πλουσίοις PR.

τιμὰς ἀπέδοσαν αὐτῷ πρεπούσας, ἀλλὰ καὶ κατ᾽ ἰδίαν οἱ
φυγάδες εἰκόνα χαλκῆν ἀναστήσαντες ἐπέγραψαν τόδε
τὸ ἐλεγεῖον.

4   βουλαὶ μὲν καὶ ἄεθλα καὶ ἁ περὶ Ἑλλάδος ἀλκά
τοῦδ᾽ ἀνδρὸς *στάλαις πλάθεται Ἡρακλέους·
ἄμμες δ᾽ εἰκόν᾽ Ἄρατε τεὰν νόστοιο τυχόντες
στάσαμεν ἀντ᾽ ἀρετᾶς ἠδὲ δικαιοσύνας,
d   σωτῆρος σωτῆρσι θεοῖς, ὅτι πατρίδι τᾷ σᾷ
*δαιμόνιον θείαν τ᾽ ὤπασας εὐνομίαν.

15. Ταῦτα διαπραξάμενος ὁ Ἄρατος τοῦ μὲν πολι-
τικοῦ φθόνου μείζων ἐγεγόνει διὰ τὰς χάριτας· Ἀντίγονος δ᾽ ὁ βασιλεὺς ἀνιώμενος ἐπ᾽ αὐτῷ, καὶ βουλόμενος
ἢ μετάγειν ὅλως τῇ φιλίᾳ πρὸς αὐτὸν ἢ διαβάλλειν πρὸς
τὸν Πτολεμαῖον, ἄλλας τε φιλανθρωπίας ἐνεδείκνυτο
μὴ πάνυ προσιεμένῳ, καὶ θύων θεοῖς ἐν Κορίνθῳ
2 μερίδας εἰς Σικυῶνα τῷ Ἀράτῳ διέπεμπε. καὶ παρὰ
τὸ δεῖπνον ἑστιωμένων πολλῶν εἰς μέσον φθεγξά-
μενος "ᾤμην" ἔφη "τόν Σικυώνιον τοῦτον νεανί-
e σκον ἐλευθέριον εἶναι τῇ φύσει μόνον καὶ φιλοπολίτην·
ὁ δὲ καὶ βίων ἔοικε καὶ πραγμάτων βασιλικῶν ἱκανὸς
3 εἶναι κριτής. πρότερον γὰρ ἡμᾶς ὑπερεώρα, ταῖς ἐλπίσιν ἔξω βλέπων, καὶ τὸν Αἰγύπτιον ἐθαύμαζε πλοῦτον,
ἐλέφαντας καὶ στόλους καὶ αὐλὰς ἀκούων, νυνὶ δ᾽ ὑπὸ
σκηνὴν ἑωρακὼς πάντα τὰ ἐκεῖ πράγματα τραγῳδίαν
ὄντα καὶ σκηνογραφίαν, ὅλος ἡμῖν προσκεχώρηκεν.
αὐτὸς τ᾽ οὖν ἀποδέχομαι τὸ μειράκιον ἐγνωκὼς εἰς
4 ἅπαντα χρῆσθαι, καὶ ὑμᾶς ἀξιῶ φίλον νομίζειν." τούτους τοὺς λόγους ὑπόθεσιν λαβόντες οἱ φθονεροὶ καὶ
κακοήθεις, διημιλλῶντο ταῖς ἐπιστολαῖς <πρὸς> ἀλλή-
f λους, πολλὰ καὶ δυσχερῆ κατὰ τοῦ Ἀράτου τῷ Πτολεμαίῳ
5 γράφοντες, ὥστε κἀκεῖνον ἐγκαλοῦντα πέμψαι. ταῖς μὲν
οὖν περιμαχήτοις καὶ διαπύροις τοξευομέναις *ἔρωσι

---

3. ἐπέγραφον G¹.   4. στάλαις Anon : στᾶλαι PRL² τάλαι G¹ τἆλλα L¹G².
ἄμμες GL ἅμεις PR¹ ἅμμεις R². ἀρετῆς GP. δαιμόνιον Zeitz : δαίμονισον G¹P²
δαίμονι σὸν R¹ δαίμον᾽ ἴσον LP² δαίμον᾽ ἴσον G² δαίμονι σω R². εὐνομίαν G²PRL
εὐδαιμονίαν G¹. 15. 4. <πρὸς> ἀλλήλους Reiske : ἀλλήλους GL καὶ ἀλλήλους
P (καὶ erased in R): ἀλλήλοις Stephanus. 5. ἔρωσι Anon ἔρωτι.

φιλίαις βασιλέων καὶ τυράννων τοσοῦτον προσῆν φθόνου καὶ κακοηθείας.

16. Ὁ δ᾽ Ἄρατος αἱρεθεὶς στρατηγὸς τὸ πρῶτον ὑπὸ τῶν Ἀχαιῶν, τὴν μὲν ἀντιπέρας Λοκρίδα καὶ Καλυδωνίαν ἐπόρθησε, Βοιωτοῖς δὲ μετὰ μυρίων στρατιωτῶν βοηθῶν ὑστέρησε τῆς μάχης, ἣν ὑπ᾽ Αἰτωλῶν περὶ Χαιρώνειαν ἡττήθησαν, Ἀβοιωκρίτου τε τοῦ βοιωτάρχου καὶ χιλίων 1034 σὺν αὐτῷ πεσόντων.

Ἐνιαυτῷ δ᾽ ὕστερον αὖθις στρατηγῶν, ἐνίστατο τὴν 2 περὶ τὸν Ἀκροκόρινθον πρᾶξιν, οὐ Σικυωνίων οὐδ᾽ Ἀχαιῶν κηδόμενος, ἀλλὰ κοινήν τινα τῆς Ἑλλάδος ὅλης τυραννίδα, τὴν Μακεδόνων φρουράν, ἐκεῖθεν ἐξελάσαι διανοούμενος. Χάρης μὲν γὰρ ὁ Ἀθηναῖος ἔν τινι μάχῃ πρὸς τοὺς 3 βασιλέως στρατηγοὺς εὐτυχήσας, ἔγραψε τῷ δήμῳ τῶν Ἀθηναίων, ὡς νενικήκοι τῆς ἐν Μαραθῶνι μάχης ἀδελφήν· ταύτην δὲ τὴν πρᾶξιν οὐκ ἂν ἁμάρτοι τις ἀδελφὴν προσει- 4 πὼν τῆς Πελοπίδου τοῦ Θηβαίου καὶ Θρασυβούλου τοῦ b Ἀθηναίου τυραννοκτονίας, πλὴν ὅτι τῷ μὴ πρὸς Ἕλληνας ἀλλ᾽ ἐπακτὸν ἀρχὴν γεγονέναι καὶ ἀλλόφυλον αὕτη διή- νεγκεν. ὁ μὲν γὰρ Ἰσθμὸς ἐμφράσσων τὰς θαλάσσας 5 εἰς ταὐτὸ συνάγει τῷ τόπῳ καὶ συνάπτει τὴν ἤπειρον ἡμῶν, ὁ δ᾽ Ἀκροκόρινθος ὑψηλὸν ὄρος ἐκ μέσης ἀναπε- φυκὸς τῆς Ἑλλάδος, ὅταν λάβῃ φρουράν, ἐνίσταται καὶ ἀποκόπτει τὴν ἐντὸς Ἰσθμοῦ πᾶσαν ἐπιμειξιῶν τε καὶ παρόδων καὶ στρατειῶν ἐργασίας τε κατὰ γῆν καὶ κατὰ θάλατταν, καὶ ἕνα κύριον ποιεῖ *καὶ ἄρχοντα τὸν κατέ- 6 χοντα φρουρᾷ τὸ χωρίον, ὥστε μὴ παίζοντα δοκεῖν τὸν c νεώτερον Φίλιππον ἀλλ᾽ ἀληθῶς ἑκάστοτε πέδας τῆς Ἑλλάδος τὴν Κορινθίων πόλιν προσαγορεύειν.

17. Πᾶσι μὲν οὖν περιμάχητος ἦν ὁ τόπος ἀεὶ *καὶ βασιλεῦσι καὶ δυνάσταις, ἡ δ᾽ Ἀντιγόνου σπουδὴ περὶ αὐτὸν οὐδὲν ἀπέλιπε πάθει τῶν ἐμμανεστάτων ἐρώτων, ἀλλ᾽ ὅλος ἀνήρτητο ταῖς φροντίσιν, ὅπως ἀφαιρήσεται δόλῳ τοὺς ἔχοντας, ἐπεὶ φανερῶς ἀνέλπιστος ἦν ἡ ἐπι-

---

2 χείρησις. Ἀλεξάνδρου γὰρ ὑφ᾽ ὃν τὸ χωρίον ἦν
ἀποθανόντος (ὡς λέγεται) φαρμάκοις ὑπ᾽ αὐτοῦ, Νικαίας
δὲ τῆς ἐκείνου γυναικὸς ἐπὶ τῶν πραγμάτων γενομένης
καὶ φυλαττούσης τὸν Ἀκροκόρινθον, εὐθὺς ὑποπέμπων
d Δημήτριον τὸν υἱὸν αὐτῇ, καὶ γλυκείας ἐλπίδας ἐνδιδοὺς
γάμων βασιλικῶν καὶ συμβιώσεως πρὸς οὐκ ἀηδὲς
ἐντυχεῖν γυναικὶ πρεσβυτέρᾳ μειράκιον, αὐτὴν μὲν
ᾑρήκει, τῷ παιδὶ χρησάμενος ὥσπερ ἄλλῳ τινὶ τῶν
δελεασμάτων ἐπ᾽ αὐτῇ, τὸν δὲ τόπον οὐ προϊεμένης ἀλλ᾽
3 ἐγκρατῶς φυλαττούσης, ἀμελεῖν προσποιούμενος ἔθυε
γάμους αὐτῶν ἐν Κορίνθῳ, καὶ θέας ἐπετέλει καὶ πότους
συνῆγε καθ᾽ ἡμέραν, ὡς ἄν τις μάλιστα παίζειν καὶ
σχολάζειν τὴν διάνοιαν ὑφ᾽ ἡδονῆς καὶ φιλοφροσύνης
4 ἀφεικώς. ἐπεὶ δὲ καιρὸς ἦν, ᾄδοντος Ἀμοιβέως ἐν τῷ
e θεάτρῳ, παρέπεμπε τὴν Νίκαιαν αὐτὸς ἐπὶ τὴν θέαν ἐν
φορείῳ κεκοσμημένῳ βασιλικῶς, ἀγαλλομένην τε τῇ
5 τιμῇ καὶ πορρωτάτω τοῦ μέλλοντος οὖσαν. γενόμενος
δὲ τῆς ὁδοῦ κατὰ τὴν ἐκτροπὴν τὴν ἄνω φέρουσαν,
ἐκείνην μὲν ἐκέλευσε προάγειν εἰς τὸ θέατρον, αὐτὸς δὲ
χαίρειν μὲν Ἀμοιβέα χαίρειν δὲ τοὺς γάμους ἐάσας,
ἀνῄει πρὸς τὸν Ἀκροκόρινθον ἁμιλλώμενος παρ᾽ ἡλικίαν·
καὶ κεκλεισμένην τὴν πύλην εὑρών, ἔκοπτε τῇ βακτηρίᾳ
κελεύων ἀνοίγειν· οἱ δ᾽ ἔνδον ἀνέῳξαν καταπλαγέντες.
6 οὕτω δὲ τοῦ τόπου κρατήσας, οὐ κατέσχεν αὐτὸν ἀλλ᾽
f ἔπινε παίζων ὑπὸ χαρᾶς ἐν τοῖς στενωποῖς, καὶ δι᾽ ἀγορᾶς
αὐλητρίδας ἔχων καὶ στεφάνους περικείμενος, ἀνὴρ γέρων
καὶ τηλικαύταις πραγμάτων μεταβολαῖς κεχρημένος,
ἐκώμαζε δεξιούμενος καὶ προσαγορεύων τοὺς ἀπαντῶντας.
7 οὕτως ἄρα καὶ λύπης καὶ φόβου μᾶλλον ἐξίστησι καὶ
σάλον παρέχει τῇ ψυχῇ τὸ χαίρειν ἄνευ λογισμοῦ
παραγινόμενον.

18. Ἀλλὰ γὰρ Ἀντίγονος μὲν ὥσπερ εἴρηται
κτησάμενος τὸν Ἀκροκόρινθον, ἐφύλαττε μετὰ τῶν ἄλλων
οἷς ἐπίστευε μάλιστα καὶ Περσαῖον ἐπιστήσας ἄρχοντα

---

2. εὐτυχεῖν.
ἀμοιβαίου P.
ἀνίει PR¹.

4. ἀμοιβέως R² ἀμοιβαίως R¹ ἀμοιβέου GL ἀμοιβέου or
5. ἀμοιβέα PR² ἀμοιβαῖα R¹ ἀμοιβέαν GL. ἀνῄει GLR²

τὸν φιλόσοφον. ὁ δ᾽ Ἄρατος ἔτι μὲν καὶ Ἀλεξάνδρου 21035
ζῶντος ἐπεχείρησε τῇ *πράξει, γενομένης δὲ συμμαχίας
τοῖς Ἀχαιοῖς πρὸς τὸν Ἀλέξανδρον ἐπαύσατο. τότε δ᾽
αὖθις ἐξ ὑπαρχῆς ἑτέραν ἔλαβε τῆς πράξεως ὑπόθεσιν
τοιαύτην.
Ἦσαν ἐν Κορίνθῳ τέσσαρες ἀδελφοὶ Σύροι τὸ γένος, 3
ὧν εἷς ὄνομα Διοκλῆς ἐν τῷ φρουρίῳ μισθοφορῶν διέτρι-
βεν. οἱ δὲ τρεῖς κλέψαντες βασιλικὸν χρυσίον, ἦλθον εἰς 4
Σικυῶνα πρὸς Αἰγίαν τινὰ τραπεζίτην, ᾧ διὰ τὴν ἐργασίαν
ὁ Ἄρατος ἐχρῆτο. καὶ μέρος μὲν εὐθὺς διέθεντο τοῦ
χρυσίου, τὸ δὲ λοιπὸν εἰς αὐτῶν Ἐργῖνος ἐπιφοιτῶν
ἡσυχῇ κατήλλαττεν. ἐκ δὲ τούτου γενόμενος τῷ Αἰγίᾳ 5
συνήθης, καὶ προαχθεὶς εἰς λόγον ὑπ᾽ αὐτοῦ περὶ τῆς b
φρουρᾶς, ἔφη πρὸς τὸν ἀδελφὸν ἀναβαίνων *παρὰ τὸ
κρημνῶδες ἐντομὴν καθεωρακέναι πλαγίαν, ἄγουσαν ᾗ
χθαμαλώτατον ἐπῳκοδόμηται τῷ φρουρίῳ τὸ τεῖχος.
προσπαίξαντος δ᾽ αὐτῷ τοῦ Αἰγίου καὶ εἰπόντος· "εἶτ᾽ 6
ὦ βέλτιστε διὰ σμικρὸν οὕτω χρυσίον ἀνασπᾶτε τὰς
βασιλικὰς <εἰσ>πράξεις, δυνάμενοι μίαν ὥραν πολλῶν
ἀποδόσθαι χρημάτων ; ἢ γὰρ οὐχὶ καὶ τοιχωρύχοις καὶ
προδόταις ἁλοῦσιν ἅπαξ ἀποθανεῖν ὑπάρχει ;" γελάσας 7
ὁ Ἐργῖνος τότε μὲν ὡμολόγησεν ἀποπειρᾶσθαι τοῦ Διοκλέους, τοῖς γὰρ ἄλλοις ἀδελφοῖς μὴ πάνυ τι πιστεύειν, c
ὀλίγαις δ᾽ ὕστερον ἡμέραις ἐπανελθὼν συντίθεται τὸν
Ἄρατον ἄξειν πρὸς τὸ τεῖχος, ὅπου τὸ ὕψος οὐ μεῖζον
ἦν πεντεκαίδεκα ποδῶν, καὶ τἆλλα συμπράξειν μετὰ
τοῦ Διοκλέους. 19. ὁ δ᾽ Ἄρατος ἐκείνοις μὲν ἑξήκοντα
τάλαντα δώσειν κατορθώσας ὡμολόγησεν, ἢν δ᾽ ἀποτύχῃ
σωθῇ δὲ μετ᾽ ἐκείνων, οἰκίαν ἑκατέρῳ καὶ τάλαντον. ἐπεὶ 2
δ᾽ ἔδει παρὰ τῷ Αἰγίᾳ τὰ ἑξήκοντα τάλαντα κεῖσθαι τοῖς
περὶ τὸν Ἐργῖνον, ὁ δ᾽ Ἄρατος οὔτ᾽ αὐτὸς εἶχεν οὔτ᾽
ἐβούλετο δανειζόμενος αἴσθησιν ἑτέρῳ τῆς πράξεως
παρασχεῖν, λαβὼν τῶν ἐκπωμάτων τὰ πολλὰ καὶ τὰ
χρυσία τῆς γυναικὸς ὑπέθηκε τῷ Αἰγίᾳ πρὸς τὸ ἀργύ-

18. 2. πράξει Anon: πατρίδι.   4. εἰς σικυῶνα πρὸς αἰγίαν GL πρὸς αἰγίαν
εἰς σικυῶνα PR.   5. παρὰ Ed. from Polyaen. 6, 5 πρὸς.   6. εἰσπράξεις
Henry : πράξεις. ἢ γὰρ.   7. ἢ G¹.   ποδῶν G¹PR πῆχων L and G² (margin).

B

3 ριον. [ὁ δὲ] οὕτω γὰρ ἐπῆρτο τῇ ψυχῇ, καὶ τοσοῦτον
d ἔρωτα τῶν καλῶν πράξεων εἶχεν, ὥστε τὸν Φωκίωνα καὶ
τὸν Ἐπαμεινώνδαν ἐπιστάμενος Ἑλλήνων δικαιοτάτους
καὶ κρατίστους γεγονέναι δοκοῦντας ἐπὶ τῷ διώσασθαι
δωρεὰς μεγάλας καὶ μὴ προέσθαι χρημάτων τὸ καλόν,
αὐτὸς εἰς ταῦτα δαπανᾶσθαι κρύφα καὶ προεισφέρειν, ἐν
οἷς ἐκινδύνευε μόνος ὑπὲρ πάντων οὐδ' εἰδότων τὰ πραττό-
4 μενα. [ᾑρεῖτο] τίς γὰρ οὐκ ἂν θαυμάσειε καὶ συναγωνί-
σαιτ' ἔτι νῦν τῇ μεγαλοψυχίᾳ τοῦ ἀνδρός, ὠνουμένου
χρημάτων τοσούτων κίνδυνον τηλικοῦτον καὶ τὰ τιμιώ-
τατα δοκοῦντα τῶν κτημάτων ὑποτιθέντος, ὅπως παρει-
e σαχθεὶς νυκτὸς εἰς τοὺς πολεμίους διαγωνίσηται περὶ
τῆς ψυχῆς, ἐνέχυρον λαβὼν τὴν ἐλπίδα τοῦ καλοῦ παρ'
αὐτῶν ἄλλο δ' οὐδέν;

20. Οὖσαν δὲ καθ' αὑτὴν ἐπισφαλῆ τὴν πρᾶξιν
ἐπισφαλεστέραν ἐποίησεν ἁμαρτία τις εὐθὺς ἐν ἀρχῇ
2 συμβᾶσα δι' ἄγνοιαν. ὁ γὰρ οἰκέτης τοῦ Ἀράτου
Τέχνων ἐπέμφθη μὲν ὡς μετὰ τοῦ Διοκλέους κατα-
σκεψόμενος τὸ τεῖχος, οὔπω δ' ἦν τῷ Διοκλεῖ πρότερον
ἐντετυχηκὼς κατ' ὄψιν, ἀλλὰ τὴν μορφὴν αὐτοῦ καὶ τὸ
εἶδος δοκῶν κατέχειν ἐξ ὧν ὁ Ἐργῖνος ἐπεσήμηνεν,
f 3 οὐλοκόμην καὶ μελάγχρουν καὶ ἀγένειον· ἐλθὼν οὖν
ὅπου συνετέτακτο, τὸν Ἐργῖνον ὡς ἀφιξόμενον μετὰ τοῦ
Διοκλέους ἀνέμενε πρὸ τῆς πόλεως πρὸ τοῦ καλουμένου
4 Ὄρνιθος. ἐν δὲ τούτῳ πρῶτος ἀδελφὸς Ἐργίνου καὶ
Διοκλέους ὄνομα Διονύσιος, οὐ συνειδὼς τὴν πρᾶξιν
οὐδὲ κοινωνῶν ὅμοιος δὲ τῷ Διοκλεῖ, προσῄει κατὰ
τύχην. ὁ δὲ Τέχνων πρὸς τὰ σημεῖα τῆς μορφῆς τῇ
ὁμοιότητι κινηθείς, ἠρώτησε τὸν ἄνθρωπον εἴ τι
5 συμβόλαιον αὐτῷ πρὸς Ἐργῖνον εἴη. φήσαντος δ'
1036 ἀδελφὸν εἶναι, παντάπασιν ὁ Τέχνων ἐπείσθη τῷ Διοκλεῖ
διαλέγεσθαι· καὶ μήτε τοὔνομα πυθόμενος μήτ' ἄλλο
μηδὲν προσμείνας τεκμήριον, ἐμβάλλει τε τὴν δεξιὰν
αὐτῷ καὶ περὶ τῶν συγκειμένων πρὸς τὸν Ἐργῖνον ἐλάλει
6 κἀκεῖνον ἀνέκρινεν. ὁ δὲ δεξάμενος αὐτοῦ τὴν ἁμαρτίαν,

---

19. 3. [ὁ δὲ] Xylander. προσεισφέρειν R : in G the first σ has been erased
[ᾑρεῖτο] Ziegler.

πανούργως ὡμολόγει τε πάντα καὶ πρὸς τὴν πόλιν
ἀναστρέψας ὑπῆγεν ἀνυπόπτως διαλεγόμενος. ἤδη δὲ 7
πλησίον ὄντος αὐτοῦ καὶ μέλλοντος ὅσον οὔπω τὸν
Τέχνωνα διαλαμβάνειν, ἀπὸ τύχης αὖ πάλιν ὁ Ἐργῖνος
αὐτοῖς ἀπήντησεν. αἰσθόμενος δὲ τὴν ἀπάτην καὶ τὸν
κίνδυνον, διὰ νεύματος ἐδήλωσε τῷ Τέχνωνι φεύγειν· b
καὶ ἀποπηδήσαντες ἀμφότεροι δρόμῳ πρὸς τὸν Ἄρατον
ἀπεσώθησαν. οὐ μὴν ἀπέκαμε ταῖς ἐλπίσιν ἐκεῖνος, 8
ἀλλ᾽ ἔπεμψεν εὐθὺς τὸν Ἐργῖνον, χρυσίον τε τῷ
Διονυσίῳ κομίζοντα καὶ δεησόμενον αὐτοῦ σιωπᾶν. ὁ
δὲ καὶ τοῦτ᾽ ἐποίησε καὶ τὸν Διονύσιον ἄγων μεθ᾽ ἑαυτοῦ
πρὸς τὸν Ἄρατον ἦλθεν. ἐλθόντα δ᾽ αὐτὸν οὐκέτι 9
διῆκαν, ἀλλὰ δήσαντες ἐφύλαττον ἐν οἰκίσκῳ κατακεκλει-
σμένον· αὐτοὶ δὲ παρεσκευάζοντο πρὸς τὴν ἐπίθεσιν.

21. Ἐπεὶ δ᾽ ἦν ἕτοιμα πάντα, τὴν μὲν ἄλλην
δύναμιν ἐκέλευσεν ἐπὶ τῶν ὅπλων νυκτερεύειν, ἀναλαβὼν c
δὲ λογάδας τετρακοσίους, οὐδ᾽ αὐτοὺς εἰδότας τὰ
πραττόμενα πλὴν ὀλίγων, ἦγε πρὸς τὰς πύλας, παρὰ τὸ
Ἡραῖον. ἦν δὲ τοῦ ἔτους ἡ περὶ θέρος ἀκμάζον ὥρα, 2
τοῦ δὲ μηνὸς πανσέληνος, ἡ δὲ νὺξ ἀνέφελος καὶ κατα-
φανής, ὥστε καὶ φόβον τὰ ὅπλα παρέχειν ἀντιλάμποντα
πρὸς τὴν σελήνην, μὴ τοὺς φύλακας οὐ λάθωσιν. ἤδη
δὲ τῶν πρώτων ἐγγὺς ὄντων, ἀπὸ θαλάσσης ἀνέδραμε
νέφη καὶ κατέσχε τήν τε πόλιν αὐτὴν καὶ τὸν ἔξω τόπον
ἐπίσκιον γενόμενον. ἐνταῦθα δ᾽ οἱ μὲν ἄλλοι συγκα- 3
θίσαντες ὑπελύοντο τὰς κρηπῖδας· οὔτε γὰρ ψόφον
ποιοῦσι πολὺν οὔτ᾽ ὀλισθήματα λαμβάνουσιν <οἱ> γυμ- d
νοῖς τοῖς ποσὶν ἀντιλαμβανόμενοι τῶν κλιμάκων· ὁ δ᾽
Ἐργῖνος ἑπτὰ λαβὼν νεανίσκους ἐσταλμένους ὁδοι-
πορικῶς ἔλαθε τῇ πύλῃ προσμείξας, καὶ τὸν πυλωρὸν
ἀποκτιννύουσι καὶ τοὺς μετ᾽ αὐτοῦ φύλακας. ἅμα δ᾽ αἵ 4
τε κλίμακες προσετίθεντο, καὶ κατὰ σπουδὴν ὁ Ἄρατος
ὑπερβιβάσας ἑκατὸν ἄνδρας, τοὺς δ᾽ ἄλλους ἕπεσθαι
κελεύσας ὡς ἂν δύνωνται τάχιστα, τὰς κλίμακας

---

20. 9. κατακεκλειμένον PR¹L¹.   **21.** 2. παρέχειν G: κατέχειν PRL.
3. πολὺ GR¹ <οἱ> Schaefer.   4. ἕπεσθαι κελεύσας Paris. 1673 κελεύσας
ἕπεσθαι (involving hiatus) GPRL. ἀνασπάσας Paris 1673: ἀναρπάσας GPRL.

B 2

ἀνασπάσας ἐχώρει διὰ τῆς πόλεως μετὰ τῶν ἑκατὸν ἐπὶ
τὴν ἄκραν, ἤδη περιχαρὴς διὰ τὸ λανθάνειν ὡς κατορθῶν.
5 καί πως ἔτι πρόσωθεν αὐτοῖς ἀπήντα σὺν φωτὶ φυλακὴ
τεσσάρων ἀνδρῶν οὐ καθορωμένοις· ἔτι γὰρ ἦσαν ἐν
e τῷ σκιαζομένῳ τῆς σελήνης· ἐκείνους δὲ προσιόντας ἐξ
6 ἐναντίας καθορῶσι. μικρὸν οὖν ὑποστείλας τειχίοις τισὶ
καὶ οἰκοπέδοις, ἐνέδραν ἐπὶ τοὺς ἄνδρας καθίζει· καὶ
τρεῖς μὲν αὐτῶν ἐμπεσόντες ἀποθνήσκουσιν, ὁ δὲ
τέταρτος πληγεὶς ξίφει τὴν κεφαλήν, ἔφυγε βοῶν ἔνδον
7 εἶναι τοὺς πολεμίους. καὶ μετὰ μικρὸν αἵ τε σάλπιγγες
ἐπεσήμαινον, ἥ τε πόλις ἐξανίστατο πρὸς τὰ γινόμενα,
πλήρεις τ᾽ ἦσαν οἱ [τε] στενωποὶ διαθεόντων, καὶ φῶτα
πολλὰ τὰ μὲν κάτωθεν ἤδη τὰ δ᾽ ἄνωθεν ἀπὸ τῆς ἄκρας
περιέλαμπε, καὶ κραυγὴ συνερρήγνυτο πανταχόθεν
ἄσημος. 22. ἐν τούτῳ δ᾽ ὁ μὲν Ἄρατος ἐμφὺς τῇ
πορείᾳ παρὰ τὸ κρημνῶδες ἡμιλλᾶτο, βραδέως καὶ
f ταλαιπώρως τὸ πρῶτον, οὐ κατακρατῶν ἀλλ᾽ ἀποπλα-
νώμενος τοῦ τρίβου παντάπασιν ἐνδεδυκότος καὶ
περισκιαζομενου ταῖς τραχύτησι, καὶ διὰ [τῶν] πολλῶν
ἑλιγμῶν καὶ παραβολῶν περαίνοντος πρὸς τὸ τεῖχος.
2 εἶτα θαυμάσιον οἷον ἡ σελήνη λέγεται διαστέλλουσα
τὰ νέφη καὶ *ὑπολάμπουσα τῆς ὁδοῦ τὸ χαλεπώτατον
σαφηνίζειν, ἕως ἥψατο τοῦ τείχους καθ᾽ ὃν ἔδει τόπον·
ἐκεῖ δὲ πάλιν συνεσκίασε καὶ ἀπέκρυψε νεφῶν συνελ-
3 θόντων. οἱ δὲ περὶ τὰς πύλας ἔξω περὶ τὸ Ἡραῖον
ἀπολειφθέντες τοῦ Ἀράτου στρατιῶται τριακόσιοι τὸ
πλῆθος ὄντες, ὥς ποτε παρεισέπεσον εἰς τὴν πόλιν
1037 θορύβου *τε παντοδαποῦ καὶ φώτων γέμουσαν, οὐ
δυνηθέντες ἐξανευρεῖν τὸν αὐτὸν τρίβον, οὐδ᾽ εἰς ἴχνος
ἐμβῆναι τῆς ἐκείνων πορείας, ἔπτηξαν ἀθρόοι πρός τινι
παλινσκίῳ λαγόνι τοῦ κρημνοῦ συστείλαντες ἑαυτούς,
καὶ διεκαρτέρουν ἐνταῦθα περιπαθοῦντες καὶ δυσα-
4 νασχετοῦντες. βαλλομένων γὰρ ἀπὸ τῆς ἄκρας ἤδη τῶν

---

5. προιόντας G¹.   7. ὑπεσήμαινον G. [τε] Sintenis.   22. 1. βραχύτησι
LG². [τῶν] Juntine.   2. ὑπολάμπουσα Anon: ὑπολαβοῦσα.   3. τε (before
παντοδαποῦ) Juntine δὲ: τὸν αὐτῶν P τὴν αὐτῶν L περιπαθοῦντες G²PRL
προσκαρτεροῦντες G¹.

περὶ τὸν Ἄρατον καὶ μαχομένων, ἀλαλαγμὸς ἐναγώνιος
ἐχώρει κάτω, καὶ κραυγὴ περιήχει διὰ τὴν ἀπὸ τῶν
ὀρῶν ἀνάκλασιν συγκεχυμένη καὶ ἄδηλος ὅθεν εἴληφε
τὴν ἀρχήν. διαπορούντων δ' αὐτῶν ἐφ' ὅτι χρὴ 5
τραπέσθαι μέρος, Ἀρχέλαος ὁ τῶν βασιλικῶν ἡγεμὼν ъ
στρατιώτας ἔχων πολλοὺς μετὰ κραυγῆς ἀνέβαινε καὶ
σαλπίγγων, ἐπιφερόμενος τοῖς περὶ τὸν Ἄρατον, καὶ
παρήλλαττε τοὺς τριακοσίους. οἱ δ' ὥσπερ ἐξ ἐνέδρας 6
ἀναστάντες, ἐμβάλλουσιν αὐτῷ καὶ διαφθείρουσιν οἷς
ἐπέθεντο πρώτοις, τοὺς δ' ἄλλους καὶ τὸν Ἀρχέλαον
φοβήσαντες ἐτρέψαντο καὶ κατεδίωξαν ἄχρι τοῦ
σκεδασθῆναι περὶ τὴν πόλιν διαλυθέντας. ἄρτι δὲ 7
τούτων νενικηκότων, Ἐργῖνος ἀπὸ τῶν ἄνω μαχομένων
ἦλθεν, ἀγγέλλων συμπεπλέχθαι τοῖς πολεμίοις τὸν
Ἄρατον ἀμυνομένοις εὐρώστως, καὶ μέγαν ἀγῶνα περὶ c
αὐτὸ τὸ τεῖχος εἶναι, καὶ τάχους δεῖν τῆς βοηθείας. οἱ 8
δ' εὐθὺς ἐκέλευον ἡγεῖσθαι· καὶ προσβαίνοντες ἅμα
φωνῇ διεσήμαινον ἑαυτούς, ἐπιθαρρύνοντες τοὺς φίλους·
ᾗ τε πανσέληνος ἀπέφαινε τὰ ὅπλα πλείονα φαινόμενα
τοῖς πολεμίοις διὰ τὸ μῆκος τῆς πορείας, καὶ τὸ τῆς
νυκτὸς ἠχῶδες τὸν ἀλαλαγμὸν ἀπὸ πολλαπλασιόνων ἢ
τοσούτων ἐποίει δοκεῖν φέρεσθαι. τέλος δὲ συνε- 9
ρείσαντες ἐξωθοῦσι τοὺς πολεμίους, καὶ καθυπέρτεροι
τῆς ἄκρας ἦσαν, καὶ τὸ φρούριον εἶχον· ἡμέρας <δ'> ἤδη
διαυγούσης, ὅ θ' ἥλιος εὐθὺς ἐπέλαμπε τῷ ἔργῳ, καὶ
παρῆν ἐκ Σικυῶνος ἡ λοιπὴ δύναμις τῷ Ἀράτῳ, d
δεχομένων κατὰ πύλας τῶν Κορινθίων προθύμως καὶ
τοὺς βασιλικοὺς συλλαμβανόντων.

23. Ἐπεὶ δ' ἀσφαλῶς ἐδόκει πάντ' ἔχειν, κατέβαινεν
εἰς τὸ θέατρον ἀπὸ τῆς ἄκρας, πλήθους ἀπείρου
συρρέοντος ἐπιθυμίᾳ τῆς τ' ὄψεως αὐτοῦ καὶ τῶν λόγων
οἷς ἔμελλε χρῆσθαι πρὸς τοὺς Κορινθίους. ἐπιστήσας 2
δὲ ταῖς παρόδοις ἑκατέρωθεν τοὺς Ἀχαιούς, αὐτὸς ἀπὸ
τῆς σκηνῆς εἰς μέσον προῆλθε, τεθωρακισμένος καὶ τῷ
προσώπῳ διὰ τὸν κόπον καὶ τὴν ἀγρυπνίαν ἠλλοιωμένος,

7. ἦλθεν G : ἧκεν PRL.   8. ἀπέφαινε G¹ ἀπέφηνε RLG², ἀπέφηνιε P.
9. <δ'> Emperius.

ὥστε τῆς ψυχῆς τὸ γαυρούμενον καὶ χαῖρον ὑπὸ τῆς περὶ
3 τὸ σῶμα βαρύτητος κατακρατεῖσθαι. τῶν δ᾽ ἀνθρώπων
e ἅμα τῷ προ[σ]ελθεῖν αὐτὸν ἐκχυθέντων ταῖς φιλοφροσύναις, μεταλαβὼν εἰς τὴν δεξιὰν τὸ δόρυ, καὶ τὸ
γόνυ καὶ τὸ σῶμα τῇ ῥοπῇ μικρὸν ἐγκλίνας καὶ
ἀπερεισάμενος, εἱστήκει πολὺν χρόνον σιωπῇ δεχόμενος
αὐτῶν τοὺς κρότους καὶ τὰς ἐπιβοήσεις, ἐπαινούντων
4 μὲν τὴν ἀρετήν ζηλούντων δὲ τὴν τύχην. ὡς δ᾽
ἐπαύσαντο καὶ κατέστησαν, συναγαγὼν ἑαυτὸν διεξῆλθε
λόγον ὑπὲρ τῶν Ἀχαιῶν τῇ πράξει πρέποντα, καὶ
συνέπεισε τοὺς Κορινθίους Ἀχαιοὺς γενέσθαι, καὶ τῶν
πυλῶν τὰς κλεῖς ἀπέδωκε, τότε πρῶτον ἀπὸ τῶν Φιλιπ-
5 πικῶν καιρῶν ὑπ᾽ ἐκείνοις γενομένας. τῶν δ᾽ Ἀντιγόνου
f *στρατηγῶν Ἀρχέλαον μὲν ἀφῆκεν ὑποχείριον γενόμενον, Θεόφραστον δ᾽ ἀνεῖλεν οὐ βουλόμενον ἀπαλ-
λάττεσθαι· Περσαῖος δὲ τῆς ἄκρας ἁλισκομένης εἰς
6 Κεγχρεὰς διεξέπεσεν. ὕστερον δὲ λέγεται σχολάζων
πρὸς τὸν εἰπόντα μόνον αὐτῷ δοκεῖν στρατηγὸν εἶναι τὸν
σοφόν "ἀλλὰ νὴ θεούς" φάναι "τοῦτο μάλιστα κἀμοί
ποτε τῶν Ζήνωνος ἤρεσκε δογμάτων· νῦν δὲ μετα-
βάλλομαι, νουθετηθεὶς ὑπὸ τοῦ Σικυωνίου νεανίου."
ταῦτα μὲν περὶ Περσαίου πλείονες ἱστοροῦσιν. 24. ὁ
1038 δ᾽ Ἄρατος εὐθὺς τό θ᾽ Ἡραῖον ὑφ᾽ ἑαυτῷ καὶ τὸ Λέχαιον
ἐποιήσατο· καὶ νεῶν μὲν εἰκοσιπέντε βασιλικῶν
ἐκυρίευσεν, ἵππους δὲ πεντακοσίους καὶ Σύρους τετρακοσίους ἀπέδοτο· τόν τ᾽ Ἀκροκόρινθον ἐφύλαττον οἱ
Ἀχαιοί τετρακοσίοις ὁπλίταις καὶ πεντήκοντα κυσὶ καὶ
κυνηγοῖς ἴσοις ἐν τῷ φρουρίῳ τρεφομένοις.
2   Οἱ μὲν οὖν Ῥωμαῖοι τὸν Φιλοποίμενα θαυμάζοντες
Ἑλλήνων ἔσχατον προσηγόρευον, ὡς μηδενὸς μεγάλου
μετ᾽ ἐκεῖνον ἐν τοῖς Ἕλλησι γενομένου· ἐγὼ δὲ τῶν
Ἑλληνικῶν πράξεων ταύτην ἐσχάτην καὶ νεωτάτην φαίην
ἂν πεπρᾶχθαι, τοῦτο μὲν τόλμῃ τοῦτο δὲ τύχῃ ταῖς
ἀρίσταις ἐνάμιλλον, ὡς ἐδήλωσεν εὐθὺς τὰ γινόμενα.
3 Μεγαρεῖς τε γὰρ ἀποστάντες Ἀντιγόνου τῷ Ἀράτῳ
b προσέθεντο, καὶ Τροιζήνιοι μετ᾽ Ἐπιδαυρίων συνέταχ-

---

23. 3. προ[σ]ελθεῖν Ziegler.   5. στρατηγῶν Aldine στρατιωτῶν.   6. μὲν G
μὲν οὖν PRL.

θησαν εἰς τοὺς Ἀχαιούς, ἔξοδόν τε πρώτην θέμενος εἰς
τὴν Ἀττικὴν ἐνέβαλε, καὶ τὴν Σαλαμῖνα διαβὰς ἐλεηλά-
τησεν, ὥσπερ ἐξ εἱρκτῆς λελυμένῃ τῇ δυνάμει τῶν Ἀχαιῶν
ἐφ᾽ ὅτι βούλοιτο χρώμενος. Ἀθηναίοις δὲ τοὺς ἐλευθέρους 4
ἀφῆκεν ἄνευ λύτρων, ἀρχὰς ἀποστάσεως ἐνδιδοὺς αὐτοῖς.
Πτολεμαῖον δὲ σύμμαχον ἐποίησε, τῶν Ἀχαιῶν ἡγεμονίαν ἔχοντα πολέμου καὶ κατὰ γῆν καὶ κατὰ θάλατταν.
οὕτω δ᾽ ἴσχυσεν ἐν τοῖς Ἀχαιοῖς, ὥστ᾽ εἰ μὴ κατ᾽ ἐνιαυ- 5
τὸν ἐξῆν, παρ᾽ ἐνιαυτὸν αἱρεῖσθαι στρατηγὸν αὐτόν, ἔργῳ c
δὲ καὶ γνώμῃ διὰ παντὸς ἄρχειν. ἑώρων γὰρ αὐτὸν οὐ
πλοῦτον, οὐ δόξαν, οὐ φιλίαν βασιλικήν, οὐ τὸ τῆς αὐτοῦ
πατρίδος συμφέρον, οὐκ ἄλλο τι τῆς αὐξήσεως τῶν Ἀχαιῶν
ἐπίπροσθεν ποιούμενον. ἡγεῖτο γὰρ ἀσθενεῖς ἰδίᾳ τὰς 6
πόλεις ὑπαρχούσας σῴζεσθαι δι᾽ ἀλλήλων ὥσπερ ἐνδεδε-
μένας τῷ κοινῷ συμφέροντι, καὶ καθάπερ τὰ μέρη τοῦ
σώματος, ζῶντα καὶ συμπνέοντα διὰ τὴν πρὸς ἄλληλα
συμφυΐαν, ὅταν ἀποσπασθῇ καὶ γένηται χωρίς, ἀτροφεῖ
καὶ σήπεται, παραπλησίως τὰς πόλεις ἀπόλλυσθαι μὲν
ὑπὸ τῶν διασπώντων τὸ κοινόν, αὔξεσθαι δ᾽ ὑπ᾽ ἀλλήλων,
ὅταν *ὅλου τινὸς μεγάλου μέρη γενόμεναι κοινῆς προ-
νοίας τυγχάνωσιν.

25. Ὁρῶν *δὲ τοὺς ἀρίστους τῶν προσοίκων αὐτονο- d
μουμένους, Ἀργείοις δὲ δουλεύουσιν ἀχθόμενος, ἐπεβούλευεν ἀνελεῖν τὸν τύραννον αὐτῶν Ἀριστόμαχον, ἅμα τῇ
τε πόλει θρεπτήρια τὴν ἐλευθερίαν ἀποδοῦναι φιλοτιμούμενος καὶ τοῖς Ἀχαιοῖς προσκομίσαι τὴν πόλιν. οἱ 2
μὲν οὖν τολμῶντες εὑρέθησαν, ὧν Αἰσχύλος προειστήκει
καὶ Χαριμένης ὁ μάντις, ξίφη δ᾽ οὐκ εἶχον ἀλλ᾽ ἀπείρητο
κεκτῆσθαι, καὶ ζημίαι μεγάλαι τοῖς κεκτημένοις ἐπῆσαν
ὑπὸ τοῦ τυράννου. κατασκευάσας οὖν ὁ Ἄρατος αὐτοῖς
ἐν Κορίνθῳ μικρὰς παραξιφίδας ἐνέρραψεν εἰς σάγματα·
καὶ ταῦτα περιθεὶς ὑποζυγίοις σκεύη τινὰ παρημελημένα e
κομίζουσιν εἰς Ἄργος ἀπέστειλε. Χαριμένους δὲ τοῦ 3
μάντεως προσλαβόντος ἐπὶ τὴν πρᾶξιν <ἄδοξον> ἄνθρω-

---

24. 5. <ἐπ>εὶ μὴ Coraes.   6. ὅλου Solanus : ἄλλου.   25. 1. δὲ Anon : τε.
3. <ἄδοξον> Ed. ἀνάξιον Kronenberg ἄλλον Richards. ἠγανάκτουν G¹PR ἠγανάκ-
τησαν G²L.

πον, οἱ περὶ τὸν Αἰσχύλον ἠγανάκτουν καὶ δι᾽ ἑαυτῶν
ἔπραττον, τοῦ Χαριμένους καταγνόντες. αἰσθόμενος δ᾽
ἐκεῖνος ὀργῇ κατεμήνυσε τοὺς ἄνδρας ἤδη βαδίζοντας
ἐπὶ τὸν τύραννον· ὧν οἱ πλεῖστοι φθάσαντες ἐξ ἀγορᾶς
4 ἀπέφυγον καὶ διεξέπεσον εἰς Κόρινθον. οὐ μὴν ἀλλὰ
χρόνου βραχέος διελθόντος, ἀποθνῄσκει μὲν ὑπὸ δούλων
f Ἀριστόμαχος, ὑπολαμβάνει δὲ τὴν ἀρχὴν φθάσας Ἀρίστιππος, ἐξωλέστερος ἐκείνου τύραννος. ὅσοι δὴ τῶν
Ἀχαιῶν ἐν ἡλικίᾳ παρόντες ἔτυχον, τούτους ἀναλαβὼν
ὁ Ἄρατος ἐβοήθει πρὸς τὴν πόλιν ὀξέως, οἰόμενος εὑρή-
5 σειν τὰ τῶν Ἀργείων πρόθυμα. τῶν δὲ πολλῶν ἤδη διὰ
συνήθειαν ἐθελοδούλως ἐχόντων, καὶ μηδενὸς ἀφιστα-
μένου πρὸς αὐτόν, ἀνεχώρησεν ἔγκλημα κατεσκευακὼς
τοῖς Ἀχαιοῖς, ὡς ἐν εἰρήνῃ πόλεμον ἐξενηνοχόσι. καὶ
1039 δίκην ἔσχον ἐπὶ τούτῳ παρὰ Μαντινεῦσιν, ἣν Ἀράτου
μὴ παρόντος Ἀρίστιππος εἷλε διώκων, καὶ μνῶν ἐτιμήθη
6 τριάκοντα. τὸν δ᾽ Ἄρατον αὐτὸν ἅμα καὶ μισῶν καὶ
δεδοικώς, ἐπεβούλευεν ἀνελεῖν. συνεργοῦντος Ἀντιγόνου
τοῦ βασιλέως· καὶ πανταχοῦ σχεδὸν ἦσαν οἱ τοῦτο
7 πράττοντες αὐτοῖς καὶ καιρὸν ἐπιτηροῦντες. ἀλλ᾽ οὐδὲν
οἷον ἀληθινὴ καὶ βέβαιος εὔνοια φυλακτήριον ἀνδρὸς
ἄρχοντος. ὅταν γὰρ ἐθισθῶσιν οἵ τε πολλοὶ καὶ οἱ
δυνατοὶ μὴ τὸν ἡγούμενον ἀλλ᾽ ὑπὲρ τοῦ ἡγουμένου
δεδιέναι, πολλοῖς μὲν ὄμμασιν ὁρᾷ, διὰ πολλῶν δ᾽ ὤτων
ἀκούει καὶ προαισθάνεται τὰ γινόμενα.

8 Διὸ καὶ βούλομαι τὸν λόγον ἐπιστήσας ἐνταῦθά που
b διεξελθεῖν περὶ τῆς Ἀριστίππου διαίτης, ἣν ἡ ζηλοτυπου-
μένη τυραννὶς αὐτῷ καὶ ὁ τῆς μακαρίας καὶ περιβοήτου
μοναρχίας ὄγκος περιέθηκεν. 26. ἐκεῖνος γὰρ Ἀντίγονον μὲν ἔχων σύμμαχον, τρέφων δὲ πολλοὺς ἕνεκα τῆς
τοῦ σώματος ἀσφαλείας, οὐδένα δ᾽ ἐν τῇ πόλει ζῶντα
τῶν ἐχθρῶν ὑπολελοιπώς, τοὺς μὲν δορυφόρους καὶ
φύλακας ἔξω παρεμβάλλειν ἐκέλευεν ἐν τῷ περιστύλῳ,
2 τοὺς δ᾽ οἰκέτας ὁπότε δειπνῆσαι τάχιστα πάντας
ἐξελαύνων, καὶ τὴν μέταυλον ἀποκλείων, μετὰ τῆς

---

26. 2. δειπνῆσαι GL² δειπνήσειεν L¹ δειπνήσαιεν PR. καταρράκτηι G¹.

ἐρωμένης αὐτὸς εἰς οἴκημα κατεδύετο μικρὸν ὑπερῷον,
θύρᾳ καταρρακτῇ κλειόμενον· ἧς ὑπεράνω τὴν κλίνην c
ἐπιτιθεὶς ἐκάθευδεν, ὡς εἰκὸς καθεύδειν τὸν οὕτως ἔχοντα,
ταραχωδῶς καὶ περιφόβως. τὸ δὲ κλιμάκιον ἡ τῆς 3
ἐρωμένης μήτηρ ὑφαιροῦσα κατέκλειεν εἰς ἕτερον οἴκημα,
καὶ πάλιν ἅμ᾽ ἡμέρᾳ προσετίθει καὶ κατεκάλει τὸν
θαυμαστὸν τύραννον, ὥσπερ ἑρπετόν ἐκ φωλεοῦ κατερ-
χόμενον. ὁ δ᾽ οὐχ ὅπλοις κατὰ βίαν, νόμῳ δ᾽ ὑπ᾽ 4
ἀρετῆς ἀκατάπαυστον ἀρχὴν περιπεποιημένος, ἐν ἱματίῳ
καὶ χλαμυδίῳ τῷ τυχόντι, τῶν πώποτε τυράννων κοινὸς
ἀποδεδειγμένος ἐχθρός, ἄχρι τῆς τήμερον ἡμέρας γένος
εὐδοκιμώτατον ἀπολέλοιπεν ἐν τοῖς Ἕλλησιν. ἐκείνων 5
δὲ τῶν τὰς ἄκρας καταλαμβανόντων καὶ τοὺς δορυφόρους
τρεφόντων καὶ τὰ ὅπλα καὶ τὰς πύλας καὶ τοὺς
καταρράκτας προβαλλομένων ὑπὲρ τῆς τοῦ σώματος
ἀσφαλείας ὀλίγοι τὸν ἐκ πληγῆς θάνατον ὥσπερ οἱ
λαγωοὶ διέφυγον· οἶκος δ᾽ ἢ γένος ἢ τάφος ἔχων
τιμωμένην μνήμην οὐδενὸς λέλειπται.

27. Πρὸς δ᾽ οὖν τὸν Ἀρίστιππον ὁ Ἄρατος καὶ
κρύφα πολλάκις καὶ φανερῶς προσέπταισεν, ἐπιχειρήσας
καταλαμβάνειν τὸ Ἄργος. ἅπαξ δὲ κλίμακας προσθεὶς
μετ᾽ ὀλίγων ἐπὶ τὸ τεῖχος ἀνέβη παραβόλως, καὶ τοὺς
βοηθοῦντας ἐνταῦθα τῶν φυλάκων ἀπέκτεινεν. εἶθ᾽ 2
ἡμέρας ἐπιφανείσης, καὶ τοῦ τυράννου πανταχόθεν αὐτῷ e
προσβάλλοντος, οἱ μὲν Ἀργεῖοι, καθάπερ οὐχ ὑπὲρ τῆς
ἐκείνων ἐλευθερίας τῆς μάχης οὔσης, ἀλλ᾽ ὡς τὸν ἀγῶνα
τῶν Νεμείων βραβεύοντες, ἴσοι καὶ δίκαιοι θεαταὶ
καθῆντο τῶν γινομένων, πολλὴν ἡσυχίαν ἄγοντες, ὁ δ᾽ 3
Ἄρατος εὐρώστως ἀμυνόμενος λόγχῃ μὲν ἐκ χειρὸς
διελαύνεται τὸν μηρόν, ἐκράτησε δὲ τῶν τόπων ἐν οἷς ἦν
καὶ οὐκ ἐξεώσθη μέχρι νυκτὸς ἐνοχλούμενος ὑπὸ τῶν
πολεμίων. εἰ δὲ καὶ τὴν νύκτα τῷ πόνῳ προσετα- 4
λαιπώρησεν, οὐκ ἂν διήμαρτεν· ὁ γὰρ τύραννος ἤδη
περὶ δρασμὸν εἶχε, καὶ πολλὰ τῶν ἰδίων ἐπὶ θάλασσαν
προεξέπεμψε. νῦν δὲ τοῦτο μὲν οὐδενὸς ἐξαγγείλαντος f
πρὸς τὸν Ἄρατον, ὕδατος δ᾽ ἐπιλιπόντος, ἑαυτῷ δὲ
χρήσασθαι διὰ τὸ τραῦμα μὴ δυνάμενος, ἀπήγαγε τοὺς
στρατιώτας.

28. Ἐπεὶ δὲ ταύτην ἀπέγνω τὴν ὁδόν, ἐμβαλὼν φανερῶς τῷ στρατοπέδῳ τὴν Ἀργολίδα χώραν ἐπόρθει· καὶ περὶ τὸν *Χάραδρον ποταμὸν ἰσχυρᾶς μάχης γενο-μένης πρὸς Ἀρίστιππον, αἰτίαν ἔσχεν ὡς ἐγκαταλιπὼν

2 τὸν ἀγῶνα καὶ προέμενος τὸ νίκημα. τῆς γὰρ ἄλλης

1040 δυνάμεως ὁμολογουμένως ἐπικρατούσης καὶ τῷ διωγμῷ πολὺ προελθούσης εἰς τοὔμπροσθεν, αὐτὸς οὐχ οὕτως ἐκβιασθεὶς ὑπὸ τῶν καθ᾽ αὑτόν, ὡς ἀπιστῶν τῷ κατορ-θώματι καὶ φοβηθείς, ἀνεχώρησε τεταραγμένος εἰς τὸ

3 στρατόπεδον. ἐπεὶ δ᾽ ἀπὸ τῆς διώξεως ἐπανελθόντες οἱ λοιποὶ χαλεπῶς ἔφερον, ὅτι τρεψάμενοι τοὺς πολεμίους καὶ πολὺ πλείονας ἐκείνων καταβαλόντες ἢ σφῶν αὐτῶν ἀπολέσαντες παραλελοίπασι τοῖς ἡττημένοις στῆσαι κατ᾽ αὐτῶν τρόπαιον, αἰσχυνθεὶς πάλιν ἔγνω διαμάχεσθαι περὶ τοῦ τροπαίου, καὶ μίαν ἡμέραν διαλιπὼν αὖθις ἐξέταττε

4 τὴν στρατιάν. ὡς δ᾽ ᾔσθετο πλείονας γεγονότας καὶ

b θαρραλεώτερον ἀνθισταμένους τοὺς περὶ τὸν τύραννον, οὐκ ἐτόλμησεν ἀλλ᾽ ἀπῆλθε, τοὺς νεκροὺς ὑποσπόνδους

5 ἀνελόμενος. οὐ μὴν ἀλλὰ τῇ περὶ τὴν ὁμιλίαν καὶ πολιτείαν ἐμπειρίᾳ καὶ χάριτι τὴν διαμαρτίαν ταύτην ἀναμαχόμενος, προσηγάγετο τὰς Κλεωνὰς τοῖς Ἀχαιοῖς, καὶ τὸν ἀγῶνα τῶν Νεμείων ἤγαγεν ἐν Κλεωναῖς, ὡς

6 πάτριον ὄντα καὶ μᾶλλον προσήκοντα τούτοις. ἤγαγον δὲ καὶ Ἀργεῖοι, καὶ συνεχύθη τότε πρῶτον ἡ δεδομένη τοῖς ἀγωνισταῖς ἀσυλία καὶ ἀσφάλεια, πάντας τῶν Ἀχαιῶν, ὅσους ἔλαβον ἠγωνισμένους ἐν Ἄργει, διὰ τῆς χώρας πορευομένους ὡς πολεμίους ἀποδομένων. οὕτω

c σφοδρὸς ἦν καὶ ἀπαραίτητος ἐν τῷ μισεῖν τοὺς τυράννους.

29. ὀλίγῳ δ᾽ ὕστερον ἀκούσας τὸν Ἀρίστιππον ἐπιβου-λεύειν μὲν ταῖς Κλεωναῖς, φοβεῖσθαι δ᾽ ἐκεῖνον ἐν Κορίνθῳ

2 καθεζόμενον, ἤθροισεν ἐκ παραγγέλματος στρατιάν. καὶ σιτία κελεύσας πλειόνων ἡμερῶν κομίζειν εἰς Κεγχρεὰς κατῆλθεν, ἐκκαλούμενος δι᾽ ἀπάτης τὸν Ἀρίστιππον ὡς αὑτοῦ μὴ παρόντος ἐπιθέσθαι τοῖς Κλεωναίοις. ὃ καὶ συνέβη· παρῆν γὰρ εὐθὺς ἐξ Ἄργους ἔχων τὴν

---

28. 1. Χάραδρον Herwerden : Χάρητα.   3. ἐξέταττε G¹ ἐξέτασσε G²PRL.
29. 1. στρατιάν R² στρατείαν GR¹PL.   2. P has ἀθροίζειν for κομίζειν.

δύναμιν. ὁ δ' Ἄρατος εἰς Κόρινθον ἤδη σκοταῖος ἐκ 3
Κεγχρεῶν ὑποστρέψας, καὶ τὰς ὁδοὺς φυλακαῖς δια-
λαβών, ἦγε τοὺς Ἀχαιοὺς ἑπομένους οὕτω μὲν εὐτάκτως d
οὕτω δὲ ταχέως καὶ προθύμως, ὥστε μὴ μόνον ὁδεύοντας
ἀλλὰ καὶ παρελθόντας εἰς τὰς Κλεωνὰς ἔτι νυκτὸς οὔσης
καὶ συνταξαμένους ἐπὶ μάχην ἀγνοεῖσθαι καὶ λανθάνειν
τὸν Ἀρίστιππον. ἅμα δ' ἡμέρᾳ τῶν πυλῶν ἀνοιχθεισῶν 4
καὶ τῆς σάλπιγγος ἐγκελευσαμένης, δρόμῳ καὶ ἀλα-
λαγμῷ προσπεσὼν τοῖς πολεμίοις εὐθὺς ἐτρέψατο, καὶ
κατεῖχε διώκων ᾗ μάλιστα φεύγειν ὑπενόει τὸν
Ἀρίστιππον, ἐκτροπὰς πολλὰς τῶν χωρίων ἐχόντων.
γενομένης δὲ τῆς διώξεως ἄχρι Μυκηνῶν, ὁ μὲν τύραννος 5
ὑπὸ Κρητός τινος, ὡς Δεινίας ἱστορεῖ, τοὔνομα Τραγίσκου
καταληφθεὶς ἀποσφάττεται, τῶν δ' ἄλλων ἔπεσον ὑπὲρ e
χιλίους πεντακοσίους. ὁ δ' Ἄρατος οὕτως λαμπρῶς 6
εὐτυχήσας, καὶ μηδένα τῶν αὐτοῦ στρατιωτῶν ἀπο-
βαλών, ὅμως οὐκ ἔλαβε τὸ Ἄργος οὐδ' ἠλευθέρωσε τοὺς
ἐν αὐτῷ, τῶν περὶ Ἀγίαν καὶ τὸν νεώτερον Ἀριστόμαχον
μετὰ δυνάμεως βασιλικῆς παρεισπεσόντων καὶ κατα-
σχόντων τὰ πράγματα.

τὸ μὲν οὖν πολὺ τῆς διαβολῆς καὶ λόγους καὶ 7
σκώμματα καὶ βωμολοχίας παρείλετο τῶν κολακευόντων
τοὺς τυράννους, καὶ διεξιόντων ἐκείνοις χαριζομένων, ὡς
τοῦ στρατηγοῦ τῶν Ἀχαιῶν ἐκταράττοιτο μὲν ἡ κοιλία
παρὰ τὰς μάχας, κάρος δὲ προσπίπτοι καὶ ἴλιγγος ἅμα f
τῷ παραστῆναι τὸν σαλπιγκτήν, ἐκτάξας δὲ τὴν δύναμιν
καὶ τὸ σύνθημα παρεγγυήσας, καὶ πυθόμενος τῶν
ὑποστρατήγων καὶ λοχαγῶν, μή τις αὐτοῦ χρεία παρόντος—βεβλῆσθαι γὰρ τοὺς ἀστραγάλους—, ἀπέρχοιτο
καραδοκήσων πόρρωθεν τὸ συμβησόμενον. ταῦτα γὰρ 8
οὕτως ἴσχυσεν, ὥστε καὶ τοὺς φιλοσόφους ἐν ταῖς
σχολαῖς ζητοῦντας, εἰ τὸ πάλλεσθαι τὴν καρδίαν καὶ τὸ
χρῶμα τρέπεσθαι καὶ τὴν κοιλίαν ἐξυγραίνεσθαι παρὰ

---

3. Before τοὺς Ἀχαιοὺς P, R have πρὸς.   4. ἐκκελευσαμένης G.
29. 5–8 are in Photius, *Bibl.*, p. 398.   6. τοὺς ἐν αὐτῷ added in Photius.
7. κάρος δὲ καὶ ἴλιγγος προσπίπτοι Phot. εἴλιγγος R¹. καὶ λοχαγῶν om. Phot.
8. ζητοῦντας om. G¹, ζητεῖν Phot. cod. A. καὶ τὴν κοιλίαν ἐξυγραίνεσθαι add. Phot.

τὰ φαινόμενα δεινὰ δειλίας ἐστὶν ἢ δυσκρασίας τινὸς
περὶ τὸ σῶμα καὶ ψυχρότητος, ὀνομάζειν ἀεὶ τὸν Ἄρατον,
ὡς ἀγαθὸν μὲν ὄντα στρατηγόν, ἀεὶ δὲ ταῦτα πάσχοντα
παρὰ τοὺς ἀγῶνας. 30. Ὡς δ' οὖν τὸν Ἀρίστιππον ἀνεῖλεν, εὐθὺς
ἐπεβούλευσε Λυδιάδῃ τῷ Μεγαλοπολίτῃ τυραννοῦντι
2 τῆς ἑαυτοῦ πατρίδος. ὁ δ' οὐκ ὢν ἀγεννὴς οὐδ'
ἀφιλότιμος τὴν φύσιν, οὐδ' ὥσπερ οἱ πολλοὶ τῶν
μοναρχων ἀκρασίᾳ καὶ πλεονεξίᾳ πρὸς ταύτην ῥυεὶς τὴν
ἀδικίαν, ἀλλ' ἐπαρθεὶς ἔρωτι δόξης ἔτι νέος καὶ λόγους
ψευδεῖς καὶ κενοὺς λεγομένους περὶ τυραννίδος, ὡς
μακαρίου καὶ θαυμαστοῦ πράγματος, εἰς μέγα φρόνημα
παραδεξάμενος ἀνοήτως καὶ καταστήσας ἑαυτὸν τύραν-
3 νον, ταχὺ μεστὸς ἦν τῆς ἐκ μοναρχίας βαρύτητος. ἅμα
b δὲ ζηλῶν εὐημεροῦντα καὶ δεδοικὼς ἐπιβουλεύοντα τὸν
Ἄρατον, ὥρμησε καλλίστην ὁρμὴν μεταβαλόμενος,
πρῶτον μὲν ἑαυτὸν ἐλευθερῶσαι μίσους καὶ φόβου καὶ
φρουρᾶς καὶ δορυφόρων, εἶτα τῆς πατρίδος εὐεργέτης
4 γενέσθαι. καὶ μεταπεμψάμενος τὸν Ἄρατον ἀφῆκε τὴν
ἀρχήν, καὶ τὴν πόλιν εἰς τοὺς Ἀχαιοὺς μετεκόμισεν. ἐφ'
οἷς μεγαλύνοντες αὐτὸν οἱ Ἀχαιοὶ στρατηγὸν εἵλοντο.
5 φιλοτιμούμενος δ' εὐθὺς ὑπερβαλεῖν δόξῃ τὸν Ἄρατον,
ἄλλας τε πολλὰς πράξεις οὐκ ἀναγκαίας εἶναι δοκούσας
6 καὶ στρατείαν ἐπὶ Λακεδαιμονίους παρήγγελλεν. ἐνιστά-
μενος δ' ὁ Ἄρατος αὐτῷ φθονεῖν ἐδόκει· καὶ τό γε
c δεύτερον ὁ Λυδιάδης στρατηγὸς ᾑρέθη, ἀντιπράττοντος
ἄντικρυς Ἀράτου καὶ σπουδάζοντος ἑτέρῳ παραδοθῆναι
τὴν ἀρχήν. αὐτὸς μὲν γὰρ ὡς εἴρηται παρ' ἐνιαυτὸν
7 ἦρχε. μέχρι μὲν οὖν τρίτης στρατηγίας ὁ Λυδιάδης εὖ
φερόμενος διετέλει, καὶ παρ' ἐνιαυτὸν ἦρχεν [μὲν]
ἐναλλὰξ τῷ Ἀράτῳ στρατηγῶν· φανερὰν δ' ἐξενεγκά-
μενος ἔχθραν καὶ πολλάκις αὐτοῦ κατηγορήσας ἐν τοῖς
Ἀχαιοῖς, ἀπερρίφη καὶ *παρώφθη, πεπλασμένῳ δοκῶν

---

8. ψυχρότητος· τὸν γὰρ Ἄρατον ἀεὶ μὲν ἀγαθὸν ἡγεῖσθαι στρατηγόν, ἀεὶ δὲ κτλ.
Phot.   30. 3. μεταβαλόμενος L (after erasure) μεταβαλλόμενος GPR and L
(before erasure).   4. μετεκοίμισεν GL¹ μετεκόσμησεν PRL².   5. παρήγγελλεν
PRG² παρήγγελεν G¹ παρήγγειλεν L.   7. [μὲν] Anon: παρώφθη l'flugk :
γὰρ ὤφθη.

ἤθει πρὸς ἀληθινὴν καὶ ἀκέραιον ἀρετὴν ἁμιλλᾶσθαι.
καὶ καθάπερ τῷ κόκκυγί φησιν Αἴσωπος ἐρωτῶντι τοὺς 8
λεπτοὺς ὄρνιθας, ὅ τι φεύγοιεν αὐτόν, εἰπεῖν ἐκείνους, ὡς
ἔσται ποθ᾽ ἱέραξ, οὕτως ἔοικε τῷ Λυδιάδῃ παρακολουθεῖν d
ἐκ τῆς τυραννίδος ὑποψία, βλάπτουσα τὴν *πίστιν
αὐτοῦ τῆς μεταβολῆς. 31. Ὁ δ᾽ Ἄρατος εὐδοκίμησε καὶ περὶ τὰς
Αἰτωλικὰς πράξεις, ὅτε συμβαλεῖν μὲν αὐτοῖς πρὸ τῆς
Μεγαρικῆς ὡρμημένων τῶν Ἀχαιῶν, καὶ τοῦ βασιλέως
τῶν Λακεδαιμονίων Ἄγιδος ἀφικομένου μετὰ δυνάμεως
καὶ συνεξορμῶντος ἐπὶ τὴν μάχην τοὺς Ἀχαιούς,
ἐναντιωθεὶς καὶ πολλὰ μὲν ὀνείδη πολλὰ δ᾽ εἰς μαλακίαν 2
καὶ ἀτολμίαν [καὶ] σκώμματα καὶ χλευασμὸν ὑπομείνας,
οὐ προήκατο τὸν τοῦ συμφέροντος λογισμὸν διὰ τὸ
φαινόμενον αἰσχρόν, ἀλλὰ παρεχώρησε τοῖς πολεμίοις
ὑπερβαλοῦσι τὴν Γεράνειαν ἀμαχεὶ παρελθεῖν εἰς
Πελοπόννησον. ὡς μέντοι παρελθόντες ἐξαίφνης Πελλή- e 3
νην κατέλαβον, οὐκέτ᾽ ἦν ὁ αὐτός, οὐδ᾽ ἔμελλε διατρίβων
καὶ περιμένων ἀθροισθῆναι καὶ συνελθεῖν εἰς ταὐτὸ πανταχόθεν τὴν δύναμιν, ἀλλ᾽ εὐθὺς ὥρμησε μετὰ τῶν παρόντων ἐπὶ τοὺς πολεμίους, ἐν τῷ κρατεῖν ἀσθενεστάτους δι᾽
ἀταξίαν καὶ ὕβριν ὄντας. ἅμα γὰρ τῷ παρελθεῖν εἰς τὴν 4
πόλιν, οἱ μὲν στρατιῶται διασπαρέντες ἐν ταῖς οἰκίαις
ἦσαν, ἐξωθοῦντες ἀλλήλους καὶ διαμαχόμενοι περὶ τῶν
χρημάτων, ἡγεμόνες δὲ καὶ λοχαγοὶ τὰς γυναῖκας καὶ
τὰς θυγατέρας τῶν Πελληνέων περιιόντες ἥρπαζον, καὶ f
τὰ κράνη τὰ αὑτῶν ἀφαιροῦντες ἐκείναις περιετίθεσαν
τοῦ μηδένα λαβεῖν ἄλλον, ἀλλὰ τῷ κράνει δῆλον εἶναι
τὸν δεσπότην ἑκάστης. οὕτω δὲ διακειμένοις αὐτοῖς καὶ 5
ταῦτα πράττουσιν ἐξαίφνης ὁ Ἄρατος ἐπιπεσὼν προσηγ-
γέλθη. καὶ γενομένης ἐκπλήξεως, οἵαν εἰκὸς ἐν ἀταξίᾳ 1042
τοιαύτῃ, πρὶν ἢ πάντας πυθέσθαι τὸν κίνδυνον, οἱ πρῶτοι
περὶ τὰς πύλας τοῖς Ἀχαιοῖς καὶ τὰ προάστεια συμπε-
σόντες ἔφευγον ἤδη νενικημένοι, καὶ κατεπίμπλασαν
ἐλαυνόμενοι προτροπάδην ἀπορίας τοὺς συνισταμένους

---

8. πίστιν Anon : φύσιν.   31. I. ἀφικομένου Paris 1673 ἀφικνουμένου
GPRL.   2. [καὶ]Reiske. πελληνέων GPR² πελληναίαν LR¹.   4. ἔφυγον G¹.

καὶ προσβοηθοῦντας. **32.** ἐν τούτῳ δὲ τῷ ταράχῳ
μία τῶν αἰχμαλώτων, Ἐπιγήθους ἀνδρὸς ἐνδόξου θυγά-
τηρ, αὐτὴ δὲ κάλλει καὶ μεγέθει σώματος εὐπρεπής,
ἔτυχε μὲν ἐν τῷ ἱερῷ καθεζομένη τῆς Ἀρτέμιδος, οὗ
κατέστησεν αὐτὴν ὁ ἐπιλεκτάρχης, ἑλὼν ἑαυτῷ καὶ
περιθεὶς τὴν τριλοφίαν, ἄφνω δ' ἐκδραμοῦσα πρὸς τὸν
2 θόρυβον, ὡς ἔστη πρὸ τῶν θυρῶν τοῦ ἱεροῦ καὶ κατέ-
b βλεψεν εἰς τοὺς μαχομένους ἄνωθεν ἔχουσα τὴν τριλοφίαν, αὐτοῖς τε τοῖς πολίταις θέαμα σεμνότερον ἢ κατ'
ἄνθρωπον ἐφάνη, καὶ τοῖς πολεμίοις φάσμα θεῖον ὁρᾶν
δοκοῦσι φρίκην ἐνέβαλε καὶ θάμβος, ὥστε μηδένα τρέ-
3 πεσθαι πρὸς ἀλκήν. αὐτοὶ δὲ Πελληνεῖς λέγουσι τὸ
βρέτας τῆς θεοῦ τὸν μὲν ἄλλον ἀποκεῖσθαι χρόνον
ἄψαυστον, ὅταν δὲ κινηθὲν ὑπὸ τῆς ἱερείας ἐκφέρηται,
μηδένα προσβλέπειν ἐναντίον ἀλλ' ἀποτρέπεσθαι πάντας·
οὐ γὰρ ἀνθρώποις μόνον ὅραμα φρικτὸν εἶναι καὶ χαλε-
πόν, ἀλλὰ <καὶ> δένδρα ποιεῖν ἄφορα καὶ καρποὺς
4 ἀπαμβλίσκειν δι' ὧν ἂν κομίζηται. τοῦτο δὴ τότε τὴν
c ἱέρειαν ἐξενεγκαμένην καὶ τρέπουσαν ἀεὶ κατὰ τοὺς
Αἰτωλοὺς ἀντιπρόσωπον, ἔκφρονας καταστῆσαι καὶ
5 παρελέσθαι τὸν λογισμόν. ὁ δ' Ἄρατος οὐδὲν ἐν τοῖς
ὑπομνήμασιν εἴρηκε τοιοῦτον, ἀλλά φησι τρεψάμενος
τοὺς Αἰτωλοὺς καὶ φεύγουσι συνεισπεσὼν εἰς τὴν πόλιν
6 ἐξελάσαι κατὰ κράτος, ἑπτακοσίους δ' ἀποκτεῖναι. τὸ
δ' ἔργον ἐν τοῖς μεγίστοις διεβοήθη, καὶ Τιμάνθης ὁ
ζωγράφος ἐποίησεν ἐμφαντικῶς τῇ διαθέσει τὴν μάχην
ἔχουσαν.

33. Οὐ μὴν ἀλλὰ πολλῶν ἐθνῶν καὶ δυναστῶν ἐπὶ
τοὺς Ἀχαιοὺς συνισταμένων, εὐθὺς ὁ Ἄρατος ἔπραττε
φιλίαν πρὸς τοὺς Αἰτωλούς, καὶ Πανταλέοντι τῷ πλεῖστον
d Αἰτωλῶν δυναμένῳ συνεργῷ χρησάμενος, οὐ μόνον εἰρήνην ἀλλὰ καὶ συμμαχίαν τοῖς Ἀχαιοῖς πρὸς τοὺς
Αἰτωλοὺς ἐποίησε.

2 Τοὺς δ' Ἀθηναίους σπουδάζων ἐλευθερῶσαι, διεβλήθη
καὶ κακῶς ἤκουσεν ὑπὸ τῶν Ἀχαιῶν, ὅτι σπονδὰς πεποι-

---

32. 3. <καὶ> Reiske (in Paris 1673 it is inserted above the line). 6. ἐμφα-
τικῶς G¹.

ἡμένων αὐτῶν πρὸς τοὺς Μακεδόνας καὶ ἀνοχὰς ἀγόντων,
ἐπεχείρησε τὸν Πειραιᾶ καταλαβεῖν. αὐτὸς δ' ἀρνού- 3
μενος ἐν τοῖς ὑπομνήμασιν οἷς ἀπολέλοιπεν Ἐργῖνον
αἰτιᾶται, μεθ' οὗ τὰ περὶ τὸν Ἀκροκόρινθον ἔπραξεν.
ἐκεῖνον γὰρ ἰδίᾳ τῷ Πειραιεῖ προσβα[λ]λόντα καὶ τῆς
κλίμακος συντριβείσης διωκόμενον ὀνομάζειν καὶ καλεῖν
συνεχῶς Ἄρατον ὥσπερ παρόντα, καὶ διαφυγεῖν οὕτως ε
ἐξαπατήσαντα τοὺς πολεμίους. οὐ μὴν δοκεῖ πιθανῶς 4
ἀπολογεῖσθαι. τὸν γὰρ Εργῖνον, ἄνθρωπον ἰδιώτην καὶ
Σύρον, ἀπ' οὐδενὸς ἦν εἰκότος ἐπὶ νοῦν βαλέσθαι τηλικαύτην πρᾶξιν, εἰ μὴ τὸν Ἄρατον εἶχεν ἡγεμόνα καὶ παρ'
ἐκείνου τὴν δύναμιν καὶ τὸν καιρὸν εἰλήφει πρὸς τὴν
ἐπίθεσιν. ἐδήλωσε δὲ καὶ αὐτὸς ὁ Ἄρατος, οὐ δὶς οὐδὲ 5
τρίς, ἀλλὰ πολλάκις, ὥσπερ οἱ δυσέρωτες, ἐπιχειρήσας
τῷ Πειραιεῖ καὶ πρὸς τὰς διαμαρτίας οὐκ ἀποκαμών,
ἀλλὰ τῷ παρὰ μικρὸν ἀεὶ καὶ σύνεγγυς ἀποσφάλλεσθαι
τῶν ἐλπίδων πρὸς τὸ θαρρεῖν ἀνακαλούμενος ἅπαξ
δὲ καὶ τὸ σκέλος ἔσπασε διὰ τοῦ Θριασίου φεύγων·
καὶ τομὰς ἔλαβε πολλὰς θεραπευόμενος, καὶ πολὺν
χρόνον ἐν φορείῳ κομιζόμενος ἐποιεῖτο τὰς στρατείας.
34. Ἀντιγόνου δ' ἀποθανόντος καὶ Δημητρίου τὴν βασιλείαν παραλαβόντος ἔτι μᾶλλον ἐνέκειτο ταῖς Ἀθήναις,
καὶ ὅλως κατεφρόνει τῶν Μακεδόνων. διὸ καὶ κρατη- 2
θέντος αὐτοῦ μάχῃ περὶ Φυλακίαν ὑπὸ Βίθυος τοῦ
Δημητρίου στρατηγοῦ, καὶ λόγου γενομένου πολλοῦ
μὲν ὡς ἑάλωκε πολλοῦ δ' ὡς τέθνηκεν, ὁ μὲν τὸν
Πειραιᾶ φρουρῶν Διογένης ἔπεμψεν ἐπιστολὴν εἰς 1043
Κόρινθον, ἐξίστασθαι τῆς πόλεως κελεύων τοὺς Ἀχαιούς, ἐπειδή<περ> Ἄρατος ἀπέθανεν· ἔτυχε δὲ τῶν 3
γραμμάτων κομισθέντων παρὼν αὐτὸς ἐν Κορίνθῳ,
καὶ διατριβὴν οἱ τοῦ Διογένους καὶ γέλωτα πολὺν
παρασχόντες ἀπηλλάγησαν. αὐτὸς δ' ὁ βασιλεὺς ἐκ
Μακεδονίας ναῦν ἔπεμψεν, ἐφ' ἧς κομισθήσεται πρὸς
αὐτὸν ὁ Ἄρατος δεδεμένος. πᾶσαν δ' Ἀθηναῖοι 4

---

33. 3. προσβα[λ]λόντα Coraes.   5. καὶ αὐτὸς G¹RP καὶ αὖθις R (marg.)
αὖθις P (marg.).   τῶν ἐλπίδων LG² τὴν ἐλπίδα G¹PR.   **34.** 2. ἐπειδήπερ Ed.
ἐπεί γ' Benseler ἐπειδή GRL ἐπεὶ δὲ P.

κουφότητα *κολακεία τῇ πρὸς Μακεδόνας ὑπερβάλλοντες, ἐστεφανηφόρησαν ὅτε πρῶτον ἠγγέλθη τεθνηκώς.
b διὸ καὶ πρὸς ὀργὴν εὐθὺς ἐκστρατεύσας ἐπ᾽ αὐτούς, ἄχρι
5 τῆς Ἀκαδημείας προῆλθεν· εἶτα πεισθεὶς οὐδὲν ἠδίκησεν.
οἱ δ᾽ Ἀθηναῖοι συμφρονήσαντες αὐτοῦ τὴν ἀρετήν, ἐπεὶ
Δημητρίου τελευτήσαντος ὥρμησαν ἐπὶ τὴν ἐλευθερίαν,
6 ἐκεῖνον ἐκάλουν. ὁ δέ, καίπερ ἑτέρου μὲν ἄρχοντος
τότε τῶν Ἀχαιῶν, αὐτὸς δὲ δι᾽ ἀρρωστίαν τινὰ μακρὰν
κλινήρης ὑπάρχων, ὅμως ἐν φορείῳ κομιζόμενος ὑπήντησε
τῇ πόλει πρὸς τὴν χρείαν, καὶ τὸν ἐπὶ τῆς φρουρᾶς Διο-
γένη συνέπεισεν ἀποδοῦναι τόν τε Πειραιᾶ καὶ τὴν
Μουνυχίαν καὶ τὴν Σαλαμῖνα καὶ τὸ Σούνιον τοῖς Ἀθηναίοις ἐπὶ πεντήκοντα καὶ ἑκατὸν ταλάντοις, ὧν αὐτὸς
c 7 ὁ Ἄρατος εἴκοσι τῇ πόλει συνεβάλετο. προσεχώρησαν
δ᾽ εὐθὺς Αἰγινῆται καὶ Ἑρμιονεῖς τοῖς Ἀχαιοῖς, ἥ τε
πλείστη τῆς Ἀρκαδίας αὐτοῖς συνετέλει. καὶ Μακεδόνων μὲν ἀσχόλων ὄντων διά τινας προσοίκους καὶ
ὁμόρους πολέμους, Αἰτωλῶν δὲ συμμαχούντων, ἐπίδοσιν
μεγάλην ἡ τῶν Ἀχαιῶν ἐλάμβανε δύναμις.

35. Ὁ δ᾽ Ἄρατος ἐξεργαζόμενος τὴν παλαιὰν *ὑπόθεσιν, καὶ δυσανασχετῶν τὴν ἐν Ἄργει τυραννίδα γειτνι-
ῶσαν αὐτοῖς, ἔπειθε πέμπων τὸν Ἀριστόμαχον εἰς μέσον
θεῖναι καὶ προσαγαγεῖν τοῖς Ἀχαιοῖς τὴν πόλιν, καὶ
ζηλώσαντα Λυδιάδην ἔθνους τηλικούτου μετ᾽ εὐφημίας
καὶ τιμῆς στρατηγὸν εἶναι μᾶλλον, ἢ μιᾶς πόλεως κινδυ-
2 νεύοντα καὶ μισούμενον τύραννον. ὑπακούσαντος δὲ τοῦ
Ἀριστομάχου καὶ κελεύσαντος αὐτῷ πεντήκοντα τάλαντα
πέμψαι τὸν Ἄρατον, ὅπως ἀπαλλάξῃ καὶ διαλύσηται τοὺς
παρ᾽ αὐτῷ στρατευομένους, καὶ τῶν χρημάτων ποριζο-
3 μένων, ὁ Λυδιάδης ἔτι στρατηγῶν καὶ φιλοτιμούμενος
ἴδιον αὐτοῦ πολίτευμα τοῦτο πρὸς τοὺς Ἀχαιοὺς
γενέσθαι, τοῦ μὲν Ἀράτου κατηγόρει πρὸς Ἀριστόμαχον,
ὡς δυσμενῶς καὶ ἀδιαλλάκτως ἀεὶ πρὸς τοὺς τυράννους

---

4. κολακείᾳ τῇ Madvig: κολακείας τῆς. Ἀκαδημείας Sintenis: ἀκαδημίας.
6. δι᾽ ἀρρωστίαν τινὰ μακραν PRL: ἀρρωστία μακρᾶι G. συνεπείσθη PR. συνεβάλετο GL² συνεβάλλετο. 35. 1. ὑπόθεσιν Anon ὑπόσχεσιν: λυδιάδην G¹
λυσιάδην G²PL. 2. πεντήκοντα P: τὰ πεντήκοντα GRL.

ἔχοντος, αὐτῷ δὲ πείσας τὴν πρᾶξιν ἐπιτρέψαι προσήγαγε
τοῖς Ἀχαιοῖς τὸν ἄνθρωπον. ἔνθα δὴ μάλιστα φανερὰν 4 e
ἐποίησαν οἱ σύνεδροι τῶν Ἀχαιῶν τὴν πρὸς τὸν Ἄρατον
εὔνοιαν καὶ πίστιν. ἀντειπόντος μὲν γὰρ αὐτοῦ δι'
ὀργήν, ἀπήλασαν τοὺς περὶ τὸν Ἀριστόμαχον· ἐπεὶ δὲ 5
συμπεισθεὶς πάλιν αὐτὸς ἤρξατο περὶ αὐτῶν διαλέγεσθαι
παρών, πάντα ταχέως καὶ προθύμως ἐψηφίσαντο, καὶ
προσεδέξαντο μὲν τοὺς Ἀργείους καὶ Φλιασίους εἰς
τὴν πολιτείαν, ἐνιαυτῷ δ' ὕστερον καὶ τὸν Ἀριστόμαχον
εἵλοντο στρατηγόν.

Ὁ δ' εὐημερῶν παρὰ τοῖς Ἀχαιοῖς καὶ βουλόμενος εἰς 6
τὴν Λακωνικὴν ἐμβαλεῖν, ἐκάλει τὸν Ἄρατον ἐξ Ἀθηνῶν.
ὁ δ' ἔγραφε μὲν αὐτῷ τὴν στρατείαν ἀπαγορεύων [καὶ]
τῷ Κλεομένει θράσος ἔχοντι καὶ παραβόλως αὐξανομένῳ f
συμπλέκεσθαι τοὺς Ἀχαιοὺς μὴ βουλόμενος. ὡρμημένου
δὲ πάντως ὑπήκουσε καὶ παρὼν συνεστράτευεν. ὅτε δὴ 7
καὶ κωλύσας, περὶ τὸ Παλλάντιον τοῦ Κλεομένους
ἐπιφανέντος αὐτοῖς, μάχην συνάψαι τὸν Ἀριστόμαχον,
ὑπὸ Λυδιάδου κατηγορήθη, καὶ περὶ τῆς στρατηγίας εἰς
ἀγῶνα καὶ ἀντιπαραγγελίαν αὐτῷ καταστάς, ἐκράτησε
τῇ χειροτονίᾳ καὶ τὸ δωδέκατον ᾑρέθη στρατηγός.

36. Ἐν ταύτῃ τῇ στρατηγίᾳ περὶ τὸ Λύκαιον
ἡττηθεὶς ὑπὸ τοῦ Κλεομένους ἔφευγε· καὶ πλανηθεὶς 1044
νυκτὸς ἔδοξε μὲν τεθνάναι, καὶ πάλιν οὗτος ὁ λόγος κατ'
αὐτοῦ πολὺς ἐξεφοίτησεν εἰς τοὺς Ἕλληνας· ἀνασωθεὶς 2
δὲ καὶ τοὺς στρατιώτας συναγαγών, οὐκ ἠγάπησεν
ἀσφαλῶς ἀπελθεῖν, ἀλλ' ἄριστα τῷ καιρῷ χρησάμενος,
οὐδενὸς προσδοκῶντος οὐδὲ συλλογιζομένου τὸ μέλλον,
ἐξαίφνης ἐπέπεσε Μαντινεῦσι συμμάχοις οὖσι τοῦ
Κλεομένους. καὶ τὴν πόλιν ἑλών, φρουρὰν ἐνέβαλε καὶ 3
τοὺς μετοίκους πολίτας ἐποίησεν αὐτῶν, καὶ μόνος, ἃ
νικῶντες οὐκ ἂν ῥᾳδίως ἔσχον, ἐκτήσατο νενικημένοις
τοῖς Ἀχαιοῖς.

Αὖθις δὲ τῶν Λακεδαιμονίων ἐπὶ Μεγάλην πόλιν 4
στρατευσάντων, βοηθήσας ὤκνει μὲν ἀψιμαχοῦντι τῷ b
Κλεομένει λαβὴν παρασχεῖν, καὶ τοῖς Μεγαλοπολίταις

---

6. [καὶ] Sintenis.

C

5 βιαζομένοις ἀντεῖχεν, οὔτ᾽ ἄλλως πρὸς τὰς κατὰ στόμα
μάχας εὖ πεφυκώς, καὶ τότε λειπόμενός τε πλήθει καὶ
πρὸς ἄνδρα τολμητὴν καὶ νέον ἤδη παρακμάζοντι τῷ
θυμῷ καὶ κεκολασμένῃ τῇ φιλοτιμίᾳ συνεστηκώς, καὶ
νομίζων, ἣν διὰ τοῦ τολμᾶν ἐκεῖνος ἐξ οὐχ ὑπαρχόντων
ἐκτᾶτο δόξαν, αὐτῷ κεκτημένῳ φυλακτέον εἶναι διὰ τῆς
εὐλαβείας. 37. οὐ μὴν ἀλλὰ τῶν ψιλῶν ἐκδραμόντων
καὶ ὠσαμένων τοὺς Σπαρτιάτας ἄχρι τοῦ στρατοπέδου
καὶ περὶ τὰς σκηνὰς διασπαρέντων, ὁ μὲν Ἄρατος οὐδ᾽
c ὡς ἐπήγαγεν, ἀλλ᾽ ἐν μέσῳ λαβὼν χαράδραν ἐπέστησε
2 καὶ κατεκώλυσε διαβῆναι τοὺς *ὁπλίτας· ὁ δὲ Λυδιάδης
περιπαθῶν πρὸς τὰ γιγνόμενα καὶ τὸν Ἄρατον κακίζων,
ἀνεκαλεῖτο τοὺς ἱππεῖς ὡς *αὐτόν, ἀξιῶν ἐπιφανῆναι τοῖς
διώκουσι καὶ μὴ προέσθαι τὸ νίκημα, μήδ᾽ ἐγκαταλιπεῖν
3 αὐτὸν ὑπὲρ τῆς πατρίδος ἀγωνιζόμενον. πολλῶν δὲ
συστραφέντων καὶ ἀγαθῶν, ἐπιρρωσθεὶς ἐνέβαλε τῷ
δεξιῷ τῶν πολεμίων, καὶ τρεψάμενος ἐδίωκεν, ὑπὸ θυμοῦ
καὶ φιλοτιμίας ἀταμιεύτως ἐπισπασθεὶς εἰς χωρία σκολιὰ
καὶ μεστὰ δένδρων πεφυτευμένων καὶ τάφρων πλατειῶν,
d ἐν οἷς ἐπιθεμένου τοῦ Κλεομένους, ἔπεσε λαμπρῶς ἀγωνι-
σάμενος τὸν κάλλιστον τῶν ἀγώνων ἐπὶ θύραις τῆς πατρί-
4 δος. οἱ δ᾽ ἄλλοι φεύγοντες εἰς τὴν φάλαγγα καὶ συντα-
ράξαντες τοὺς ὁπλίτας, ὅλον τὸ στράτευμα τῆς ἥττης
5 ἀνέπλησαν. αἰτίαν δὲ μεγάλην ὁ Ἄρατος ἔλαβε, δόξας
προέσθαι τὸν Λυδιάδην· καὶ βιασθεὶς ὑπὸ τῶν Ἀχαιῶν
ἀπερχομένων πρὸς ὀργήν, ἠκολούθησεν αὐτοῖς εἰς Αἴγιον.
ἐκεῖ δὲ συνελθόντες ἐψηφίσαντο μὴ διδόναι χρήματ᾽ αὐτῷ
μηδὲ μισθοφόρους τρέφειν, ἀλλ᾽ αὐτῷ πορίζειν εἰ δέοιτο
πολεμεῖν. 38. οὕτω δὲ προπηλακισθείς, ἐβουλεύσατο
μὲν εὐθὺς ἀποθέσθαι τὴν σφραγῖδα καὶ τὴν στρατηγίαν
e ἀφεῖναι, λογισμῷ δὲ χρησάμενος τότε μὲν ὑπέμεινε, καὶ
πρὸς Ὀρχομενὸν ἐξαγαγὼν τοὺς Ἀχαιούς, μάχην ἔθετο
πρὸς Μεγιστόνουν τὸν Κλεομένους πατρῷον, ἐν ᾗ κρατήσας τριακοσίους μὲν ἀπέκτεινε, ζῶντα δὲ τὸν Μεγιστόνουν συνέλαβεν.

---

37. 1. ὁπλίτας Bryan πολίτας.   2. αὐτὸν Coraes: αὐτὸς (ὡς αὐτὸς ἄξων
Reiske).

Εἰωθὼς δὲ στρατηγεῖν παρ' ἐνιαυτόν, ὡς ἡ τάξις αὐτῷ 2 περιῆλθε, καλούμενος ἐξωμόσατο, καὶ Τιμόξενος ᾑρέθη στρατηγός. ἐδόκει δ' ἡ μὲν πρὸς τοὺς ὄχλους ὀργὴ 3 πρόφασις εἶναι λεγομένη τῆς ἐξωμοσίας ἀπίθανος, αἰτία δ' ἀληθὴς τὰ περιεστῶτα τοὺς Ἀχαιούς, οὐκέθ' ὡς πρότερον ἀτρέμα καὶ σχέδην τοῦ Κλεομένους ἐπιβαίνοντος f 4 οὐδ' ἐμπλεκομένου ταῖς πολιτικαῖς ἀρχαῖς, ἀλλ' ἐπεὶ τοὺς ἐφόρους ἀποκτείνας καὶ τὴν χώραν ἀναδασάμενος καὶ πολλοὺς τῶν μετοίκων ἐμβαλὼν εἰς τὴν πολιτείαν ἔσχεν ἰσχὺν ἀνυπεύθυνον, εὐθὺς ἐπικειμένου τοῖς Ἀχαιοῖς καὶ τῆς ἡγεμονίας ἑαυτὸν ἀξιοῦντος.

Διὸ καὶ μέμφονται τὸν Ἄρατον, ἐν σάλῳ μεγάλῳ καὶ 5 χειμῶνι τῶν πραγμάτων φερομένων, ὥσπερ κυβερνήτην ἀφέντα καὶ προέμενον ἑτέρῳ τοὺς οἴακας, ὅτε καλῶς εἶχε 1045 καὶ ἀκόντων ἐπιστάντα σῴζειν τὸ κοινόν· <εἰ δ'> ἀπεγνώ- 6 κει τὰ πράγματα καὶ τὴν δύναμιν τῶν Ἀχαιῶν, εἶξαι τῷ Κλεομένει, καὶ μὴ πάλιν τὴν Πελοπόννησον ἐκβαρβαρῶσαι φρουραῖς Μακεδόνων, *μηδὲ πληρῶσαι τὸν Ἀκροκόρινθον Ἰλλυρικῶν ὅπλων καὶ Γαλατικῶν, μηδ' οὓς αὐτὸς ἐν ταῖς πράξεσι καταστρατηγῶν καὶ καταπολιτευόμενος, ἐν δὲ τοῖς ὑπομνήμασι λοιδορῶν διετέλει, τούτους ἐπάγεσθαι δεσπότας ταῖς πόλεσι, συμμάχους ὑποκοριζόμενον. εἰ δὲ Κλεομένης ἦν — λεγέσθω γὰρ οὕτως — 7 παράνομος καὶ τυραννικός, ἀλλ' Ἡρακλεῖδαι πατέρες αὐτῷ καὶ Σπάρτη πατρίς, ἧς τὸν ἀφανέστατον ἠξίουν <ἂν> ἀντὶ τοῦ πρώτου Μακεδόνων ἡγεμόνα ποιεῖσθαι b τοὺς ἔν τινι λόγῳ τὴν Ἑλληνικὴν τιθεμένους εὐγένειαν. καίτοι Κλεομένης ᾔτει τὴν ἀρχὴν παρὰ τῶν Ἀχαιῶν 8 ὡς πολλὰ ποιήσων ἀγαθὰ τὰς πόλεις ἀντὶ τῆς τιμῆς καὶ τῆς προσηγορίας ἐκείνης· Ἀντίγονος δὲ καὶ κατὰ γῆν 9 καὶ κατὰ θάλατταν αὐτοκράτωρ ἡγεμὼν ἀναγορευθείς, οὐχ ὑπήκουσε πρὶν τὸν μισθὸν αὐτῷ τῆς ἡγεμονίας ὁμολογηθῆναι τὸν Ἀκροκόρινθον, ἀτεχνῶς τὸν Αἰσώπου μιμησάμενος κυνηγόν. οὐ γὰρ πρότερον ἐπέβη τοῖς 10

---

38. 6. <εἰ δ'> Anon. μηδὲ Coraes μήτε. ὑποκοριζόμενον LG² : ὑποκοριζόμενος R ὑποκοριζόμενος P ὑποκοριζομένους G¹.　　7. οὗτος G. ἠξίουν <ἂν> Reiske : ἠξίουν PRL ἠξίου G ἄξιον Solanus.

'Αχαιοῖς δεομένοις καὶ ὑποβάλλουσιν αὐτοὺς διὰ τῶν
πρεσβειῶν καὶ τῶν ψηφισμάτων, ἢ τῇ φρουρᾷ καὶ τοῖς
11 c ὁμήροις ὥσπερ χαλινουμένους ἀνασχέσθαι. καίτοι
πᾶσαν ὁ Ἄρατος ἀφίησι φωνὴν ἀπολογιζόμενος τὴν
ἀνάγκην. ὁ Πολύβιος δ᾽ αὐτὸν ἐκ πολλοῦ φησι καὶ
πρὸ τῆς ἀνάγκης, ὑφορώμενον τὸ θράσος τὸ τοῦ
Κλεομένους, κρύφα τῷ Ἀντιγόνῳ διαλέγεσθαι, καὶ τοὺς
Μεγαλοπολίτας προκαθιέναι δεομένους Ἀχαιῶν ἐπι-
καλεῖσθαι τὸν Ἀντίγονον· οὗτοι γὰρ ἐπιέζοντο τῷ
πολέμῳ μάλιστα, συνεχῶς ἄγοντος αὐτοὺς καὶ φέροντος
12 τοῦ Κλεομένους. ὁμοίως δὲ καὶ Φύλαρχος ἱστόρηκε
περὶ τούτων, ᾧ μὴ τοῦ Πολυβίου μαρτυροῦντος οὐ πάνυ
τι πιστεύειν ἄξιον ἦν· ἐνθουσιᾷ γὰρ ὅταν ἅψηται τοῦ
Κλεομένους ὑπ᾽ εὐνοίας, καὶ καθάπερ ἐν δίκῃ τῇ ἱστορίᾳ
d τῷ μὲν ἀντιδικῶν διατελεῖ τῷ δὲ συναγορεύων.

39. Ἀπέβαλον δ᾽ οὖν οἱ Ἀχαιοὶ τὴν Μαντίνειαν,
πάλιν ἑλόντος αὐτὴν τοῦ Κλεομένους, καὶ μάχῃ μεγάλῃ
περὶ τὸ Ἑκατόμβαιον ἡττηθέντες οὕτω κατεπλάγησαν,
ὥστε πέμπειν εὐθὺς ἐφ᾽ ἡγεμονίᾳ τὸν Κλεομένη
2 καλοῦντες εἰς Ἄργος. ὁ δ᾽ Ἄρατος ὡς ᾔσθετο
βαδίζοντα καὶ περὶ Λέρναν ὄντα μετὰ τῆς δυνάμεως,
φοβηθεὶς ἀπέστελλε πρέσβεις τοὺς ἀξιοῦντας, ὡς παρὰ
φίλους καὶ συμμάχους αὐτὸν ἥκειν μετὰ τριακοσίων· εἰ
3 δ᾽ ἀπιστεῖ λαβεῖν ὁμήρους. ταῦθ᾽ ὕβριν εἶναι καὶ
χλευασμὸν αὐτοῦ φήσας ὁ Κλεομένης ἀνέζευξεν, ἐπιστο-
e λὴν γράψας τοῖς Ἀχαιοῖς, ἐγκλήματα πολλὰ κατὰ τοῦ
Ἀράτου καὶ διαβολὰς ἔχουσαν· γέγραφε δὲ κἀκεῖνος
ἐπιστολὰς κατὰ τοῦ Κλεομένους, καὶ ἐφέροντο λοιδορίαι
καὶ βλασφημίαι, μέχρι γάμων καὶ γυναικῶν ἀλλήλους
κακῶς λεγόντων.

4 Ἐκ τούτου κήρυκα πέμψας ὁ Κλεομένης πόλεμον
προεροῦντα τοῖς Ἀχαιοῖς, μικροῦ μὲν ἔλαθε τὴν Σικυωνίων πόλιν ἁρπάσας διὰ προδοσίας, ἔγγυθεν δ᾽ ἀποτρα-

---

11. τῷ πολέμῳ μάλιστα συνεχῶς G, μάλιστα συνεχῶς τῷ πολέμῳ PRL.

12. ὁμοίως PL ὁμοίως R ὡς G. καὶ om. in G.   **39.** 1. ἀπέβαλον GL² ἀπεβά-
λοντο R² ἀπεβάλλοντο PR¹L². 2. ἀπέστελλε G ἀπέστειλε PRL.   3. ταῦτα
ὕβριν αὐτοῦ εἶναι καὶ χλευασμὸν φήσας L.

πεὶς Πελλήνῃ προσέβαλε, καὶ τοῦ στρατηγοῦ τῶν Ἀχαιῶν
ἐκπεσόντος, ἔσχε τὴν πόλιν· ὀλίγῳ δ' ὕστερον καὶ Φενεὸν
ἔλαβε καὶ Πεντέλειον. εἶτ' εὐθὺς Ἀργεῖοι προσεχώρησαν 5
αὐτῷ, καὶ Φλιάσιοι φρουρὰν ἐδέξαντο· καὶ ὅλως οὐδὲν ἔτι f
τῶν ἐπικτήτων βέβαιον ἦν τοῖς Ἀχαιοῖς, ἀλλὰ θόρυβος
πολὺς ἄ<φ>νω περιειστήκει τὸν Ἄρατον, ὁρῶντα τὴν
Πελοπόννησον κραδαινομένην καὶ τὰς πόλεις ἐξανιστα-
μένας ὑπὸ τῶν νεωτεριζόντων πανταχόθεν. 40. ἠτρέμει
γὰρ οὐδὲν οὐδ' ἔστεργεν ἐπὶ τοῖς παροῦσιν, ἀλλὰ καὶ 1046
Σικυωνίων αὐτῶν καὶ Κορινθίων ἐγένοντο πολλοὶ κατα-
φανεῖς διειλεγμένοι τῷ Κλεομένει, καὶ πάλαι πρὸς τὸ
κοινὸν ἰδίων ἐπιθυμίᾳ δυναστειῶν ὑπούλως ἔχοντες. ἐπὶ 2
τούτους ἐξουσίαν ἀνυπεύθυνον ὁ Ἄρατος λαβών, τοὺς
μὲν ἐν *Σικυῶνι διεφθαρμένους ἀπέκτεινε, τοὺς δ' ἐν
Κορίνθῳ πειρώμενος ἀναζητεῖν καὶ κολάζειν, ἐξηγρίαινε
τὸ πλῆθος, ἤδη νοσοῦν καὶ βαρυνόμενον τὴν ὑπὸ τοῖς
Ἀχαιοῖς πολιτείαν. συνδραμόντες οὖν εἰς τὸ τοῦ Ἀπόλ- 3
λωνος ἱερόν, μετεπέμποντο τὸν Ἄρατον, ἀνελεῖν ἢ συλ-
λαβεῖν πρὸ τῆς ἀποστάσεως ἐγνωκότες. ὁ δ' ἧκε μὲν αὐτὸς 4
ἐφελκόμενος τὸν ἵππον, ὡς οὐκ ἀπιστῶν οὐδ' ὑποπτεύων, b
ἀναπηδησάντων δὲ πολλῶν καὶ λοιδορουμένων αὐτῷ καὶ
κατηγορούντων, εὖ πως καθεστῶτι τῷ προσώπῳ καὶ τῷ
λόγῳ πράως ἐκέλευε καθίσαι καὶ μὴ βοᾶν ἀτάκτως ἑστῶ-
τας, ἀλλὰ καὶ τοὺς περὶ θύρας ὄντας εἴσω παριέναι· καὶ
ταῦθ' ἅμα λέγων ὑπεξῄει βάδην ὡς παραδώσων τινὶ τὸν
ἵππον. οὕτως δ' ὑπεκδύς, καὶ τοῖς ἀπαντῶσι τῶν Κο- 5
ρινθίων ἀθορύβως διαλεγόμενος καὶ κελεύων πρὸς τὸ
Ἀπολλώνιον βαδίζειν, ὡς ἔλαθε πλησίον τῆς ἄκρας γενόμενος, ἀναπηδήσας ἐπὶ τὸν ἵππον καὶ Κλεοπάτρῳ τῷ
ἄρχοντι τῆς φρουρᾶς διακελευσάμενος ἐγκρατῶς φυλάτ-
τειν, ἀφίππευσεν εἰς Σικυῶνα, τριάκοντα μὲν αὐτῷ στρα- c
τιωτῶν ἑπομένων, τῶν δ' ἄλλων ἐγκαταλιπόντων καὶ
διαρρυέντων. αἰσθόμενοι δ' οἱ Κορίνθιοι μετ' ὀλίγον 6
τὴν ἀπόδρασιν αὐτοῦ καὶ διώξαντες, ὡς οὐ κατέλαβον,

---

5. ἄφνω Bryan ἄνω.   40. I. ἠρέμει GP (the Attic equivalent).   2. Σικυῶνι
διεφθαρμένους Sintenis: σικυωνίαι ἐφθαρμένους.   4. ἀπαντῶσι G¹ ὑπαντῶσι
G²PRL.

μετεπέμψαντο τὸν Κλεομένη καὶ παρέδοσαν τὴν πόλιν,
οὐδὲν οἰομένῳ λαμβάνειν παρ᾽ αὐτῶν τοσοῦτον, ὅσου
7 *διήμαρτεν ἀφέντων Ἄρατον. οὗτος μὲν οὖν, προσγε-
νομένων αὐτῷ τῶν τὴν λεγομένην Ἀκτὴν κατοικούντων
καὶ τὰς πόλεις ἐγχειρισάντων, ἀπεσταύρου καὶ περιετείχιζε τὸν Ἀκροκόρινθον. 41. Τῷ δ᾽ Ἀράτῳ συνῆλθον εἰς Σικυῶνα τῶν Ἀχαιων
d οὐ πολλοί· καὶ γενομένης ἐκκλησίας, ᾑρέθη στρατηγὸς
2 αὐτοκράτωρ. καὶ περιεστήσατο φρουρὰν ἐκ τῶν ἑαυτοῦ
πολιτῶν, τριάκοντα μὲν ἔτη καὶ τρία πεπολιτευμένος ἐν
τοῖς Ἀχαιοῖς, πεπρωτευκὼς δὲ καὶ δυνάμει καὶ δόξῃ τῶν
Ἑλλήνων, τότε δ᾽ ἔρημος καὶ ἄπορος συντετριμμένος,
ὥσπερ ἐπὶ ναυαγίου τῆς πατρίδος ἐν τοσούτῳ σάλῳ
3 καὶ κινδύνῳ διαφερόμενος. καὶ γὰρ Αἰτωλοὶ δεομένου
βοηθεῖν ἀπείπαντο, καὶ τὴν Ἀθηναίων πόλιν χάριτι
τοῦ Ἀράτου πρόθυμον οὖσαν οἱ περὶ Εὐ<ρυ>κλείδην καὶ
4 Μικίωνα διεκώλυσαν. ὄντων δὲ τῷ Ἀράτῳ καὶ χρημάτων
ἐν Κορίνθῳ καὶ οἰκίας, ὁ Κλεομένης ἥψατο μὲν οὐδενός,
e οὐδ᾽ ἄλλον εἴασε, μεταπεμψάμενος δὲ τοὺς φίλους αὐτοῦ
καὶ τοὺς διοικητάς, ἐκέλευε πάντα *διοικεῖν καὶ φυλάσ-
5 σειν ὡς Ἀράτῳ λόγον ὑφέξοντας· ἰδίᾳ δὲ πρὸς αὐτὸν
ἔπεμψε Τρίπυλον καὶ πάλιν Μεγιστόνουν τὸν πατρῷόν,
ὑπισχνούμενος ἄλλα τε πολλὰ καὶ δώδεκα τάλαντα σύνταξιν ἐνιαύσιον, ὑπερβαλλόμενος τῷ <ἥ>μίσει Πτολε-
μαῖον· ἐκεῖνος γὰρ ἓξ τάλαντα τῷ Ἀράτῳ κατ᾽ ἐνιαυτὸν
6 ἀπέστελλεν. ἠξίου δὲ τῶν Ἀχαιῶν ἡγεμὼν ἀναγορευθῆ-
ναι καὶ κοινῇ μετ᾽ αὐτῶν φυλάσσειν τὸν Ἀκροκόρινθον.
7 f τοῦ δ᾽ Ἀράτου φήσαντος, ὡς οὐκ ἔχοι τὰ πράγματα,
μᾶλλον δ᾽ ὑπ᾽ αὐτῶν ἔχοιτο, καὶ κατειρωνεύσασθαι
δόξαντος, ἐμβαλὼν εὐθὺς τὴν Σικυωνίαν ἐπόρθει καὶ
κατέφθειρε, καὶ προσεκάθητο τῇ πόλει τρεῖς μῆνας,
ἐγκαρτεροῦντος τοῦ Ἀράτου καὶ διαποροῦντος, εἰ δέξεται
τὸν Ἀντίγονον ἐπὶ τῷ παραδοῦναι τὸν Ἀκροκόρινθον·
ἄλλως γὰρ οὐκ ἐβούλετο βοηθεῖν. 42. οἱ μὲν οὖν

.6. ὅσου R ὅσον GPL.   7. διήμαρτεν Aldine διήμαρτον : ἀφέντων PRL
ἀφέντες τὸν G: αὐτῷ PRL αὐτόθι G.   41. 1. οὐ GL οἱ PR.   3. Εὐ<ρυ>κλείδην
Bergk.   4. διοικεῖν Sintenis, cf. Cleom. 19: ποιεῖν.   5. <ἥ>μίσει, Aldine.

Ἀχαιοὶ συνεληλυθότες εἰς Αἴγιον, ἐκεῖ τὸν Ἄρατον
ἐκάλουν. ἦν δὲ κίνδυνος, τοῦ Κλεομένους πρὸς τῇ πόλει
στρατοπεδεύοντος, διελθεῖν. καὶ κατεῖχον οἱ πολῖται, 1047
δεόμενοι καὶ προήσεσθαι τὸ σῶμα τῶν πολεμίων ἐγγὺς
ὄντων οὐ φάσκοντες· ἐξήρτηντο δ᾽ αὐτοῦ καὶ γυναῖκες
ἤδη καὶ παῖδες ὥσπερ πατρὸς κοινοῦ καὶ σωτῆρος
περιεχόμενοι καὶ δακρύοντες. οὐ μὴν ἀλλὰ θαρρύνας 2
καὶ παραμυθησάμενος αὐτούς, ἐξίππευσεν ἐπὶ τὴν
θάλατταν, ἔχων δέκα φίλους καὶ τὸν υἱὸν ἤδη νεανίαν
ὄντα· καὶ παρορμούντων ἐκεῖ πλοίων, ἐπιβάντες εἰς
Αἴγιον παρεκομίσθησαν ἐπὶ τὴν ἐκκλησίαν, ἐν ᾗ καλεῖν
τὸν Ἀντίγονον ἐψηφίσαντο καὶ παραδιδόναι τὸν Ἀκροκόρινθον. ἔπεμψε δὲ καὶ τὸν υἱὸν Ἄρατος πρὸς αὐτὸν 3
μετὰ τῶν ἄλλων ὁμήρων. ἐφ᾽ οἷς οἱ Κορίνθιοι χαλεπῶς
φέροντες, τά τε χρήματα διήρπασαν αὐτοῦ, καὶ τὴν b
οἰκίαν τῷ Κλεομένει δωρεὰν ἔδωκαν.

43. Τοῦ δ᾽ Ἀντιγόνου προσιόντος ἤδη μετὰ τῆς
δυνάμεως—ἦγε δὲ πεζοὺς δισμυρίους Μακεδόνας, ἱππεῖς
δὲ χιλίους καὶ τριακοσίους—, ἀπήντα μετὰ τῶν δημιουργῶν ὁ Ἄρατος αὐτῷ κατὰ θάλατταν εἰς Πηγάς, λαθὼν
τοὺς πολεμίους, οὐ πάνυ τι θαρρῶν τὸν Ἀντίγονον οὐδὲ
πιστεύων τοῖς Μακεδόσιν. ᾔδει γὰρ ηὐξημένον ἑαυτὸν 2
ἐξ ὧν ἐκείνους κακῶς ἐποίησε, καὶ πρώτην εἰληφότα με-
γίστην ὑπόθεσιν τῆς πολιτείας τὴν πρὸς Ἀντίγονον τὸν
παλαιὸν ἔχθραν. ἀλλ᾽ ὁρῶν ἀπαραίτητον ἐπικειμένην
<τὴν>ἀνάγκην καὶ τὸν καιρόν ᾧ δουλεύουσιν οἱ δοκοῦντες
ἄρχειν, ἐχώρει πρὸς τὸ δεινόν. ὁ δ᾽ Ἀντίγονος, ὥς τις 3
αὐτῷ προσιόντα τὸν Ἄρατον ἔφρασε, τοὺς μὲν ἄλλους
ἠσπάσατο μετρίως καὶ κοινῶς, ἐκεῖνον δὲ καὶ περὶ τὴν
πρώτην ἀπάντησιν ἐδέξατο τῇ τιμῇ περιττῶς, καὶ τἆλλα
πειρώμενος ἀνδρὸς ἀγαθοῦ καὶ νοῦν ἔχοντος, ἐνδοτέρω
τῆς χρείας προσηγάγετο.

Καὶ γὰρ ἦν ὁ Ἄρατος οὐ μόνον ἐν πράγμασι μεγάλοις 4
ὠφέλιμος, ἀλλὰ καὶ σχολάζοντι βασιλεῖ συγγενέσθαι
παρ᾽ ὁντινοῦν ἐπίχαρις. διό, καίπερ ὢν νέος ὁ Ἀντίγονος, 5

---

43. 2. εἰληφότα G, εἰληφότι PRL. <τὴν> Ziegler. ὥστις R²L², ἵστις GPR¹L¹.
3. καὶ τἆλλα Paris 1671, 1672, καὶ κατ᾽ ἄλλα GL κατἆλλα PR¹ καὶ κατὰ τ᾽ ἄλλα R².

ὡς κατενόησε τὴν φύσιν τοῦ ἀνδρὸς μηδὲν ἀργὸν εἰς φιλίαν βασιλικὴν οὖσαν, οὐ μόνον Ἀχαιῶν <μᾶλλον> ἀλλὰ
d καὶ Μακεδόνων τῶν σὺν αὐτῷ πάντα χρώμενος ἐκεί-
6 νῳ διετέλει. καὶ τὸ σημεῖον ἀπέβαινεν, ὡς ὁ θεὸς ἐπὶ
τῶν ἱερῶν ἔδειξε. λέγεται γὰρ οὐ πρὸ πολλοῦ θύοντι τῷ
Ἀράτῳ δύο χολὰς ἐν ἥπατι φανῆναι, μιᾷ πιμελῇ περιε-
χομένας· καὶ τὸν μάντιν εἰπεῖν, ὡς ταχὺ πρὸς τὰ ἔχθιστα
7 καὶ πολεμιώτατα σύνεισιν εἰς ἄκραν φιλίαν. τότε μὲν
οὖν παρήνεγκε τὸ ῥηθέν, οὐδ᾽ ἄλλως πολὺ νέμων πίστεως
8 ἱεροῖς καὶ μαντεύμασιν, ἀλλὰ τῷ λογισμῷ χρώμενος. ἐπεὶ
δ᾽ ὕστερον εὖ χωροῦντι τῷ πολέμῳ συναγαγὼν ὁ Ἀντίγονος ἑστίασιν ἐν Κορίνθῳ, καὶ πολλοὺς ὑποδεχόμενος
e τὸν Ἄρατον ἐπάνω κατέκλινεν ἑαυτοῦ, καὶ μετὰ μικρὸν
αἰτήσας περιβόλαιον ἠρώτησεν, εἰ δοκεῖ κἀκείνῳ ψῦχος
εἶναι, τοῦ δὲ καὶ πάνυ ῥιγοῦν φήσαντος, ἐκέλευσε προσ-
χωρεῖν ἐγγυτέρω, καὶ δάπιδος κομισθείσης ἀμφοτέρους
9 ὁμοῦ περιέβαλον οἱ παῖδες, τότε δὴ τὸν Ἄρατον ἀνα-
μνησθέντα τῶν ἱερῶν ἐκείνων γέλως ἔλαβε, καὶ διηγεῖτο
τῷ βασιλεῖ τὸ σημεῖον καὶ τὴν προαγόρευσιν. ἀλλὰ
ταῦτα μὲν ἐπράχθη χρόνοις ὕστερον.

44. Ἐν δὲ ταῖς Πηγαῖς δόντες καὶ λαβόντες ὅρκους,
εὐθὺς ἐβάδιζον ἐπὶ τοὺς πολεμίους. καὶ περὶ τὴν πόλιν
ἀγῶνες ἦσαν, εὖ πεφραγμένου τοῦ Κλεομένους καὶ τῶν
2 Κορινθίων ἀμυνομένων προθύμως. ἐν τούτῳ δ᾽ Ἀρι-
f στοτέλης ὁ Ἀργεῖος φίλος ὢν Ἀράτου διαπέμπεται κρύφα
πρὸς αὐτόν, ὡς ἀποστήσων τὴν πόλιν, εἰ στρατιώτας ἐκεῖ-
3 νος ἔχων ἔλθοι. τοῦ δ᾽ Ἀράτου φράσαντος τῷ Ἀντιγόνῳ
καὶ μετὰ χιλίων καὶ πεντακοσίων εἰς Ἐπίδαυρον ἐξ Ἰσθμοῦ
πλοίοις κομιζομένου κατὰ τάχος, οἱ μὲν Ἀργεῖοι προ-
1048 εξαναστάντες ἐπέθεντο τοῖς τοῦ Κλεομένους καὶ κατ-
έκλεισαν εἰς τὴν ἀκρόπολιν, ὁ δὲ Κλεομένης πυθόμενος
ταῦτα, καὶ δείσας μὴ κατασχόντες οἱ πολέμιοι τὸ Ἄργος
ἀποκόψωσιν αὐτὸν τῆς οἴκαδε σωτηρίας, ἐκλιπὼν τὸν
4 Ἀκροκόρινθον ἔτι νυκτὸς ἐβοήθει. καὶ παρελθὼν μὲν
εἰς Ἄργος ἔφθη καὶ τροπήν τινα τῶν πολεμίων ἐποίησεν,
ὀλίγῳ δ᾽ ὕστερον Ἀράτου προσφερομένου καὶ τοῦ βασι-

---

5. <μᾶλλον> Ed.

λέως ἐπιφαινομένου μετὰ τῆς δυνάμεως, ἀπεχώρησεν εἰς Μαντίνειαν. ἐκ τούτου τοῖς μὲν Ἀχαιοῖς πάλιν αἱ πόλεις 5 ἅπασαι προσεχώρησαν, Ἀντίγονος δὲ τὸν Ἀκροκόρινθον παρέλαβεν, Ἄρατος δὲ στρατηγὸς αἱρεθεὶς ὑπ' Ἀργείων, ἔπεισεν αὐτοὺς Ἀντιγόνῳ τά τε τῶν τυράννων καὶ τὰ τῶν b προδοτῶν χρήματα δωρεὰν δοῦναι.

Τὸν δ' Ἀριστόμαχον ἐν Κεγχρεαῖς στρεβλώσαντες 6 κατεπόντισαν, ἐφ' ᾧ καὶ μάλιστα κακῶς ἤκουσεν ὁ Ἄρατος, ὡς ἄνθρωπον οὐ πονηρὸν ἀλλὰ καὶ κεχρημένον ἐκείνῳ καὶ πεπεισμένον ἀφεῖναι τὴν ἀρχὴν καὶ προσαγαγεῖν τοῖς Ἀχαιοῖς τὴν πόλιν, ὅμως *περιιδὼν παρανόμως ἀπολόμενον. 45. ἤδη δὲ καὶ τῶν ἄλλων ἐκείνῳ τὰς αἰτίας ἐπέφερον, οἷον ὅτι τὴν μὲν Κορινθίων πόλιν Ἀντιγόνῳ δωρεὰν ἔδωκαν, ὥσπερ κώμην τὴν τυχοῦσαν, τὸν Ὀρχομενὸν δὲ συνεχώρησαν αὐτῷ διαρπάσαντι φρουρὰν ἐμβαλεῖν Μακεδονικήν, ἐψηφίσαντο δ' ἄλλῳ μὴ γρά- c 2 φειν βασιλεῖ μηδὲ πρεσβεύειν πρὸς ἄλλον ἄκοντος Ἀντιγόνου, τρέφειν δὲ καὶ μισθοδοτεῖν ἠναγκάζοντο τοὺς Μακεδόνας, θυσίας δὲ καὶ πομπὰς καὶ ἀγῶνας Ἀντι- 3 γόνῳ συνετέλουν, ἀρξαμένων τῶν Ἀράτου πολιτῶν καὶ δεξαμένων τῇ πόλει τὸν Ἀντίγονον ὑπ' Ἀράτου ξενιζόμενον, ἠτιῶντο πάντων ἐκεῖνον, ἀγνοοῦντες ὅτι τὰς 4 ἡνίας ἐκείνῳ παραδεδωκὼς καὶ τῇ ῥύμῃ τῆς βασιλικῆς ἐφελκόμενος ἐξουσίας οὐδενὸς ἦν ἢ μόνης φωνῆς ἔτι κύριος, ἐπισφαλῆ τὴν παρρησίαν ἐχούσης. ἐπεὶ φανε- 5 ρῶς *γε πολλὰ τῶν πραττομένων ἐλύπει τὸν Ἄρατον, ὥσπερ τὸ περὶ τῶν εἰκόνων· ὁ γὰρ Ἀντίγονος τὰς μὲν τῶν ἐν Ἄργει τυράννων καταβεβλημένας ἀνέστησε, τὰς d δὲ τῶν ἑλόντων τὸν Ἀκροκόρινθον ἑστώσας ἀνέτρεψε, πλὴν μιᾶς τῆς ἐκείνου· καὶ πολλὰ περὶ τούτων δεηθεὶς ὁ Ἄρατος οὐκ ἔπεισεν. ἐδόκει δὲ καὶ τὰ περὶ Μαντίνειαν 6 οὐχ Ἑλληνικῶς διῳκῆσθαι τοῖς Ἀχαιοῖς. κρατήσαντες γὰρ αὐτῶν δι' Ἀντιγόνου, τοὺς μὲν ἐνδοξοτάτους καὶ πρώτους ἀπέκτειναν, τῶν δ' ἄλλων τοὺς μὲν ἀπέδοντο,

---

44. 6. περιιδὼν Anon: περιιδόντα: ἀπολόμενον G¹R¹P, ἀπολλόμενον LG² ἀπολούμενον R². 45. 1. οἷον ὅτε Ziegler. 2. δὲ G τε PRL. 4. <ὧν> ἠτιῶντο Schaefer. 5. γε Stephanus τε. 6. διωικῆσθαι PRL διωκεῖσθαι G¹ διοικεῖσθαι G².

τοὺς δ' εἰς Μακεδονίαν ἀπέστειλαν <ἐν> πέδαις δεδε-
μένους, παῖδας δὲ καὶ γυναῖκας ἠνδραποδίσαντο, τοῦ
δὲ συναχθέντος ἀργυρίου τὸ τρίτον αὐτοὶ διείλοντο, τὰς
7 δὲ δύο μοίρας ἔνειμαν τοῖς Μακεδόσι. καὶ ταῦτα μὲν
e ἔσχε τὸν τῆς ἀμύνης νόμον· καὶ γὰρ εἰ δεινὸν ἄνδρας
ὁμοφύλους καὶ συγγενεῖς οὕτω μεταχειρίσασθαι δι' ὀργήν, ἀλλ' ἐν ἀνάγκαις γλυκὺ γίνεται καὶ[οὐ]σκληρόν,
κατὰ Σιμωνίδην, ὥσπερ ἀλγοῦντι τῷ θυμῷ καὶ φλεγμαί-
8 νοντι θεραπείαν καὶ ἀναπλήρωσιν προσφερόντων. τὰ
δὲ μετὰ ταῦτα πραχθέντα περὶ τὴν πόλιν οὔτ' εἰς καλὴν
οὔτ' εἰς ἀναγκαίαν ἔστι θέσθαι τῷ Ἀράτῳ πρόφασιν.
τῶν γὰρ *Ἀχαιῶν τὴν πόλιν παρ' Ἀντιγόνου δωρεὰν
λαβόντων καὶ κατοικίζειν ἐγνωκότων, αὐτὸς οἰκιστὴς
αἱρεθεὶς καὶ στρατηγὸς ὢν ἐψηφίσατο μηκέτι καλεῖν
Μαντίνειαν ἀλλ' Ἀντιγόνειαν, ὃ καὶ μέχρι νῦν καλεῖται.
f 9 καὶ δοκεῖ δι' ἐκεῖνον ἡ μὲν "ἐρατεινὴ Μαντίνεια"
παντάπασιν ἐξαληλίφθαι, διαμένει δ' ἡ πόλις ἐπώνυμος
τῶν ἀπολεσάντων καὶ ἀνελόντων τοὺς πολίτας.

46. Ἐκ τούτου Κλεομένης μὲν ἡττηθεὶς μάχῃ μεγάλῃ
περὶ Σελλασίαν ἐξέλιπε τὴν Σπάρτην καὶ ἀπέπλευσεν
εἰς Αἴγυπτον, Ἀντίγονος δὲ πάντα τὰ δίκαια καὶ φιλάν-
1049 θρωπα τῷ Ἀράτῳ πεποιηκὼς ἀνέζευξεν εἰς Μακεδονίαν,
2 κἀκεῖ νοσῶν ἤδη τὸν διάδοχον τῆς βασιλείας Φίλιππον
οὔπω πάνυ μειράκιον ὄντα πέμπων εἰς Πελοπόννησον
Ἀράτῳ μάλιστα προσέχειν ἐκέλευσε καὶ δι' ἐκείνου ταῖς
3 πόλεσιν ἐντυχεῖν καὶ γνωρισθῆναι τοῖς Ἀχαιοῖς. καὶ μέντοι καὶ παραλαβὼν αὐτὸν ὁ Ἄρατος οὕτως διέθηκεν,
ὥστε πολλῆς μὲν εὐνοίας πρὸς αὐτὸν πολλῆς δὲ πρὸς
τὰς Ἑλληνικὰς πράξεις φιλοτιμίας καὶ ὁρμῆς μεστὸν εἰς
Μακεδονίαν ἀποστεῖλαι.

47. Τελευτήσαντος δ' Ἀντιγόνου, καταφρονήσαντες
Αἰτωλοὶ τῶν Ἀχαιῶν διὰ τὴν ῥαθυμίαν—ἐθισθέντες
γὰρ ἀλλοτρίαις σῴζεσθαι χερσὶ καὶ τοῖς Μακεδόνων
b ὅπλοις αὐτοὺς ὑπεσταλκότες, ἐν ἀργίᾳ πολλῇ καὶ ἀταξίᾳ
διῆγον—ἐπέθεντο τοῖς κατὰ Πελοπόννησον πράγμασι·
2 καὶ τὴν μὲν Πατρέων καὶ Δυμαίων λεηλασίαν ὁδοῦ πάρ-

6. <ἐν> Sintenis.   7. [οὐ] Bergk: ἔτι θέσθαι L.   8. Ἀχαιῶν E. Curtius
ἀργείων.   47. 2. Δυμαίων Xylander κυμαίων.

εργον ἐποιήσαντο, τὴν δὲ Μεσσήνην ἐμβαλόντες ἐπόρ-
θουν. ἐφ' οἷς ὁ Ἄρατος ἀγανακτῶν, καὶ τὸν στρατη- 3
γοῦντα τότε τῶν Ἀχαιῶν Τιμόξενον ὁρῶν ὀκνοῦντα καὶ
διατρίβοντα τὸν χρόνον, ἤδη τῆς στρατηγίας αὐτῷ τε-
λευτώσης, αὐτὸς ᾑρημένος ἄρχειν μετ' ἐκεῖνον προέλαβεν ἡμέραις πέντε τὴν ἀρχὴν ἕνεκα τοῦ βοηθῆσαι Μεσσηνίοις. καὶ συναγαγὼν τοὺς Ἀχαιούς, τοῖς τε σώμασιν 4
ἀγυμνάστους ὄντας καὶ ταῖς διανοίαις ἐκλελυμένους πρὸς
τὸν πόλεμον, ἡττᾶται περὶ Καφύας· καὶ θυμικώτερον 5 c
ἐστρατηγηκέναι δόξας, οὕτως αὖ πάλιν ἀπημβλύνθη καὶ
προήκατο τὰ πράγματα καὶ τὰς ἐλπίδας, ὥστε πολλάκις
λαβὴν τοὺς Αἰτωλοὺς παρασχόντας ἀνέχεσθαι καὶ περι-
ορᾶν ὥσπερ κωμάζοντας ἐν τῇ Πελοποννήσῳ μετὰ πολλῆς ἀσελγείας καὶ θρασύτητος. αὖθις οὖν τὰς χεῖρας 6
ὀρέγοντες εἰς Μακεδονίαν, ἐπεσπῶντο καὶ κατῆγον ἐπὶ
τὰς Ἑλληνικὰς πράξεις τὸν Φίλιππον, οὐχ ἥκιστα διὰ
τὴν πρὸς τὸν Ἄρατον εὔνοιαν αὐτοῦ καὶ πίστιν ἐλπί-
ζοντες εὐκόλῳ περὶ πάντα χρήσεσθαι καὶ χειροήθει.

48. Καὶ τότε πρῶτον Ἀπελλοῦ καὶ Μεγαλέου καί
τινων αὐλικῶν ἄλλων διαβαλλόντων τὸν Ἄρατον, ἀνα- d
πεισθεὶς ὁ βασιλεὺς καὶ συναρχαιρεσιάσας τοῖς ἀπὸ τῆς
ἐναντίας στάσεως, ἐσπούδασε τοὺς Ἀχαιοὺς ἑλέσθαι
στρατηγὸν Ἐπήρατον. ὡς δ' ἐκείνου μὲν καταφρονου- 2
μένου τελέως ὑπὸ τῶν Ἀχαιῶν, τοῦ δ' Ἀράτου παρα-
μελοῦντος, ἐγίνετο τῶν χρησίμων οὐδέν, ἔγνω διαμαρ-
τάνων τοῦ *παντὸς ὁ Φίλιππος. καὶ ἀνακρουσάμενος 3
αὖθις ἐπὶ τὸν Ἄρατον, ὅλος ἦν ἐκείνου, καὶ τῶν πραγμάτων αὐτῷ πρός τε δύναμιν καὶ πρὸς εὐδοξίαν ἐπιδόντων, ἐξήρτητο τοῦ ἀνδρός, ὡς δι' ἐκεῖνον εὐδοκιμῶν
καὶ αὐξόμενος. ἐδόκει δὲ πᾶσιν ὁ Ἄρατος οὐ μόνον δη- 4
μοκρατίας ἀλλὰ καὶ βασιλείας ἀγαθὸς εἶναι παιδαγωγός· e
ἡ γὰρ προαίρεσις αὐτοῦ καὶ τὸ ἦθος ὡς χρῶμα ταῖς 5
πράξεσι τοῦ βασιλέως ἐπεφαίνετο. καὶ γὰρ ἡ πρὸς Λακεδαιμονίους ἁμαρτόντας μετριότης τοῦ νεανίσκου, καὶ ἡ

6. τὸν Ἄρατον G, Ἄρατον PRL.   48. 1. Μεγαλέου Sintenis Μεγαλαίου.
2. παντὸς Aldine πατρὸς.   3. ἐπιδόντων G¹PR ἐπιδιδόντων LG².   4. δὲ G
τε PRL.

πρὸς Κρῆτας ὁμιλία δι᾽ ἧς ὅλην προσηγάγετο τὴν νῆσον
ἡμέραις ὀλίγαις, ἥ τε πρὸς Αἰτωλοὺς στρατεία γενομένη
θαυμαστῶς ἐνεργός, εὐπειθείας μὲν τῷ Φιλίππῳ δόξαν,
6 εὐβουλίας δὲ τῷ Ἀράτῳ προσετίθει. καὶ διὰ ταῦτα μᾶλλον οἱ βασιλικοὶ φθονοῦντες, ὡς οὐδὲν ἐπέραινον κρύφα
διαβάλλοντες, ἀναφανδὸν ἐλοιδοροῦντο καὶ προσέκρουον
αὐτῷ παρὰ τοὺς πότους μετὰ πολλῆς ἀσελγείας καὶ βω-
f μολοχίας· ἅπαξ δὲ καὶ λίθοις βάλλοντες ἀπιόντα εἰς τὴν
7 σκηνὴν μετὰ τὸ δεῖπνον κατεδίωξαν. ἐφ᾽ οἷς ὁ Φίλιππος
ὀργισθείς, εὐθὺς μὲν αὐτοὺς ἐζημίωσεν εἴκοσι ταλάντοις, ὕστερον δὲ λυμαίνεσθαι τὰ πράγματα καὶ ταράτ-
τειν δοκοῦντας ἀπέκτεινεν.

49. Ἐπεὶ δὲ τῆς τύχης εὐροούσης ἐπαιρόμενος τοῖς
πράγμασι πολλὰς μὲν ἀνέφυε καὶ μεγάλας ἐπιθυμίας,
1050 ἡ δ᾽ ἔμφυτος κακία, τὸν παρὰ φύσιν σχηματισμὸν ἐκ-
βιαζομένη καὶ ἀναδύουσα, κατὰ μικρὸν ἀπεγύμνου καὶ
2 διέφαινεν αὐτοῦ τὸ ἦθος, πρῶτον μὲν ἰδίᾳ τὸν νεώτερον
Ἄρατον ἠδίκει περὶ τὴν γυναῖκα καὶ πολὺν χρόνον
ἐλάνθανεν, ἐφέστιος ὢν καὶ ξενιζόμενος ὑπ᾽ αὐτῶν· ἔπειτα
πρὸς τὰς Ἑλληνικὰς ἐξετραχύνετο πολιτείας, καὶ φανε-
3 ρὸς ἦν ἤδη τὸν Ἄρατον ἀποσειόμενος. ἀρχὴν δ᾽ ὑποψίας
τὰ Μεσσηνιακὰ παρέσχε. στασιασάντων γὰρ αὐτῶν, ὁ
μὲν Ἄρατος ὑστέρει βοηθῶν, ὁ δὲ Φίλιππος ἡμέρᾳ μιᾷ
πρότερον ἐλθὼν εἰς τὴν πόλιν, εὐθὺς οἶστρόν τινα κατ᾽
4 b ἀλλήλων ἐνέβαλε τοῖς ἀνθρώποις, ἰδίᾳ μὲν ἐρωτῶν τοὺς
στρατηγοὺς τῶν Μεσσηνίων, εἰ νόμους κατὰ τῶν πολλῶν οὐκ ἔχουσιν, ἰδίᾳ δὲ πάλιν τοὺς τῶν *πολλῶν προ-
εστῶτας, εἰ χεῖρας κατὰ τῶν τυραννούντων οὐκ ἔχουσιν.
5 ἐκ δὲ τούτου θαρρήσαντες, οἱ μὲν ἄρχοντες ἐπελαμβά-
νοντο τῶν δημαγωγῶν, ἐκεῖνοι δὲ μετὰ τῶν πολλῶν
ἐπελθόντες τούς τ᾽ ἄρχοντας ἀπέκτειναν καὶ τῶν ἄλλων
ὀλίγον ἀπολείποντας διακοσίων. **50.** οὕτω δὲ δεινὸν ἔργον ἐξειργασμένου τοῦ Φιλίππου καὶ συγκρούοντος ἔτι
μᾶλλον ἑαυτοῖς τοὺς Μεσσηνίους, ἐπελθὼν ὁ Ἄρατος
αὐτός τε δῆλος ἦν φέρων βαρέως, καὶ τὸν υἱὸν ἐπιτι-

---

5. εὐβουλίας PRL and G² (margin) εὐλαβείας G¹.   **49.** 3. ἐνέβαλε GL
ἐνέβαλλε PR.   4. πολλῶν Bryan πόλεων.   **50.** I. αὐτοῖς G.

ΑΡΑΤΟΣ

μῶντα πικρῶς τῷ Φιλίππῳ καὶ λοιδορούμενον οὐκ ἐκώλυσεν. ἐδόκει δ' ὁ νεανίσκος ἐρᾶν τοῦ Φιλίππου· καὶ 2 c
τότε λέγων εἶπε πρὸς αὐτόν, ὡς οὐδὲ καλὸς ἔτι φαίνοιτο
τὴν ὄψιν αὐτῷ τοιαῦτα δράσας, ἀλλὰ πάντων αἴσχιστος.
ὁ δὲ Φίλιππος ἐκείνῳ μὲν οὐδὲν ἀντεῖπε, καίπερ ἐπί- 3
δοξος ὢν ὑπ' ὀργῆς καὶ πολλάκις ἐξυλακτήσας λέγοντος
αὐτοῦ, τὸν δὲ πρεσβύτερον, ὡς ἐνηνοχὼς πρᾴως τὰ λε- f
χθέντα καί τις ὢν μέτριος καὶ πολιτικὸς τὴν φύσιν,
ἀνέστησεν ἐκ τοῦ θεάτρου τὴν δεξιὰν ἐμβαλὼν καὶ
προσῆγεν εἰς τὸν Ἰθωμάταν, τῷ τε Διὶ θύσων καὶ
θεωρήσων τὸν τόπον. ἔστι γὰρ οὐχ ἧττον εὐερκὴς τοῦ 4
Ἀκροκορίνθου, καὶ λαβὼν φρουρὰν γίνεται χαλεπὸς καὶ
δυσεκβίαστος τοῖς παροικοῦσιν. ἀναβὰς δὲ καὶ θύσας, d 5
ὡς προσήνεγκεν αὐτῷ τὰ σπλάγχνα τοῦ βοὸς ὁ μάντις,
ἀμφοτέραις ταῖς χερσὶν ὑπολαβὼν ἐδείκνυε τῷ τ' Ἀράτῳ
καὶ τῷ Φαρίῳ Δημητρίῳ, παρὰ μέρος ἀποκλίνων εἰς
ἑκάτερον καὶ πυνθανόμενος, τί καθορῶσι ἐν τοῖς ἱεροῖς, κρατοῦντα τῆς ἄκρας αὐτὸν ἢ τοῖς Μεσσηνίοις
ἀποδιδόντα. γελάσας οὖν ὁ Δημήτριος "εἰ μέν" ἔφη 6
"μάντεως ἔχεις ψυχήν, ἀφήσεις τὸν τόπον· εἰ δὲ βασιλέως, ἀμφοτέρων τῶν κεράτων τὸν βοῦν καθέξεις,"
αἰνιττόμενος τὴν Πελοπόννησον, ὡς εἰ προσλάβοι τὸν
Ἰθωμάταν τῷ Ἀκροκορίνθῳ, παντάπασιν ἐσομένην ὑποχείριον καὶ ταπεινήν. ὁ δ' Ἄρατος ἐπὶ πολὺ μὲν ἡσύ- 7
χαζε, δεομένου δὲ τοῦ Φιλίππου τὸ φαινόμενον λέγειν, e
"πολλὰ μέν" εἶπεν "ὦ Φίλιππε Κρητῶν ὄρη καὶ μεγάλα,
πολλαὶ δὲ Βοιωτῶν ἄκραι καὶ Φωκέων ἐκπεφύκασι τῆς
γῆς· εἰσὶ δέ που πολλοὶ καὶ τῆς Ἀκαρνάνων, τοῦτο μὲν
χερσαῖοι τοῦτο δ' ἔναλοι τόποι, θαυμαστὰς ὀχυρότητας
ἔχοντες. ἀλλ' οὐδένα τούτων κατείληφας, καὶ πάντες 8
ἑκουσίως σοι ποιοῦσι τὸ προστασσόμενον. λῃσταὶ γὰρ
ἐμφύονται πέτραις καὶ κρημνῶν περιέχονται, βασιλεῖ δὲ
πίστεως καὶ χάριτος ἰσχυρότερον οὐδὲν οὐδ' ὀχυρώτε-
ρον· ταῦτά σοι τὸ Κρητικὸν ἀνοίγει πέλαγος, ταῦτα τὴν 9

---

2. αὐτοῦ L¹.   3. προσῆγεν GL¹ προῆγεν PRL². ἰθωμάταν PR² εἰθωμάταν
R¹ ἠθωμάταν G¹ ἰθωμάνταν G²L, but in L the first ν is written by second
hand in an erasure.   4. δυσεκβίαστος G παρεκβίαστος PRL.   6. Ἰθωμάταν
G²R² εἰθωμάντᾱν G¹R¹ ἰθωμάντα P ἰθωμάνθαν L.

f Πελοπόννησον. ἀπὸ τούτων ὁρμώμενος σὺ τοσοῦτος ἡλικίαν τῶν μὲν ἡγεμὼν τῶν δὲ κύριος ἤδη καθέστηκας.''
10 ἔτι <δὲ> λέγοντος αὐτοῦ, τὰ μὲν σπλάγχνα τῷ μάντει
παρέδωκεν ὁ Φίλιππος, ἐκεῖνον δὲ τῆς χειρὸς ἐπισπα-
σάμενος '' δεῦρο τοίνυν '' ἔφη '' τὴν αὐτὴν ὁδὸν ἴωμεν,''
ὥσπερ ἐκβεβιασμένος ὑπ' αὐτοῦ καὶ τὴν πόλιν ἀφῃρη-
μένος.

51. Ὁ δ' Ἄρατος ἀπορρέων ἤδη τῆς αὐλῆς καὶ κατὰ
μικρὸν ἑαυτὸν ἀνακομιζόμενος ἐκ τῆς πρὸς τὸν Φίλιπ-
1051 πον συνηθείας, διαβαίνοντος εἰς Ἤπειρον αὐτοῦ καὶ
δεομένου συστρατεύειν, ἀπείπατο καὶ κατέμεινε, δεδιὼς
ἀναπλησθῆναι δόξης πονηρᾶς ἀφ' ὧν ἐκεῖνος ἔπραττεν.
2 ἐπεὶ δὲ τάς τε ναῦς ὑπὸ Ῥωμαίων ἀπολέσας αἴσχιστα
καὶ ὅλως ἀποτυχὼν ταῖς πράξεσιν ἐπανῆλθεν εἰς Πελοπόννησον, καὶ τοὺς Μεσσηνίους αὖθις ἐπιχειρήσας φε-
νακίζειν καὶ μὴ λαθὼν ἠδίκει φανερῶς καὶ τὴν χώραν
3 αὐτῶν ἐπόρθει, παντάπασιν ὁ Ἄρατος ἀπεστράφη καὶ
διεβλήθη πρὸς αὐτόν, ἤδη καὶ τῶν περὶ τὴν γυναικωνῖ-
τιν ἀδικημάτων αἰσθόμενος, καὶ φέρων ἀνιαρῶς *αὐτός,
ἀποκρυπτόμενος δὲ τὸν υἱόν· εἰδέναι γὰρ ὑβρισμένον
4 b περιῆν ἄλλο δ' οὐδὲν ἀμύνασθαι μὴ δυναμένῳ. μεγί-
στην γὰρ ὁ Φίλιππος δοκεῖ καὶ παραλογωτάτην μεταβα-
λέσθαι μεταβολήν, ἐξ ἡμέρου βασιλέως καὶ μειρακίου
σώφρονος ἀνὴρ ἀσελγὴς καὶ τύραννος ἐξώλης γενόμενος.
τὸ δ' οὐκ ἦν ἄρα μεταβολὴ φύσεως ἀλλ' ἐπίδειξις ἐν
ἀδείᾳ κακίας, πολὺν χρόνον διὰ φόβον ἀγνοηθείσης.
52. ὅτι γὰρ ἦν μεμειγμένον αἰσχύνῃ καὶ φόβῳ τὸ πρὸς
τὸν Ἄρατον αὐτοῦ πάθος ἀπ' ἀρχῆς συντεθραμμένον,
2 ἐδήλωσεν οἷς ἔπραξε περὶ αὐτόν. ἐπιθυμῶν γὰρ ἀνελεῖν
τὸν ἄνδρα, καὶ νομίζων οὐδ' ἂν ἐλεύθερος ἐκείνου ζῶντος εἶναι, μή τί γε τύραννος ἢ βασιλεύς, βίᾳ μὲν οὐδὲν
c ἐπεχείρησε, Ταυρίωνα δὲ τῶν στρατηγῶν τινα καὶ φίλων
ἐκέλευσεν [ἐν] ἀδήλῳ τρόπῳ τοῦτο πρᾶξαι, μάλιστα <δὲ>
3 διὰ φαρμάκων, αὐτοῦ μὴ παρόντος. ὁ δὲ ποιησάμενος
τὸν Ἄρατον συνήθη, φάρμακον αὐτῷ δίδωσιν, οὐκ ὀξὺ καὶ
σφοδρόν, ἀλλὰ τῶν θέρμας τε μαλακὰς τὸ πρῶτον ἐν

10. <δὲ> Ziegler.   51. 3. αὐτὸς Anon: αὐτὸν.   4. τὸ G²R²PL
τῷ G¹R¹.   52. 2. [ἐν] Bryan : <δὲ> Reiske.

τῷ σώματι καὶ βῆχα κινούντων ἀμβλεῖαν, εἶθ᾿ οὕτως
κατὰ μικρὸν εἰς φθορὰν περαινόντων. οὐ μὴν ἔλαθέ γε 4
τὸν Ἄρατον· ἀλλ᾿ ὡς οὐδὲν ἦν ὄφελος ἐλέγχοντι, πρᾴως
καὶ σιωπῇ τὸ πάθος ὡς δή τινα νόσον κοινὴν καὶ συνήθη νοσῶν διήντλει· πλὴν ἑνός γε τῶν συνήθων ἐν τῷ
δωματίῳ παρόντος, ἀναπτύσας δίαιμον, ἰδόντος ἐκείνου
καὶ θαυμάσαντος, "ταῦτα" εἶπεν "ὦ Κεφάλων ἐπίχειρα d
τῆς βασιλικῆς φιλίας."

53. Οὕτω δ᾿ αὐτοῦ τελευτήσαντος ἐν Αἰγίῳ, τὸ ἑπτακαιδέκατον στρατηγοῦντος, καὶ τῶν Ἀχαιῶν φιλοτι-
μουμένων ἐκεῖ γενέσθαι ταφὰς καὶ μνήματα πρέποντα
τῷ βίῳ τοῦ ἀνδρός, Σικυώνιοι συμφορὰν ἐποιοῦντο μὴ
παρ᾿ αὐτοῖς τεθῆναι τὸ σῶμα. καὶ τοὺς μὲν Ἀχαιοὺς 2
ἔπεισαν ἐφιέναι, νόμου δ᾿ ὄντος ἀρχαίου μηδένα θά-
πτεσθαι τειχῶν ἐντός, ἰσχυρᾶς τε τῷ νόμῳ δεισιδαιμονίας προσούσης, ἔπεμψαν εἰς Δελφοὺς ὑπὲρ τούτων
ἐρησόμενοι τὴν Πυθίαν. ἡ δ᾿ αὐτοῖς ἀναιρεῖ τὸν χρη-
σμὸν τόνδε:

βουλεύῃ Σικυὼν ζωάγριον αἰὲν Ἀράτου   3 e
ἀμφ᾿ ὁσίῃ θαλίῃ τε κατοιχομένοιο ἄνακτος;
ὡς τὸ βαρυνόμενον τῷδ᾿ ἀνέρι καὶ τὸ βαρῦνον
γαίης ἔστ᾿ ἀσέβημα καὶ οὐρανοῦ ἠδὲ θαλάσσης.

κομισθείσης δὲ τῆς μαντείας, οἵ τ᾿ Ἀχαιοὶ σύμπαντες 4
ἥσθησαν, καὶ διαφερόντως οἱ Σικυώνιοι μεταβαλόντες
εἰς ἑορτὴν τὸ πένθος, εὐθὺς ἐκ τοῦ Αἰγίου τὸν νεκρὸν
ἐστεφανωμένοι καὶ λευχειμονοῦντες ὑπὸ παιάνων καὶ
χορῶν εἰς τὴν πόλιν ἀνῆγον, καὶ τόπον ἐξελόμενοι πε-
ρίοπτον ὥσπερ οἰκιστὴν καὶ σωτῆρα τῆς πόλεως ἐκή-
δευσαν. καὶ καλεῖται μέχρι νῦν Ἀράτιον, καὶ θύουσιν 5 f
αὐτῷ θυσίαν, τὴν μέν, ᾗ τὴν πόλιν ἀπήλλαξε τῆς τυραννίδος, ἡμέρᾳ πέμπτῃ Δαισίου μηνός, ὃν Ἀθηναῖοι
καλοῦσιν Ἀνθεστηριῶνα, καὶ τὴν θυσίαν ἐκείνην Σω-
τήρια προσαγορεύουσι, τὴν δὲ [τοῦ μηνὸς] ἐν ᾗ γενέσθαι
τὸν ἄνδρα διαμνημονεύουσι. τῆς μὲν οὖν προτέρας <ὁ> 6
τοῦ Διὸς τοῦ Σωτῆρος κατήρχετο θυηπόλος, τῆς δὲ 1052

---

53. 2. (From νόμου to end of 54, 4 is found in Photius, p. 399).   ἀναιρεῖ G¹RL²
ἀνερεῖ PL¹R².   4. ἅπαντες Phot.   5. δαισίου G¹L δεσίου G² δεσίου P, in R
an erasure before δαισίου. [τοῦ μηνὸς] Ed.   6. <ὁ> Reiske.

δευτέρας ὁ τοῦ Ἀράτου, στρόφιον οὐχ *ὁλόλευκον ἀλλὰ
μεσοπόρφυρον ἔχων, μέλη δ᾽ ᾖδετο πρὸς κιθάραν ὑπὸ
τῶν περὶ τὸν Διόνυσον τεχνιτῶν, καὶ συνεπόμπευεν ὁ
γυμνασίαρχος, ἡγούμενος τῶν τε παίδων καὶ τῶν ἐφή-
βων, εἶτ᾽ ἐφείπεθ᾽ ἡ βουλὴ στεφανηφοροῦσα, καὶ τῶν
7 ἄλλων πολιτῶν ὁ βουλόμενος. ὧν ἔτι δείγματα μικρὰ
ταῖς ἡμέραις ἐκείναις ἐξοσιούμενοι διαφυλάττουσιν· αἱ
δὲ πλεῖσται τῶν τιμῶν ὑπὸ χρόνου καὶ πραγμάτων ἄλλων ἐκλελοίπασιν.

54. Ἀλλὰ γὰρ ὁ μὲν πρεσβύτερος Ἄρατος οὕτω βιῶ-
b 2 σαι καὶ τοιοῦτος γενέσθαι τὴν φύσιν ἱστορεῖται. τὸν
δ᾽ υἱὸν αὐτοῦ μιαρὸς ὢν φύσει καὶ μετ᾽ ὠμότητος ὑβρι-
στὴς ὁ Φίλιππος οὐ θανασίμοις ἀλλὰ μανικοῖς ἐξέστησε
3 τοῦ λογισμοῦ φαρμάκοις· καὶ παρέτρεψεν εἰς δεινὰς καὶ
ἀλλοκότους ἐπιφοράς, πράξεων ἀτόπων καὶ σὺν αἰσχύνῃ
παθῶν ὀλεθρίων *ὀρεγόμενον, ὥστε τὸν θάνατον αὐτῷ,
καίπερ ὄντι νέῳ καὶ ἀνθοῦντι, μὴ συμφορὰν ἀλλ᾽ ἀπό-
4 λυσιν κακῶν καὶ σωτηρίαν γενέσθαι. δίκας γε μὴν ὁ
Φίλιππος οὐ μεμπτὰς Διὶ ξενίῳ καὶ φιλίῳ τῆς ἀνοσι-
5 ουργίας ταύτης τίνων διετέλεσε. καταπολεμηθεὶς μὲν
γὰρ ὑπὸ Ῥωμαίων, ἐπέτρεψεν ἐκείνοις τὰ καθ᾽ αὑτόν,
ἐκπεσὼν δὲ τῆς ἄλλης ἀρχῆς καὶ τὰς ναῦς πλὴν πέντε
c πάσας προέμενος καὶ χίλια προσεκτείσειν ὁμολογήσας
τάλαντα καὶ τὸν υἱὸν ὁμηρεύσοντα παραδούς, δι᾽ οἶκτον
6 ἔτυχε Μακεδονίας καὶ τῶν συντελούντων· ἀποκτείνων
δ᾽ ἀεὶ τοὺς ἀρίστους καὶ συγγενεστάτους, φρίκης ἐνέ-
7 πλησε καὶ μίσους ὅλην τὴν βασιλείαν πρὸς αὐτόν. ἐν δὲ
μόνον ἐν τοσούτοις κακοῖς εὐτύχημα κτησάμενος, υἱὸν
ἀρετῇ διαφέροντα, τοῦτον φθόνῳ καὶ ζηλοτυπίᾳ τῆς
παρὰ Ῥωμαίοις τιμῆς ἀνεῖλε, Περσεῖ δὲ θατέρῳ τὴν ἀρχὴν παρέδωκεν, ὃν οὐ γνήσιον ἀλλ᾽ ὑπόβλητον εἶναί
8 φασιν, ἐκ Γναθαινίου τινὸς ἀκεστρίας γενόμενον. τοῦτον Αἰμίλιος ἐθριάμβευσε· καὶ κατέστρεψεν ἐνταῦθα
d τῆς Ἀντιγονικῆς βασιλείας ἡ διαδοχή. τὸ δ᾽ Ἀράτου
γένος ἔν τε <τῇ> Σικυῶνι καὶ τῇ Πελλήνῃ διέμεινε
καθ᾽ ἡμᾶς.

---

6. ὁλόλευκον Cobet : ὅλον λευκὸν. τὸν (before Διόνυσον) omitted in G.
54. 3. ὀρεγόμενον Aldine, ὀρεγόμενος. 8. αἰμίλιος. <τῇ> Ziegler.

NOTES.

1. 1. "There is an ancient proverb, Polycrates, which the philosopher Chrysippus, fearing I suppose its ill-omened implication, quotes not in its authentic, but in what he thought an improved form." Polycrates is otherwise unknown, but the name was traditional in the family of Aratus (see note on ch. 49, 2).

Χρύσιππος (280–206 B.C.), president of the Stoa after Zeno and Cleanthes: he had such influence on later teachers that he was called the second founder of Stoicism. His fondness for poetical citations was notable. [Diog. Laert. 7, 179, Susemihl 1, pp. 75–81.]

διατίθεται, "reproduces." In *Mor.* 345 E Plut. says that, apart from Xenophon, historians ἀλλοτρίων γεγόνασιν ἔργων ὥσπερ δραμάτων ὑποκριταὶ τὰς τῶν στρατηγῶν καὶ βασιλέων πράξεις διατιθέμενοι.

τίς πατέρ᾽ αἰνήσει ; The proverb is cited by Cicero *ad Att.* 1, 19, 10.

1. 2. Διονυσόδωρος ὁ Τροιζήνιος : identified by Susemihl ii, 161 with D. of Alexandria, a third century grammarian.

1. 3. The singular ᾧ may be defended on the analogy of the familiar ᾧ τινι ἐντυγχάνοιεν πάντας ἔκτεινον (Xen. *An.* 2, 5, 32). **κατὰ Πίνδαρον,** Pyth. 8, 44, φυᾷ τὸ γενναῖον ἐπιπρέπει ἐκ πατέρων παισὶ λῆμα. **ἀκούοντας** : acc. replacing dat. as often ; cf. Plato *Phaedr.* 275 A : τοῦτο τῶν μαθόντων λήθην ἐν ψυχαῖς παρέξει ... ἅτε διὰ πίστιν γραφῆς ἀναμιμνησκομένους.

1. 4. καθηγεμόνας : combining the notions of "founder" (τοῦ γένους) and "director" (τοῦ βίου). In Polyb. 2, 4 Aratus is described as ἀρχηγὸς καὶ καθηγεμὼν (τῆς Πελοποννησίων ὁμονοίας), whereas Philopoemen was ἀγωνιστὴς καὶ τελεσιουργὸς τῆς πράξεως. In Hdt. 2, 56 we find χρηστήριον κατηγήσατο, "he established an oracle."

1. 5. δόξῃ τῇ περὶ σεαυτόν = δόξῃ τῇ σεαυτοῦ, a classical use. [οὖν] after ἅπερ is due to a copyist who fancied that the sentence ends with ἀναγινώσκοντες. The omission of ἑαυτόν is plainly an accident.

Chapters 2–3, 4. The historical facts seem to be taken from the *Memoirs*.

2. 1. In *Cleom.* 16, 6 the same comparison is applied to the Spartan constitution. We read there of Cleomenes τὴν πάτριον πολιτείαν ὥσπερ ἁρμονίαν ἐκλελυμένην ἀνακρουόμενον αὖθις ἐπὶ τὸν σώφρονα καὶ Δώριον ... νόμον καὶ βίον : on which see *Intro.*, p. xiii.

ἐκ τῆς ἀριστοκρατίας. The relevant events in Sicyonian history may be thus tabulated :

417 B.C. Oligarchical constitution imposed by Sparta (Thuc. 5, 81, 2).

368. Revolution effected by Euphron, the demagogue or tyrant (Xen. *Hell.* vii, 1–4).

before 336. Aristratus, a partisan of Philip of Macedon, becomes tyrant (Dem. *De Cor.*, p 324 ; Plut. *Arat.* 13).

after 336. "ὁ παιδοτρίβης" restored to the tyranny by the Macedonians [Dem.] 17, 16.

D

323. The younger Euphron expels the Macedonian garrison : Sicyon takes part in the Lamian War (Syll.[3] 310).

321. Euphron killed in defending the city against Antipater's forces (*Ib.* 317).

318. Death of Antipater. Polyperchon, the new regent of Macedon, reverses his policy towards the Greek states.

314. On Polyperchon becoming reconciled with his rival Cassander, his son Alexander was murdered by some Sicyonians (Diod. 19, 67). A.'s widow Cratesipolis seized Sicyon, which she held for Polyperchon.

308. Cratesipolis surrenders Sicyon to Ptolemy Soter (Diod. 20, 37, 1-2).

303. Sicyon "liberated" by Demetrius Poliorcetes, who transfers the city to the site of the former acropolis some three miles inland (Diod. 20, 102 ; Plut. *Demetr.* 25 ; Strabo 8, p. 382 ; Paus. 2, 7, 1).

For the next fifty years Sicyonian history is practically a blank.

The new city was oval in shape, lying N.E. and S.W. between the rivers Helisson and Asopus. It was three miles in length and was divided into two terraces, that to the S.W. forming the citadel which was separated from the lower town by a fall in the ground running from N.W. to S.E. for about a mile. The theatre, senate-house, and gymnasium of Cleinias (the last recently discovered by Orlandos and identified by aid of Paus. 2, 10, 7) lay on the lower terrace. Theunissen, p. 149, suggests that Aratus crossed the city wall where the Phlius road entered the city, at the S.W. corner of the upper terrace.

Κλέωνος ἀναιρεθέντος, κ.τ.λ. : Pausanias (2, 8, 2) states that "after Cleon's tyranny . . . two men, Euthydemus and Timocleidas, were actually tyrants at the same time. The people, however, put Cleinias at their head and drove out these tyrants."

At this time there actually was an important citizen of Sicyon named Euthydemus, who was hieromnemon at Delphi in the autumn of 272. If Cleon's tyranny is subsequent to 272 we might assume that Euthydemus made a bid for power shortly after Cleon's death, but was expelled by Cleinias and Timocleidas. On this hypothesis Pausanias' error was to make Timocleidas the colleague of the tyrant, whereas in reality he was the colleague of the "archon" Cleinias. Such an incident may have been recorded in the *Memoirs* but omitted by Plutarch.

2. 2. αὐτὸν for αὐτοῦ is my conjecture, to remove the hiatus, which Plut. is careful to avoid [see App.] and the presence of which indicates that the reading of the MSS. is wrong. An emphatic reflexive pron. would mark the climax. Cf. its use in *Cleom.* 16, 4, πᾶσι μὲν τοῖς βασιλεῦσιν . . . διάφορος γενόμενος τουτονὶ δ' αὐτὸν 'Αντίγονον (*this very man Antigonus*) εἰρηκὼς κακὰ μυρία. ἐπταετῆ : the Att. form is ἑπτέτης, Thompson on Plato, *Gorgias*, 471 c. Aratus was born in 271 (Polyb. 2, 43). On conditions at Argos, see *Intro.*, p. xxxi.

3. 1. μῖσος ἐπὶ τοὺς τυράννους : grammatical usage permits the omission of τὸ before ἐπὶ, since μῖσος is a verbal noun expressing action, Kühner-Gerth ii, 1, 615. στεφάνων : In addition to the pentathlon Aratus won a chariot race at Olympia (Paus. 6, 12, 5).

3. 2. ἀμέλει = Lat. *sane*, as the latter part of the sentence shows. **εἰκόσιν**: statues of Aratus, one at Sicyon on the stage of the theatre (Paus. 2, 7, 5); another at Olympia, an offering of the Corinthians (*Id.* 6, 12, 5). **ἀδηφαγίαν**: Greek athletes, like Heracles in Euripides' *Alcestis*, were usually big feeders. **σκαφεῖον**: for the use of the hoe in training, cf. Athen. 518 D, where certain Sybarites at Croton coming upon some one σκάπτοντι τὴν τῶν ἀθλούντων κόνιν expressed surprise that the Crotonians had no servant to dig their palaestra for them.

3. 3. καίτοι γεγονέναι κομψότερο<ν εἰκὸ>ς εἰπεῖν: Henry's emendation, assuming that the letters between the brackets fell out before εἰπεῖν through *haplography*. The whole passage may be translated: "And yet it is likely that he spoke more gracefully than appears to some judging by the memoirs which he left behind him, and which he had composed in haste in a casual and offhand manner (παρέργως καὶ ὑπὸ χεῖρα), in the first words that occurred." **ἀμιλλησάμενος**: the notion of competition is not necessarily present any more than in the Lat. *certatim*. Thus in ch. 175 ἀμιλλώμενος is used of Antigonus' hurried ascent of Acrocorinth. An act. form ἀμιλλᾶν with the gloss εἰς τάχος γράφειν is recorded in Hesychius. ὑπὸ χεῖρα in *Mor.* 548 F is used of punishments inflicted "on the spot."

3. 4. Source, the *Memoirs*. **οἱ περὶ Δεινίαν καὶ Ἀριστοτέλη** = Δ. καὶ Α., a post-classical idiom: cf. 41, 3, οἱ περὶ Εὐρυκλείδην καὶ Μικίωνα, and *Pyrrh.* 20, οἱ περὶ Φαβρίκιον, where the context in each case shows that the reference is simply to the persons named. Deinias is probably the Argive historian cited in ch. 29, and Aristoteles the person mentioned in ch. 44, Pausanias' description (2, 8, 2) of the assassins as *Sicyonians* notwithstanding. **σχολαζόντων**, here and in 23, 6, "engaging in philosophical discussion": in 17, 3 and 43, 4 the word means to *amuse oneself*.

3, 5. Source, Myrsilus' Ἱστορικὰ παράδοξα.

τοῦτον ἐμφερέστατον, κ.τ.λ.: In the fourth cent. cities began the practice of setting up portrait statues of distinguished men, Conon being the first so honoured at Athens in his lifetime. Later the practice extended to private persons. Theophrastus (*Char.* 2, *ad fin.*) makes the Flatterer assure his patron that his εἰκών is a speaking likeness. Portraits were produced also of historical and mythological personages, and these developed fixed characteristics. So Nicocles could be said to have resembled the sixth cent. tyrant Periander.

τὸν Πέρσην Ὀρόντην: Satrap of Aeolis and Ionia, who twice revolted from Persia, and on the second occasion (B.C. 349-8) allied himself with Athens, where a decree was passed in his honour (I G ii, 108). His statue may have been set up at the same time—a compliment paid to Evagoras of Cyprus and other friendly princes.

Μυρσίλος: a Lesbian writer, who flourished under Ptolemy Philadelphus and his son Euergetes, mentioned by Pliny (N. H. 3, 17, 3).

καταπατηθῆναι: Myrsilus, one may suppose, represented this as an accident due to the impetuous curiosity of the crowd.

Chapters 4-9, 6: source, the *Memoirs*.

4. 1. τέσσαρας μῆνας: Plut. doubtless means that four months elapsed between Nicocles' seizure of power and the liberation of the city.

ὑπ' Αἰτωλῶν ἐπιβουλευομένην: see *Intro.*, p. xxxix, note.

μειράκιον: for the accurate use of the word an upper limit is given by Hippocrates (in Philo Mech. 1, 16) as ἄχρι γενείου λαχνώσιος, ἐς τὰ τρὶς ἑπτά.

Plutarch's use is similar. Clodius Pulcher at the time of the Bona Dea scandal (*Cic.* 28) was μειράκιον καὶ μήπω γενειῶν: J. Caesar at 15 (*Caes.* 1), Philip V of Macedon at 17 (*Arat.* 46), and Octavius at 19 (*Brut.* 27), are each of them οὔπω πάνυ μειράκιον. Alexander the Great is μειράκιον at 20 (*Mor.* 327 D), and at the same age C. Gracchus (*C. Gracch.* 1), μειράκιον παντάπασιν. Hence it may be inferred that Aratus was between 19 and 20 when he liberated Sicyon. He was between 20 and 21 (ἔχων εἴκοσι ἔτη Polyb. 2, 43) when Sicyon joined the League in 251-0.

ἀπεθεώρει, "watched"; frequent in Plut. The v.l. παρεθεώρει (used by Plut. only once (*Mor.* 33 A) in sense "compare") doubtless arose from the proximity of παρεφύλαττεν. In this latter word the prep. conveys the notion of hostility: cf. 6. 4; *Timol.* 19, 3; *Eumen.* 13, 6; "kept under observation." ξένοις πατρῴοις: Ptolemy I was in Sicyon in 308, Demetrius Poliorcetes in 303.

4. 3. παρῆγε τὸν χρόνον (cf. *Ag.* 13, *Cleom.* 27, *Demetr.* 51), *was protracting the time.* PRL have παρῆκε, "had let the time slip by."

5. 1. Ἐκδήλῳ: with him is associated Demophanes in *Philop.* 1, where his name appears as Ἔκδημος (so too in Polyb. and Suidas, while in Paus. the pair are Ἔκδηλος and Μεγαλοφάνης). The forms Ἔκδηλος (cf. Ἐκφάνης, also Ἐκπρέπης, *Agis* 6: 10) and Δημοφάνης are correct, the variants having arisen from a confused recollection of the expression Ἔκδηλος καὶ Δημοφάνης οἱ Μεγαλοπολῖται. Ἀρκεσιλάου: A. became head of the Academy about 260, being then 56, and died in 241. He developed Platonism in a sceptical direction, and hence is called the founder of the Middle Academy [Diog. L. 4, 28; Susemihl 1, 122; von Arnim, P.-W. *Arkesilaos*]. So far from being himself revolutionary in politics, he held conspicuously aloof from public affairs. ἄστει, Athens, in Plut. generally Rome.

5. 2. ἐγκαταλιπεῖν: in Plut. *abandon*; in Attic, to *leave* something *in* a place. ἀπειρίᾳ πραγμάτων θρασυνόμενον: one of the forms of spurious courage enumerated in Arist. *Eth. Nic.* 3, 8, 16.

5. 3. οὐ πάνυ δυσέφικτον: all MSS. give ἀνέφικτον; but it is not in the least likely that Plut. in this passage broke through his practice of avoiding hiatus (see Appendix). Copyists unacquainted with this usage might readily have substituted ἀνέφικτον, just as in 9, 2 the first hand in G wrote ἀνήρπαζον for διήρπαζον. οὐ πάνυ even in Att. can mean either "not altogether" or "not at all." In the *Aratus* the ironical use *not at all* occurs in 15, 1; 18, 5: the qualifying use in 38, 12; 43, 1; and 46, 2. In the present passage οὐ πάνυ δυσέφικτον = "not very difficult of approach," which accords well with the servant's report (5, 5) of the place as οὐκ ἄπορος οὐδὲ χαλεπή.

6. 2. [ἐξ ὀλίγων] is thought by Ziegler to have originally been a marginal note added by a reader who was surprised at the contrast between the number of A.'s contingent and that of the others.

Ξενοφίλου πρῶτον: the transposition was made by Anon. There is no reason for the clumsy arrangement found in the MSS.

ὡς ἐπὶ τὰς ἵππους τὰς βασιλικάς: "to raid the stud of the king" (Antigonus), whose object in keeping brood mares in Sicyonia was doubtless to avail of the fertility of the district between Sicyon and Corinth, which was reputed to be the most profitable spot in Greece: Athen. v, 219 a, etc.

Πολυγνώτου πύργον: a point unidentified on the road from Argos to Nemea. Argos is about 30 miles from Sicyon, Nemea being about half way.

6. 3. ἀχάνας: τινὲς μὲν Περσικὰ μέτρα, Φανόδημος δὲ [a fourth cent. historian] κίστας(*chests*) εἰς ἃς κατετίθεντο τοὺς ἐπισιτισμοὺς οἱ ἐπὶ θεωρίας ἰόντες. (Hesychius.)

6. 4. γυμνασίῳ: prob. that named after Cyllarabis, an Argive hero, mentioned in *Cleom.* 17, 1; 26, 2; *Pyrrh.* 32; Livy 34, 26. Vollgraff, *Bull. Corr. Hell.* 31 (1907) believes he has located the site near the church of St. Constantine, S.E. of the ancient city, outside the Diamperes gate.

6. 5. οὐδὲν ἦν ἄρα τυράννου δειλότερον εἰ καὶ N. ὀρρωδεῖ . . .: N.'s conduct is *cited as evidence* of his cowardice. In such cases the use of εἰ is idiomatic; cf. Hdt. 1, 60: μηχανῶνται ἐπὶ τῇ κατόδῳ (Πεισιστράτου) πρῆγμα εὐηθέστατον μακρῷ, εἰ καὶ τότε γε οὗτοι ἐν 'Αθηναίοις . . . μηχανῶνται τοιάδε.

7. 1. ἄριστον, the midday meal: cf. Thuc. 7, 81, where the Syracusans, when day dawned and they learnt that the Athenians had gone away, κατὰ τάχος διώκοντες καταλαμβάνουσι περὶ ἀρίστου ὥραν.

7. 5-6. Cf. Brasidas' abortive attack on Potidaea in Thuc. 4, 135: "he came up by night and fixed the scaling-ladder in position; and up to this point escaped observation"; τοῦ γὰρ κώδωνος παρενεχθέντος οὕτως ἐς τὸ διάκενον πρὶν ἐπανελθεῖν τὸν παραδιδόντα αὐτὸν ἡ πρόσθεσις ἐγένετο· ἔπειτα μέντοι εὐθὺς αἰσθομένων πρὶν προσβῆναι ἀπήγαγε πάλιν τὴν στρατιάν.

ἀποπορευομένων seems to be required, as Plut. evidently intends to contrast the sentries going off duty with those coming on, as appears from the words ἄλλης φυλακῆς ἐναντίας ταύτῃ προσερχομένης. The correction is due to R. M. Henry.

τὰς ἑκατέρωθεν ὁδούς, i.e., streets within the town to right and left of the point where the assailants were scaling the wall. **διαλαβὼν**, "cutting off the roads" by posting sentries.

8. 2. πυνθάνεσθαι . . μή τι γίνεται. Here as often in post-classical Greek μή introduces an indirect question expecting the answer "yes" (i.e., = whether . . . not): cf. *Solon* 6, 5, πυθόμενον μὴ Σόλωνος ὁ τεθνηκὼς υἱὸς ὠνομάζετο; also *Arist.* 7, *Cleom.* 22, 4. In 29, 7, however, πυθόμενος τῶν ὑποστρατήγων μή τις αὐτοῦ χρεία παρόντος, the answer "no" is expected.

8. 3. <πρὸς> αὐτὸν ἀντεφώνησε. Plut. elsewhere uses neither acc. nor dat. with ἀντιφωνεῖν, and the hiatus shows that the prep. is required. **κώδωνος**, rather than the v.l. κωδώνων, because only one bell has been mentioned.

8. 6. τὸ θέατρον: on the slope leading from the acropolis to the lower city. It is mentioned only here, Paus. 2, 7, 5, and Polyb. 29, 10, 2 (holding of a syncletos there in 168 B.C.). The remains are described by Fossum, A.J.A. ix, 1905.

9. 1. See *Intro.*, p. xxxix f., for a discussion of Beloch's explanation of this passage.

9 2. εἰς μέσον ἔθηκε: *made over to* . . . as often. The original meaning was "offered for competition," as in *Il.* 23, 704, ἀνδρὶ δὲ νικηθέντι γυναῖκ' ἐς μέσσον ἔθηκε; the derived meaning appears in Hdt. 3, 80 *al.*

9. 4. ὁμοῦ τι, "approximately," not of necessity implying "less than": see L. and S. (new ed.) *s.v.* Sicyon was a member of Demetrius' Hellenic League of 303 B.C. It has been suggested (Schorn, *ap.* Freeman, p. 280, n. 1) that after the disaster at Ipsus, 301 B.C., some politician turned tyrant and expelled anti-Macedonian agitators. On the exiles cf. Cic. *De Off.* ii, 23.

9. 6. προσέμειξεν αὐτὴν τοῖς 'Α.: The year of the union is 251-0 B.C. Data in Pol. 2, 43 and *Arat.* 21, 2 (where see note) fix the capture of Corinth to

July 25 or Aug. 24, 243. The capture occurred ὀγδόῳ ἔτει after the accession of Sicyon to the League, which thus by *exclusive* reckoning falls in 251-0. We are justified in reckoning exclusively because (1) Sicyon was freed in the fourth year after the strategia of Margos, (2) Margos became strategos 25 years after the founding of the League, (3) the League was founded κατὰ τὴν Πύρρου διάβασιν εἰς Ἰταλίαν (Pol. 41, 11): Pyrrhus crossed to Italy in the Olympian year 281-280. But whereas the Olympian year ran from Aug. to Aug. the Achaean strategos-year ran from May to May, and consequently the first strategos entered office in May, 280. Thus by *exclusive* reckoning all the chronological data of Polybius are found to be consistent (Beloch 4, 2, p. 225).

(The Achaean strategos-year began in May in the years 220 and 218 (Pol. 4, 37, 2 and 5, 1, 1), and there is no ground for assuming that there had been any change in this respect.)

The liberation of Sicyon is thus recorded in Pol. 2, 43, τετάρτῳ δ' ὕστερον ἔτει τοῦ προειρημένου (Μάργου) στρατηγοῦντος Ἄρατος ὁ Σικυώνιος, ἔτη μὲν ἔχων εἴκοσι, τυραννουμένην δ' ἐλευθερώσας τὴν πατρίδα προσένειμε πρὸς τὴν τῶν Ἀχαιῶν πολιτείαν, ἀρχῆθεν εὐθὺς ἐραστὴς γενόμενος τῆς προαιρέσεως αὐτῶν.

This passage has been misunderstood by some translators. Thus Paton (Loeb *Polybius*) writes: "Four years later *during his (Margos')* term of office Aratus of Sicyon, *then only twenty years of age*, freed his city from its tyrant, . . . and, having always been a passionate admirer of the Achaean polity, made his own city a member of the League." Shuckburgh translates: "In the fourth year after this man's tenure of office Aratus . . . caused his city to join the League, which he had, *when only twenty years of age*, delivered from the yoke of its tyrant." It is to be observed (1) that in the first of the clauses italicized Paton has mistaken Polybius' meaning, and (2) that Pol. does *not* say, as both Paton and Shuckburgh make him say, that Aratus was 20 when he freed Sicyon, but when he attached the city to the League. Beloch has fallen into the same confusion in writing, "Aratos war zur Zeit der Befreiung Sikyons (251 v. Chr.) wie Polybius angibt 20 Jahre alt." There is no evidence whatever for putting "liberation" and "union" either in the same Julian or the same strategos year.

Δωριεῖς ὄντες: Sicyon was never completely Doricised. Besides Hylleis, Pamphyli, Dymanes, there was at Sicyon the non-Dorian tribe Aigialeis, who became dominant in the sixth cent. under the Orthagorid tyrants. The Aigialeis were according to tradition Ionians, i.e. a pre-Achaean folk. (The view that the Ionians were the first speakers of Greek in Peloponnesus (Hdt. 7, 94) is accepted by Myres (1931) and Nilsson (1933).) The Achaeans on the contrary spoke a "Conquest Dialect," and on that criterion would seem to have been akin to the Eleans and the nations across the Gulf (C. A. H. iii, p. 527), having little in common with Homer's Achaeans except the name.

ἑκουσίως: *voluntarily*, i.e. they gave up their independence without external coercion.

9. 6. Neumann-Partsch, Phys. Geog. v. Griechenland (p. 353), remarks: "There are on the Achaean coast no recent deposits of fertile soil. The reason is that all the streams of the district have a short course and a remarkably rapid fall; they therefore carry all their finer detritus to the sea, while beginning to drop their coarser material, resulting from the disintegration of the conglomerate, as soon as they leave the hills. They have thus built out pebbly tongues of land on both sides of their mouths, so that all along the coast the streams empty not

into bays but at the end of points. Even across the coastal plains they usually flow in raised beds between dams which they have themselves created."

10. 1–4. The contrast between Aratus' ability as a diplomatist and his courage and resource as a guerrilla leader, on the one hand, and, on the other, his feebleness and timidity ὅτε τῶν ὑπαίθρων ἀντιποιήσασθαι βουληθείη, is brought out in Polyb. 4, 8.

10. 1. ἀκριβέστερος, *more scrupulous.*

10. 2. τῷ καιρῷ μεταβαλλόμενος : *changing at the call of emergencies* ; the dat. indicating the cause or motive of the change : cf. Thuc. 3, 97, τῇ τύχῃ ἐλπίσας, *rendered sanguine by success*, where Classen describes the dat. as causal.

The passage from ὁμονοίας ἐθνῶν to the end of the section is hardly as Plut. wrote it. Probably a number of words have dropped out. The adoption of Coraes' emendation ἄλλου (for ἀλλ' ἤ) before τῶν καλῶν at any rate enables it to be construed ; but the construction ἐπηβολώτατος κλέψαι is suspect as the adj. is elsewhere followed by a genitive (e.g. *Mor.* 1142 D, ἑρμηνείας ἐπήβολον). θεάτρου : at Athens, as early as the fourth cent., the popular assembly met for some purposes in the theatre (Arist. *Ath. Pol.* 42) ; in the third it was the ordinary place of assembly, as also elsewhere, e.g. at Sicyon (*Arat.* 8) and Corinth (*Arat.* 23). κλέψαι : cf. *Alex.* 31, οὐ κλέπτω τὴν νίκην. συσκευάσασθαι, *ensnare* : cf. *Cato* 43, οὓς μὲν δεδιξάμενοι . . . τοὺς δὲ συσκευασάμενοι δωροδοκίαις.

10. 4. ξηρότητι nsed when moisture is deficient in quantity ; λεπτότητι, in substance.

μὴ φερούσης : with temporal, modal, causal, or purely attributive participles (esp. those of βούλεσθαι, δύνασθαι, and τολμᾶν) Plut. frequently uses μὴ for οὐ : in the *Lives* we find μὴ 341 times, οὐ 629 ; in the *Moralia* μὴ 211, οὐ 538 : Stegmann *ap.* Holden, *Pericl.* 3, 2.

ἐν τοῖς ὑπαιθρίοις καὶ διακεκηρυγμένοις = πολέμῳ καὶ ἀγῶνι (just above).

10. 5. περὶ τὰς εὐφυΐας, "in good natural capacities." Cf. *Otho.* 23, ἐν τῇ πρὸς πᾶσαν ἀρετὴν εὐφυΐᾳ : *Mor.* 605 D (of exiles "making good"), ἐχρήσαντο ταῖς εὐφυΐαις.

[The subject-matter of 10, 4–5 may be compared with 29, 8. Both passages seem to be taken from some collection of subjects discussed in the philosophical schools : among such subjects was the cause of Antigonus Doson's death, *Cleom.* 30, 4.]

11–12. Source, the *Memoirs.*

11. 1. The MSS. read παρεῖχεν αὐτῷ τὸν ἀεὶ στρατηγοῦντα, a strangely inverted form of expression which certainly does not come from Plut.

11. 2. παρὰ τοῦ βασιλέως : Gonatas or Philadelphus ? See *Intro.*, p. xli.

12. 2. Μοθώνης, a harbour and town in Messenia, at the extreme S.W. of Peloponnesus, *mod.* Modon. The name is spelt as here in Paus. 4, 35, 1, but Μεθώνη in Thuc. 2, 25, Diod. 11, 85, Strabo 8, p. 359.

διὰ πόρου, "by the regular passage" : Diod. 15, 3, like Pindar, *Nem.* 4, 53, uses πόρος of the Ἰόνιος πόντος between Greece and Italy ; Polyb. 1, 37 1, of the sea between Sicily and Africa. In our passage it must refer to the sea between Peloponnesus and the coast of Africa. τῷ δρόμῳ, *the run before the wind*, as in *Mor.* 76 C : οἱ πρὸς ἄχανες θέοντες ἱστίοις πέλαγος ἅμα τῷ χρόνῳ πρὸς τὴν τοῦ πνεύματος ῥώμην ἀναμετροῦνται τὸν δρόμον.

'Ανδρίας : the MSS. read 'Αδρίας, but only two places named Adria are known, one near the mouth of the Po, the other in Picenum, the modern Atri, both of which are out of the picture. 'Ανδρίας is the correction of the seventeenth century scholar, Palmerius (Le Paulmier). Omission of letters is a characteristic of the MSS. and their archetype. After "α" the letter "ν" tended to fall out when a consonant followed. Leaf on *Il.* 2, 651 cites from Hesychius ἀδρί· ἀνδρί, and adds "In the Cyprian inscriptions the nasal is regularly omitted before a consonant and so often in Mod. Greek, e.g., ἄθρωπος"; which suggests that in pronunciation there was little difference between 'Ανδρία and 'Αδρία. The use of 'Ανδρία to denote the country parts of the island as opposed to the town of Andros is sufficiently justified by Xen., *Hell.* 1, 4, 22, where Alcibiades lands his army τῆς 'Ανδυίας χώρας εἰς Γαυρίον, with which cf. Athen. v, 209 e, περὶ Λεύκολλαν τῆς Κῴας (also in Strabo 14, p. 657); cf. ἐπίκειται δὲ (Μυκάλη) τῇ Σαμίᾳ (*Ib.*, p. 686). Palmerius' emendation is accepted on geographical grounds by Hatzfeld, *Les Traffiquants italiens* (p. 19), who observes : "A ship after having doubled C. Malea, if caught by a Southern tempest, naturally reaches land in the N. Cyclades." The proximity of Andros to Euboea is a further consideration in favour of the reading 'Ανδρίας (see *Intro.*, p. xliii). πολεμίας οὔσης, *Intro.*, p. xliii.

12. 3. Τιμάνθη, doubtless to be identified with the painter of that name (ch. 32, 6).

12. 5. 'Ρωμαικῆς νεώς : the presence of a Roman ship in the Aegean so early as 251–50 B.C. has occasioned surprise. It was, no doubt, an Italian merchant-ship. In the Delian choregic inscription (IG xi, **2**, no. 115) of 259 B.C. we find in the list of actors Σέρδων· 'Ρωμαῖος, and in IG xi, 4, no. 287 A, 58 (circ. 250) there is mentioned one Νουίος (Novius). παραβαλούσης, "having put in" at the spot, which was probably a regular landing-place : for the act in this sense cf. Arist. *De Gen. Anim.* iii, 2, 31, περὶ 'Ρόδον παραβαλόντος ναυτικοῦ στόλου. The mid. is more frequent, e.g., Aristoph., *Frogs* 180, παραβαλοῦ ! ἄχρι Καρίας. If the voyage from Italy was made in stages as Hatzfeld (*loc. cit.*) suggests, it would explain the presence of the Roman ship at Andros and the possibility of Aratus' conveyance to Caria in a vessel bound for Syria. Caria was one of the territories mentioned by Euergetes (246–221 B.C.) in the Adulis inscr. as inherited by him from his father, Philadelphus.

13. Source, Polemon of Ilium (fl. c. 200 B.C.), who is mentioned in the course of the chapter. He wrote περὶ τῆς ἐν Σικυῶνι ποικίλης στοᾶς, which may be identical with the περὶ τῶν ἐν Σικυῶνι πινάκων, also attributed to him.

The Sicyonian group of painters, who flourished between the end of the Peloponnesian War and the death of Alexander the Great, constituted the first *school* of painters, making the training of pupils a regular part of the profession. Pamphilus about the middle of the fourth cent. introduced the teaching of drawing into boys' schools in Greece, and developed encaustic painting in wax (Pliny, N.H. xxxv, 76, 123). "In this process the colours were prepared in little rods, heated red-hot and laid on with the spatula; its difficulty made it suitable only for small pictures, but the brilliancy of the result gave it a place in ancient art analogous to that of oil-painting among the moderns" (Woltmann and Woermann, *Hist. of Painting*, Eng. tr.). Hence Plutarch's words, ὡς μόνης ἀδιαφθόρου ἐχούσης τὸ καλόν. Melanthus, the painter of the tyrant Aristratus, was one of Pamphilus' pupils. The school continued to exist during the third century, no less than four painters (as Skalet observes) being associated with

Aratus—Timanthes who accompanied him to Egypt and depicted the rout of the Aetolians at Pellene (ch. 31), Mnasitheus who shared in his liberation of Sicyon (ch. 7), Leontiscus who portrayed him as a victor with a trophy, accompanied by a woman playing the cithara (Pliny N.H. xxxv, 141), and Nealces who "painted out" Aristratus. This Nealces, presumably through Aratus' influence, found his way to the court of Ptolemy, where he painted a battle between Egyptians and Persians (Pliny, N.H. xxxv, 142). References in Skalet, ch. 8, who cites modern authorities.

13. 1. χρηστογραφίας : either = *fine painting* generally (cf. καλλιγραφία, artistic writing), or else it must have a technical meaning not elsewhere recorded in reference to the encaustic process which is mentioned in the words immediately following. Ἀπελλῆς (born *c.* 370 B.C.), the greatest painter of antiquity. Μέλανθον : in Pliny, N. H. xxxv, 50 and 80 (where the name appears as Melanthius), he is said to have excelled Apelles himself in *dispositio* (composition), and though using only four colours, to have been one of the best colourists among the Greek painters. His portrait of Aristratus is his only work on record.

13. 5. διήλειψεν : the aor. is required by the sense. A copyist who misread the first half of the word and gave διείληφεν proceeded to turn ψ into φ. In 14, 2 G¹ has ἐπέγραφον where the other MSS. preserve the correct ἐπέγραψαν. Cf. Athenaeus 9, 407 c for Chamaeleon's account of how Alcibiades rescued Hegemon of Thasos from a prosecution : ἧκεν εἰς τὸ Μητρῷον ὅπου τῶν δικῶν ἦσαν αἱ γραφαὶ καὶ βρέξας τὸν δάκτυλον ἐκ τοῦ στόματος διήλειψε τὴν δίκην.

παρεμβαλεῖν : the meaning required is *insert, interpolate*, which is not given by παραβαλεῖν, the reading of the MSS. So in *Lucull.* 9, 5 the MSS. give παραβεβληκότας where the meaning, *encamped*, requires Solanus' emendation παρεμβεβληκότας. In the transitive use Plut. has παρεμβάλλειν in *Mor.* 730 f. ὁ τὸν Κήυκος γάμον εἰς τὰ Ἡσιόδου παρεμβαλών in the sense required here.

13. 6. This paragraph is obviously based on the *Memoirs*. τούτων resumes the narrative from the end of ch. 12. <γνώμης>. A reference to the quality of which Aratus "gave proof" is wanting. Cf. *Dion.* 4, 1, ὕστερον δὲ τοῦ φρονεῖν διδοὺς πεῖραν ἠγαπᾶτο παρὰ τῷ τυράννῳ; *Cleom.* 32, ἐπεὶ δε γνώμης διδοὺς πεῖραν ἀνὴρ ἐφαίνετ᾽ ἔμφρων . . . αἰδὼς καὶ μετάνοια τὸν Πτολεμαῖον εἶχεν. An alternative suggestion, also due to Ziegler, is ἑαυτοῦ. δόσεις is used here in the post-classical sense of "portions" which is rare except in reference to a physician's "doses" : see exx. in L. and S.

14. The chapter is composed of Plutarch's reflections, a reference to the arbitration at Sicyon after Aratus' return [probable date, spring 250], doubtless derived from the *Memoirs*, and a copy of the verses inscribed on the base of his statue, which may be the statue seen by Pausanias in the theatre at Sicyon.

14. 2. πεντεκαίδεκα τῶν πολιτῶν : the story is told in Cic. *De Off.* 2, 23, who adds : perfecitque aestimandis possessionibus, ut persuaderent aliis ut pecuniam accipere vellent, aliis ut commodius putarent numerari sibi quod tanti esset quam suum recuperare.

14. 4. σωτῆρος : gen. in app. to the possessive pron. τεάν.

15. The subject-matter is discussed in *Intro.*, p. xlvi ; as there stated, the most probable date is the spring of 250. Possibly Antigonus had found it convenient to be at Corinth during the Isthmian games celebrated that year. Source, the *Memoirs*.

15. 1. τὸ δεῖπνον : *the* banquet held after the sacrifice.

15. 3. αὐλάς, "palaces": plural suggesting magnificence, ὑπὸ σκηνήν, "behind the curtain." σκηνή means the back-scene of the theatre with its three doors; cf. 23, 2. τραγῳδίαν καὶ σκηνογραφίαν; for the language cf. Pomp. 31, where Lucullus is said τραγῳδίαις καὶ σκιογραφίαις βασιλικαῖς πεπολεμηκέναι. Ferguson has found here a covert jibe at Philadelphus' unwillingness to take an active part in war.

15. 4. <πρὸs> ἀλλήλους : to read ἀλλήλοις would be also possible ; cf. *Caes.* 42, 2; *Them.* 5. 4.

15. 5. The order of words is τοσοῦτον φθόνου . . . προσῆν ταῖς φιλίαις τοξευομέναις περιμαχήτοις . . . ἔρωσι.

16. 1. Source, the *Memoirs.* Aratus' first strategia 245-4, his second, 243-2. The Aetolo-Boeotian war is mentioned in Pol. 20, 4. The B. had suffered a continuous loss of reputation and influence ἔχοντες στρατηγὸν Ἀμαιόκριτον (sic). They had allied themselves with the Achaeans who instigated them against Aetolia (Ἀχαιῶν γὰρ αὐτοὺς πρὸς Ἀ. ἐκπολεμωσάντων, . . . μετὰ ταῦτα κατὰ τὸ συνεχὲς ἐπολέμουν πρὸς Αἰτωλούς). After their defeat they abandoned the Achaean alliance and προσένειμαν Αἰτωλοῖς τὸ ἔθνος, i.e., entered into isopolity with them. Beloch has suggested that Alexander of Corinth as an ally of the Achaeans was also involved in the war. He further infers (4, 2, p. 402) from a study of the Amphictyony lists that Phocis at this time seceded from Aetolia and, despite the defeat of her Boeotian allies, secured her independence.

16. 1. Ἀβοιωκρίτου τοῦ βοιωτάρχου : the correct form of the name is Ἀβαιόκριτος (*Syll.*[3] 238, ii, and 446). The spelling found in Plutarch's text has evidently arisen from assimilation to Βοιωτός. A. had been "naopoios" and Delphian proxenos in Thebes. The survival of the Boeotian League from pre-Macedonian days is indicated by the mention of Boeotarchs when Thebes revolted from Alexander (Arrian I, 7), again in reference to events of 329 (Hypereides, *Contra Dem.* 18), and 313 (Diod. 19, 77, 4). See Beloch 4, 2, p. 426).

16. 2. ἐνιαυτῷ δ' ὕστερον : the interval is to be dated from the *end* of the strategia of 245, as appears from the statement in 24, 5 that a year must elapse before an Achaean strategos became eligible for re-election.

16. 3-6. Reflections of Plutarch.

16. 3-4. Χάρης μὲν γὰρ . . . ταύτην δὲ τὴν πρᾶξιν : as often, the μέν clause is logically subordinate; cf. 24, 2. γὰρ will either mean *truly, verily* if with Shilleto on Thuc. I, 25, and Kühner-Gerth ii, 2, p. 331 f. we admit an adverbial use (γὰρ being by origin γε ἄρα), or if with L. and S. we admit only a causative use an ellipse must be assumed (I say this for . . .). Obviously the clause Χάρης μὲν γὰρ . . . does not *explain* but merely *confirms* the statement contained in the previous sentence.

Diod. 16, 12, 1 relates how Chares, being short of funds, took service with Artabazus, a satrap in rebellion against Artaxerxes, and won the victory in the campaign that followed.

Πελοπίδου τυραννοκτονίας : Xen., *Hell.* 5, 47, Plut., *Pel.* 10-11. No such action is reported of the Athenian restorer of democracy, Thrasybulus.

ἀλλόφυλον : The material available for determining the character of the Macedonian speech (including the γλῶσσαι of the Macedonian Amerius) exhibits according to Hoffmann three elements : (1) Greek words in one of the intelligible dialect forms, (2) Greek words with abnormal morphology, (3) words of non-Greek origin, relating chiefly to things connected with the soil—plants or animals.

But the national name Μακεδόνες, the name of the royal house, the vast majority both of personal names and of cult names and names of deities are Greek. It has been inferred from these facts that the Macedonians were a people originally settled in N. Thessaly, which, along with other Greek stocks, Tymphaei, Orestae, Elimiotae, became detached from their home-region and settled between Bermion and Olympus in the plains which stretch from Aegae to Pella ; they subdued and incorporated the Illyrian tribes, and founded the Macedonian state in the earlier half of the seventh century. Their language—although many words of alien origin in use among the older layers of the population kept their place after the fusion—continued to be Greek. Hence the Macedonians were not foreigners in the same sense as the Romans, Thracians and Illyrians (cf. Pol. 28, 8, where Pleuratus is appointed ambassador to the Illyrian king, διὰ τὸ τὴν διάλεκτον εἰδέναι τὴν Ἰλλυρικήν) ; and the Acarnanian Lyciscus in 211 B.C. could thus address the Lacedaemonians ; " Formerly you contended for hegemony πρὸς Ἀχαιοὺς καὶ Μακεδόνας ὁμοφύλους, but now the Greeks are engaging in war πρὸς ἀλλοφύλους ἀνθρώπους " (the Romans).

But this point of view found no expression until the intervention of Rome in Greek affairs had emphasised the essential connection of the Macedonians with the pure Greeks beyond their southern border. Fellmann (p. 4) has raised the question : Did the Macedonians regard themselves as Greeks and were they regarded by the Greeks as kindred ?

The evidence, however, which may be cited to justify an answer in the negative to these questions is of very varying value. For the fifth cent. the most important is that contained in Hdt. 5, 22. Alexander of Macedon, "the Philhellene," was objected to as a competitor at the Olympian games on the ground of being a " barbarian," and though he vindicated the claim of his own family to Hellenism he did not deny the imputation that the Macedonians were "barbarians." With this accords Isocrates' reference to the founder of the Macedonian kingdom as μόνος τῶν Ἑλλήνων οὐχ ὁμοφύλου γένους ἄρχων. On the other hand it is not certain that the " Hellenic War " means the war waged by Hellenes against a non-Hellene, for in Thuc. I, 112 (a reference I owe to Dr. Parke) we find Ἑλληνικοῦ πολέμου ἔσχον οἱ Ἀθηναῖοι (" the A. held aloof from a war with Greeks ").

Fellmann's later citations are all of an *ex parte* character. In any case Hellenism was susceptible of degrees, from Athens, "Ἑλλάδος Ἑλλάς," down. The Macedonians were doubtless low in the scale, but it is incredible that the Greeks of the third cent. actually felt them to be aliens in the same sense as the Romans or Illyrians. To the English the Scots were foreigners till 1603, but not ἀλλόφυλοι in the same sense as the French or Spanish. [Beloch 4, 1, 1 ff. ; Fellmann, pp. 4-10 ; Hoffmann P.-W. Makedonia.]

16. 5. εἰς ταὐτὸ ... τῷ τόπῳ : The words τῷ τόπῳ depend on ταὐτὸ, cf. Xen., An. 3, 1, 27 : ἐν ταὐτῷ ἦσθα τούτοις ὅτε ... Tr. "the isthmus unites and links our continent with this spot " (Acrocorinth, described as τόπος also in 17, 1). On Capps' emendation τὼ τόπω (i.e., N. Greece and Peloponnesus) Dr. Henry has sent me the following criticisms : (1) you could hardly call either of these areas a τόπος, (2) neither of them is even mentioned; (3) Plut. uses the dual only of pairs of things, hands, feet, etc., (4) clearly ἤπειρον depends on both συνάγει and συνάπτει, (5) the reading of the MSS. is quite regular.

Ἀκροκόρινθος, height 1886 ft. : length of ring-wall on summit 1¼ miles : ascent about 1½ hours. The position of Acrocorinth and the Oneion Mts. makes it impossible to pass southwards except by one of three routes : (1) the western route to Sicyon, etc., (2) the route to Tenea, between Acrocorinth and the Oneion Mts., (3) a path between the Oneion Mts. and the Savronic Gulf.

16. 6. καὶ ἄρχοντα τὸν κατέχοντα : The transposition proposed by Zeitz is justified by the improvement in the sense. Variation of word-order is not infrequent in the MSS. Thus, four lines down (ch. 17) where G has ἀνέλπιστος ἦν ἡ ἐπιχείρησις, P. R. L. have ἦν ἡ ἐπιχείρησις ἀνέλπιστος. **πέδας τῆς Ἑλλάδος** : not Corinth only, but Chalcis and Demetrias as well, Polyb. 18, 11 (Hultsch).

17. The anti-Macedonian bias exhibited in this ch. (which has nothing to do with Aratus), combined with the interest displayed in Nicaea, are in keeping with what we know of Phylarchus' historiography. Polyaenus 4, 6, 1, which closely resembles Plut. in language, adds the remark that Antigonus acquired the place easily, τῶν φυλάκων . . . τὴν θέαν κατειληφότων (*had gone down to the festival*, for which use see L. and S., *s.v.*).

17. 1. καὶ βασιλεῦσι. The δέ of the MSS. is obviously wrong. Confusion between δ and κ occurs also in 47, 2, and between ε and αι in the following mis-spellings (found in one or other of the MSS.), Τριτεεύς, Περσέου, Ἀμοιβαῖα, Μαλαίας, Μεγαλαίου.

Acrocorinth was occupied successively by Philip II of Macedon (ch. 23), Alexander the Great, Polyperchon (under whom it was held by his son Alexander and A.'s widow, Cratesipolis), Ptolemy Soter, Demetrius Poliorcetes, who garrisoned it at the request of the Corinthians, μέχρις ἂν ὁ πρὸς Κάσσανδρον καταλυθῇ πόλεμος (Diod. 20, 103, 3), but the garrison was still there in 287 (Plut., *Dem.* 43), Antigonus Gonatas, represented by Craterus and after his death by his son Alexander.

ἀνήρτητο ταῖς φροντίσιν, "was kept in a state of suspense by thoughts of how to . . ."

17. 2. Ἀλεξάνδρου : on the date of his period of independent rule, see *Intro.*, p. xxxvi. **Νικαίας** : apparently a princess of some western house (Tarn). We read in Livy 35, 26 of a galley captured by the Achaeans while it was conveying Nicaea from Naupactus to Corinth. The galley was retained by the Achaeans, for Philopoemen attempted to launch it eighty years afterwards (in 192 B.C.). It follows that Nicaea's journey was made either during the Pyrrhic war (i.e., in 272) or, if Livy was speaking in round numbers (as is probable in such a case), during the Chremonidean War. In both wars the Achaeans were engaged against Macedon. If we assume with Tarn that N. on the occasion of the capture was on her way to be married at the age of sixteen, she would, if the capture had taken place in the earlier war, be now forty-three : if we refer it to the Chremonidean War, in the late thirties.

Livy (*loc. cit.*) indeed speaks of Nicaea as *Crateri uxor*, but obviously either he or a copyist is guilty of an error ; Craterus and his son are not likely both to have married women named Nicaea. (The words *filii Alexandri* have probably been dropped after *Crateri*.) The launching of the galley in 192 B.C. by Philopoemen is mentioned in Plut., *Philop.* 14, but the age of the ship is there given wrongly as forty years, no mention being made of Nicaea. Livy's eighty years is correct, since *forty* years before 192 Corinth was in the Achaean League.

N.'s fiancé Demetrius was in 245 about thirty, for his mother Phila had married Antigonus in 276. About 253 he had married his cousin Stratonice, but she appears to have recently deserted him. Agatharchides, a second cent.

historian, states that she returned to Antioch in hope of marrying her nephew Seleucus—who succeeded to the throne of Syria in 246 [F.H.G. iii, p. 196].

Tarn (p. 373) is right in holding that Demetrius' proposal of marriage to N. was a hoax; otherwise "Antigonus need have been in no hurry to secure the citadel." Of her later history we are uninformed. Euphorion of Chalcis is stated to have enjoyed her patronage; if this is the meaning of Suidas' words, Νικαίας στερξάσης αὐτόν. But whether their acquaintance belongs to the time when she reigned as queen-consort over Euboea and Corinth or to the period of her exile remains in dispute. [Beloch 4, 2, 585 in contrast with Skutsch, P.-W. vii, 1175.]

17. 3. ἔθυε γαμους ... θέας ἐπετέλει ... πότους συνῆγε: the imperfects denote repeated action. The marriage had not yet taken place. πότους συνῆγε, "kept holding drinking-parties": cf. 43, 8 συνάγειν ἑστίασιν. The vb., like our "entertain," was also used intransitively, Athen. 365 d, who adds by way of explanation that this meaning of συνάγειν is perhaps derived from the practice of bringing contributions to the entertainment (as at picnics): μήποτε δὲ (and perhaps) τοῦτ' ἔστι τὸ "ἀπὸ συμβολῶν" καλούμενον. ὡς ἄν τις μάλιστα (sc. ποιοῖ). ἀφεικώς: cf. Luc. I, ἀφῆκε τὴν διάνοιαν ἐν φιλοσοφίᾳ σχολάζειν. (Note, however, that in our passage the association of σχολάζειν with παίζειν shows that the meaning is simply, amuse oneself.)

17. 4. Ἀμοιβέως: a celebrated citharoedus, to whose performances Zeno, the founder of stoicism (who died in 261), used, as Plut. tells us (Mor. 443 A), to bring his pupils to hear οἵαν ἔντερα καὶ νεῦρα καὶ ξύλα καὶ ὀστᾶ λόγου καὶ ἀριθμοῦ μετασχόντα καὶ ταξέως ἐμμέλειαν καὶ φωνὴν ἀφίησιν. Amoebeus lived at Athens and is said to have received an Attic talent for public appearances at the theatre.

17. 5. κατὰ τὴν ἐκτροπήν: cf. plan of Corinth at end of book, from which it will be seen that the ἐκτροπή is the N.W. corner of the Agora, from which started a road called by Pausanias "the road to Sicyon." This road, he adds, led past the theatre. The distance of the theatre from the agora is three minutes' walk. Antigonus, leaving Nicaea, walked across the agora to its S.W. corner, whence the road to the summit proceeded in a S.W. direction to an entrance on the W. side. (This is the usual path at the present day.) It may be noticed that the remains of an Hellenistic villa have been found (H V on plan) in a direct line between the agora and the N.W. corner of Acrocorinthus.

18–24. Source, the Memoirs, to which Plut. adds moral reflections.

18. 1. Περσαῖος, sent by Zeno as a substitute for himself to Antigonus' court in 276, was more of a courtier than a philosopher. Among his writings were περὶ βασιλείας (Diog. Laert. 7, 36) and συμποτικὰ ὑπομνήματα (Athen. 13, 607 B). See further, Susemihl I, p. 68. ἄρχοντα: Tarn may be right in regarding P. as civil governor of Corinth, though Plut. in ch. 23 ranks him among the three στρατηγοί.

18. 2. ἔτι καὶ Ἀ. ζῶντος κ.τ.λ.: this seems to refer to a time when Sicyon was already a member of the League, but A. not yet its ally. See Intro., p. xl. The date would then be c. 249.

πράξει: the MSS. have the unmeaning πατρίδι. So in 23, 5 we find στρατιωτῶν for στρατηγῶν, in 24, 6 ἄλλου for ὅλου, in 35, 1 ὑπόσχεσιν for ὑπόθεσιν, in 48, 2 πατρός for παντός, in 49, 4 πόλεων for πολλῶν. Similarly in 30, 8 φύσιν is, I believe, an error for πίστιν.

18. 4. χρυσίον: gold pieces, to be exchanged for less compromising silver (Tarn).

18. 5. ἔφη πρὸς τὸν ἀδελφὸν ἀναβαίνων *παρὰ τὸ κρημνῶδες ἐντομὴν καθεωρακέναι πλαγίαν κ.τ.λ.: "he said that when going up to his brother along the rocky path he had noticed a sloping fissure leading to a point where . . ." I have taken the reading παρά (for πρὸς) from the parallel passage Polyaen. 6, 5, which has plainly been derived either from Plutarch or his source. Polyaenus' words are: παρὰ τὸ κρ. ἐντομὴν ἑωρακέναι πλαγίαν. That τὸ κρημνῶδες means the *path* along which Erginus was walking appears from ch. 22, 1: παρὰ τὸ κρ. ἡμιλλᾶτο.

Keeping the reading of the MSS., πρὸς τὸ κρημνῶδες, Perrin elicits the version, "he said he had noticed in the face of the cliff a slanting fissure . . ." The construction ἐντομὴ πρὸς τὸ κρ. might be justified by Aesch. *Eum.* 592, πρὸς δέρην τεμών, but it seems more likely that the πρὸς before τὸ κρημνῶδες has crept into the text from πρὸς τὸν ἀδελφόν, ousting παρά.

At some point on the regular path to the summit, Erginus saw a fissure branching off on the left to a point on the north side of the ring-wall of the citadel. Such a track still exists (Theunissen, p. 192). See plan of Corinth.

18. 6. προσπαίξαντος: the earlier form is (πυοσ)παίσαντος, but παιξοῦμαι (fut.) is found in Xen. *Conviv.* 9, 2. To this form the aor. was assimilated.

εἶτ', ὦ βέλτιστε, "so then, my excellent friend, are you men lifting the king's taxes to get so small a quantity of gold, when you might sell one short hour of your time for a large sum of money?"

ἀνασπᾶτε: "lift up and carry off," cf. ch. 21, 4 (and note), τὰς κλίμακας ἀνασπάσας; also *Mor.* 557c: Ἡρακλῆς ἀνασπάσας τὸν τρίποδα εἰς Φενεὸν ἀπήνεγκεν. <εἰσ>πράξεις: Henry's conjecture for πράξεις. εἰσπραξις properly means *collection of taxes* (as the simple πρᾶξις may in an appropriate context), e.g. Diod. 24, 8, εἰσπραξις τῶν εἰσφορῶν, but could also stand for the taxes themselves. The grammarian Pollux, Plutarch's contemporary, has the gloss, μίσθος· ἀργύριον, χρήματα . . . χρημάτων φυρὰ, τέλος, εἴσπραξις, τέλεσμα, εἰσφορά. So in English "collection" may mean the objects collected.

ὥραν = Lat. horam. This use came into vogue from the astronomers of Alexandria about 150 B.C. To Aratus and his contemporaries ὥρα meant a division of the day (ὄρθρος, μεσημβρία, δειλινὸς καιρός, ἑσπέρα) or night. Cf. Xen. *Mem.* 4, 3, 4.

ἦ γὰρ οὐχί; *is it not a fact that?* ἅπαξ: Circe to Odysseus (*Od.* 12, 22): δισθανέες, ὅτε τ' ἄλλοι ἅπαξ θνήσκουσ' ἄνθρωποι.

18. 7. μὴ πάνυ τι: see on ch. 5, 4.

ἦν: in strict grammar either ἐστί or εἴη is required, but exceptions occur; e.g. Thuc. 3, 3², ἔλεγον οὐ καλῶς τὴν Ἑλλάδα ἐλευθεροῦν αὐτὸν, εἰ ἄνδρας διέφθειρον οὔτε χεῖρας ἀνταιρομένους οὔτε πολεμίους: *Dem.* 48, 16, ἃ μὲν εἰλήφει τῆς πόλεως ἀποδώσειν (ἡγούμην): Xen. *Mem.* 1, 3, 3. In such irregular passages the subordinate clause is treated as if it contained the words or thought of the writer or reporter, whereas in fact it contains the words or thought of its own subject. In ch. 34, 2 *infra*, we find the regular and irregular constructions in the same sentence.

Aratus' capture of Acrocorinth is mentioned in Polyb. 2, 43, 4; Strabo 8, p. 385; Paus. 2, 8, 4, and 7, 8, 3; Athen. 4, 162 D; Diog. Laert. 7, 36; Prol. *Trag.* 26; Polyaen. 6, 5.

19–23. For these chapters the source is still the *Memoirs*. Here and there Plut. moralises on the events. Ch. 23, 5 seems taken from a collection of anecdotes of philosophers.

19. 3. Some copyist, failing to construe this passage, has tried unsuccessfully to improve it. The first words ὁ δὲ are out of construction; at the end appears ᾔρεῖτο, which is not required by the sense and introduces hiatus: hence it is rightly deleted by Ziegler.

20. 2. Τέχνων: cf. 5, 4. οὔπω δ' ἦν τῷ Δ. . . . ἐντετυχηκὼς . . . ἀλλὰ τὴν μορφὴν αὐτοῦ δοκῶν κατέχειν: "he had not yet met D. . . . but supposed . . ." The periphrasis (οὔπω) ἦν ἐντετυχηκὼς *emphasises the continuance* of the non-acquaintance of the two men up to the incident about to be recorded. Cf. Lysias I, 34: οἱ νόμοι οὐ μόνον ἀπεγνωκότες εἰσὶ μὴ ἀδικεῖν ἀλλὰ καὶ κεκελευκότες ταύτην τὴν δίκην λαμβάνειν. Demosth. 21, 104: ἐτόλμα λέγειν ὡς ἐγὼ τὸ πρᾶγμ' εἰμὶ τοῦτο δεδρακώς. (Goodwin, *Moods and Tenses*, p. 14.)

The pres. part. δοκῶν balances and points the contrast with ἐντυχηκώς. With ἦν δοκῶν = ἐδόκει, cf. *Them.* 29, 1, ἦν προσιών = προσῄει; *Mor.* 374 B, ὁρώμενόν ἐστιν = ὁρᾶται.

οὐλοκόμην: "a curly-headed man, sallow and beardless"; accusative in loose apposition to μορφήν and εἶδος.

20. 3. πρὸ τῆς πόλεως, πρὸ τοῦ καλουμένου Ὄρνιθος: in Paus. 2, 2, 4 Craneum is described as πρὸ τῆς πόλεως κυπαρίσσων ἄλσος. As Craneum was a place lying outside the city to the east, so Ornis probably lay outside the gates on the west. De Waele has identified it with the hill of Aetopetra (Eagle Rock), about forty-five minutes' walk from the Agora, near the point where roads from Sicyon to Corinth and from Cleonae to Corinth converge. The remarkable appearance of the hillock (see photograph in Theunissen *ad fin.*) and the modern name alike suggest that this is the spot mentioned by Plut. (De Waele, P.-W. Suppt., vol. vi, p. 200). On the "hiatus licitus," see App.

20. 4. συμβόλαιον: any form of connection or association, not necessarily commercial: cf. *Alex.* 30, τί γὰρ εὐπρεπὲς ἀνδρὶ νέῳ πρὸς ἐχθροῦ γυναῖκα συμβόλαιον;

20. 5. μήτε: see on ch. 10, 4.

21. 1. ἦγε πρὸς τὰς πύλας: see plan of Corinth at end of book. The regular road from Sicyon apparently entered Corinth at G S I on the plan, where a gate has actually been found. Pausanias describes the theatre (Th.) as situated on the road to Sicyon. Another road may have left Corinth for Sicyon at G S 2, where the remains of a tower have been discovered. It is plain that neither of these gates would have suited Aratus' purpose. The distance to be covered inside the city would have made surprise impossible. On the other hand a street from the gate G P would lead to the ordinary route to the summit. Proceeding by that ordinary route for some little distance, one may suppose, he reached the point where the ἐντομή turned off at an angle on the left and led to the weak point in the ring-wall of the citadel. G P may be identified with τὰς πύλας τὰς ἐπὶ Φλειοῦντα ἰόντι (Xen., *Hell.* vii, 1, 18-19), where the reference to Corinthians ἀναβάντες ἐπὶ τὰ μνήματα καὶ τὰ ὑπερέχοντα χωρία in order to resist the Thebans, suggests an irregular *terrain*.

παρὰ τὸ Ἡραῖον: *past the Heraeum*. No remains of a temple outside the walls have so far been discovered, but that such a temple existed as early as the sixth cent. appears from Hdt. 5, 92, where a Corinthian speaker tells the story of Periander's outrage upon the women of Corinth, whom as a preliminary he ordered ἐξιέναι ἐς τὸ Ἡραῖον.

[On Corinthian topography see P.-W. Suppt., vol. iv, p. 1004 (Byvanck); vi, 184-200 (De Waele); O'Neill, ch. 2; Theunissen, pp. 184-197.]

21. 2. ἦν τοῦ ἔτους ἡ περὶ θέρος ἀκμάζον ὥρα, τοῦ δὲ μηνὸς πανσέληνος. This passage, combined with Polyb. 2, 43, gives the date of the liberation of Corinth [see Beloch 4, 2, p. 225]. Polybius states that Corinth was taken in the year before the battle of the Aegatian Isles between Rome and Carthage, which was fought on a date = May 16, 241 (Eutrop. ii, 27), i.e., in the Olympian year 134, 3 (= July, 242–1). The year of the capture of Corinth is accordingly Ol. 134, 2 (= July, 243–2). Since the Achaean strategos year began in May, and Aratus, who held office every alternate year (ch. 24, 5), was strategos during a Nemean festival (ch. 28), and since the Nemean games were held in July in the uneven years B.C., it is to be inferred that he was strategos in 243–2 (May to May). As Corinth was taken in the midsummer period of the Olympian year corresponding to July, 243–242, and as in the summer of 242 Aratus was out of office, the capture must have taken place on or about one of the nights of full moon during the summer period of 243, the 25th of July or 24th of August.

21. 3. λαμβάνουσιν <οἱ> ... ἀντιλαμβανόμενοι. The change from past to present (ψόφον ποιοῦσι) shows that the sentence contains a general statement which requires a subject. Hence Schaefer inserts οἱ.

21. 4. ἀνασπάσας, the reading of Paris, 1673, whether due to conjecture or tradition, gives an obviously better sense than ἀναρπάσας given by G P R L.

διὰ τῆς πόλεως, i.e., between the gate and the point on the regular path to the summit where the ἐντομή branched off to the left. This point is conjectured by Theunissen to have been about 200 yards S. of the church of the Anargyroi. [See plan of Corinth.] The distance of this point from the gate would be about 500 yards.

21. 5. ἐν τῷ σκιαζομένῳ τῆς σελήνης = ἐν τῇ σκιᾷ τῆς σελήνης: cf. 23, 2 τῆς ψυχῆς τὸ γαυρούμενον καὶ χαῖρον. In 21, 2 "clouds rose from the sea and covered with shadow the city and the parts adjacent"; not till 22, 2 does the sky become clear again. Aratus' men can see the guard, because the guard carry a light. The scene of the encounter was the main path to the summit. In chapter 22, 1 Aratus has entered the ἐντομή, as the context shows. It is to be noted that in 18, 5 τὸ κρημνῶδες means not the ἐντομή but the regular path from which the ἐντομή branched off. The appellation is equally applicable to either.

21. 7. στενωποὶ (τόποι): τοὺς ὑπ' Ἀθηναίων καλουμένους στενωποὺς ἀγυιὰς ὀνομάζουσιν οἱ Ἡλεῖοι (Paus. 5, 15, 2).

22. I. "And meanwhile A. had thrown his energies into the march, and was struggling up the precipice path slowly and painfully at first, not winning his way, but wandering from the track." This path = Erginus' ἐντομή: cf. the words, περαίνοντος εἰς τὸ τεῖχος and those in 22, 2, ἕως ἥψατο τοῦ τείχους καθ' ὃν ἔδει τόπον.

With ἐμφὺς τῇ πορείᾳ cf. Themistocles' advice to the Athenians (Them. 9) to stick to their ships, ἐμφῦναι ταῖς ναυσίν. τοῦ τρίβου, more often fem., but cf. Eur. Or. 1251. περαίνοντος εἰς: for the constr. cf. Cato Maj. 13. τραχύτησι, projecting crags, as in Flam. 4.

22. 2. ὑπολάμπουσα: ὑπολαβοῦσα (MSS.) would mean "having withdrawn the clouds": cf. with Solanus Artax. 29, 5, τὴν αὐλαίαν ὑπολαβὼν ἀνεχώρησεν, but the aor. part. is hardly appropriate in collocation with the pres. διαστέλλουσα.

22. 3. τὸν αὐτὸν τρίβον, i.e. the ἐντομή. The second division of A.'s forces was already on the main path to the summit, for in 22, 5 Archelaus passes them on the way up; in 22, 7 Erginus descends from the summit to guide them.

Theunissen suggests the following hypothetical time-table for Aratus' expedition: departing from Sicyon at dark, and marching to Aetopetra (Ornis), and thence across country to the Phlius gate, he might have reached it at 1 a.m. (14 miles); leaving the gate at 2 a.m. he could reach the weak point in the ring-wall of the citadel at 4 a.m. At 5 a.m. the work was done.

22. 4. ἀλαλαγμὸς ἐναγώνιος: the din *of battle*, in this sense first in Polybius.

22. 9. καθυπέρτεροι = ἐγκρατεῖς. ἡμέρας <δ'> ἤδη διαυγούσης: Emperius' insertion enables the previous sentence to end at εἶχον and gives an improved sense.

23. 1. τὸ θέατρον: it lay about a furlong N.W. of the temple of Apollo. To reach it Aratus, descending by the main path, passed through the agora at its W. extremity. The Roman theatre of the restored city was built on the site of the fourth century structure known to Aratus. It has been calculated that the *Greek* theatre contained 36 rows of seats giving space for 20,000 spectators. The auditorium is built on a slope stretching from S. to N. The stage faced S., and when Aratus addressed the people, he had Acrocorinthus, the scene of his triumph, full in view.

23. 2. Was this description of Aratus, it has been asked, taken by Plut. from the *Memoirs*, or from some other source? It is natural to suppose that, writing at the close of his career, Aratus recalled with full details the occurrences of that glorious day. We may also presume that, like Caesar's *Commentaries* or Xenophon's *Anabasis*, the *Memoirs* of Aratus were written in the third person. Some heightening touches may have been added by Plut.

23. 3. ἐκχυθέντων ταῖς φιλοφροσύναις: *when the people had welcomed him with effusive demonstrations of goodwill.*

τὸ γόνυ καὶ τὸ σῶμα τῇ ῥοπῇ μικρὸν ἐγκλίνας καὶ ἀπερεισάμενος εἱστήκει: Perrin's version, "slightly inclining his knee and his body he supported himself upon it (the spear) and stood . . .," conveniently omits any explicit rendering of τῇ ῥοπῇ! The word ῥοπή can mean a small weight inserted in a scale-pan to produce equilibrium. Examples: Herodotus Med. (a contemporary of Plut.) 7, 33, οὐδ' ὅσον ῥοπή; LXX *Isaiah* 40, 15, ὡς ῥοπὴ ζυγοῦ ἐλογίσθησαν, where the English version has "as dust in the balance"; IG. ii² 1013. 35, τὸ πεντάμνουν τὸ ἐμπορικὸν ἐχέτω ῥοπὴν ἐμπορικὴν μνᾶν ὅπως ἰσορρόπου τοῦ πήχεως γενομένου ἄγῃ ἐμπορικὰς μνᾶς ἕξ. Metaphorically we find the same use in Polyb. 16, 14, 6, δεῖ ῥοπὰς διδόναι ταῖς αὐτῶν πατρίσι τοὺς συγγραφέας, where L. and S. transl. "give the casting-weight." Cf. Plut. *Artax.* 30; ἦν ἐπὶ ῥοπῆς μικρᾶς ὁ Ἀ. διὰ τὸ γῆρας.

In the present passage τῇ ῥοπῇ seems to mean *casting-weight, make-weight*, and to be a metaphorical synonym for τὸ δόρυ, the point of the comparison being that, as a make-weight preserves the equilibrium of a scale, so the spear enabled the tired Aratus to maintain his balance, as he stood to address the audience. Tr., "when he had rested and supported knee and body upon the make-weight he stood a long time silent."

23. 4. ἀπὸ τῶν Φιλιππικῶν καιρῶν: this passage is our sole authority for the occupation of Acrocorinthus by Philip II of Macedon.

23. 5. Περσαῖος is stated in *Ind. Stoic. Herc.*, col. xv, followed by Paus, 2, 8, 4; 7, 5, 3, to have perished in the fighting; but Plutarch's account based on the *Memoirs* is obviously preferable.

24. Source, the *Memoirs*, except sects. 2 and 6, which contain reflections of Plutarch.

E

24. 1. Ἡραῖον, not, it would seem, the temple outside the Phlius gate, but that of Hera Acraea in the Peraea (mod. Perachora), situated on a promontory in the Corinthian Gulf (Theunissen).

24. 4. Πτολεμαῖον: he allowed Aratus a pension of six talents per annum (ch. 41, 5), but about 225 B.C. transferred his patronage to Cleomenes (Polyb. 2, 51).

24. 5. εἰ μὴ κατ᾽ ἐνιαυτὸν ἐξῆν: see *Intro.*, sect. 7, note 9.

24. 6. συμπνέοντα, metaphorically as often, "working in harmony with …": Polyb. 30, 2 συμπνεύσαντες καὶ μιᾷ γνώμῃ χρώμενοι.

25. Source, the *Memoirs*, except sects. 5–6, which are probably derived from Deinias.

25. 1. τοὺς ἀρίστους τῶν προσοίκων: Sparta, Messenia, Elis, and Arcadian cities not included in the dominions of the tyrant Lydiades.

25. 2. Aeschylus and Charimenes are otherwise unknown.

25. 3. <ἄδοξον>: Richards first saw that some word had fallen out here, but his <ἄλλον> does not suggest why the action gave such offence to Aeschylus. <ἄδοξον> might have fallen out after πρᾶξιν: Kronenberg, *Mnemosyne*, 1933–4, p. 172, proposed ἀνάξιον. In ἄνθρωπος)(ἀνήρ there is, as usual, a note of contempt, while in 44, 6 its use implies pity.

καταγνόντες, "having *blamed* C." as in Plato, *Demod.* 382 E.

25. 4. ἀποθνήσκει Ἀριστόμαχος, B.C. 241–0.

Ἀρίστιππος: the connection of these persons (suggested by Thirlwall) as set out below is generally accepted:

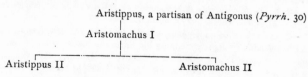

Aristippus, a partisan of Antigonus (*Pyrrh.* 30)

Aristomachus I

Aristippus II   Aristomachus II

25. 5. Ἀράτου μὴ παρόντος: for the use of μή see on 10, 4. Aratus was absent doubtless because out of office: hence the date may be presumed to be 240-239.

ἐτιμήθη: if we understand Ἄρατος as subj. we are involved in the absurdity that the Achaeans were prosecuted but Aratus fined. *Sc.* ἡ δίκη and transl. "the penalty was assessed at 30 minae," and cf. Antiphon 145, 4: καὶ ἐγὼ τοὺς ταῦτα μηχανωμένους εἰσάγων εἰς τὸ δικαστήριον εἷλον ἅπαντας, καὶ ἐτιμήθη αὐτοῖς ὧν ἐπίστασθε (the penalty was assessed for them at the amount known to you). The 30 minae presumably represented nominal damages.

25. 6. αὐτὸν: the pron. would be meaningless if in the previous sentence Ἄρατος is subj. to ἐτιμήθη. There is a contrast indicated between the Achaeans against whom Aristippus won his case, and Aratus whom he planned to assassinate.

Ἀντιγόνου: A. died in spring 240 B.C.

26. This ch. has nothing to do with Aratus, but treats of Aristippus of Argos, and probably comes from Deinias' *Argolica*. Plut. tells the same story in Mor. 781 E. of "Aristodemus," substituted for Aristippus by a lapse of memory: Ἀριστόδημος ὁ Ἀργεῖος εἰς ὑπερῷον οἴκημα (ἐνδυόμενος) θύραν ἔχον ἐπιρρακτήν …

26. 1. παρεμβάλλειν, bivouac.

26. 2. καταρρακτῇ (sc. θύρᾳ) from κατα-ρρακτός verbal of κατα-ρράσσω : cf. ἐπιρρακτήν in the passage just cited. In 26, 5 τοὺς καταρράκτας is from the noun καταρράκτης. Tr. in each case *trap-door*.

26. 4. τῶν πώποτε τυράννων, of all the tyrants that ever were, but the context limits the reference to *contemporaries*. In Attic the idiom with πώποτε occurs only (1) after a neg., (2) in a rhetorical question, (3) after εἰ. οὓς in Plato, *Rep.* 352 c = εἴ τινας.

27. Principal source, the *Memoirs* : Deinias may also have been consulted. Date, 235 or possibly 237.

28. 5. τὸν ἀγῶνα τῶν Νεμείων ἤγαγεν ἐν Κλεωναῖς : That the Nemean games for some 300 years were held by the folk of Cleonae under Argive patronage, but that shortly before 235 (the date of Cleonae's entry into the League) the festival had been transferred to Argos, appears from the following evidence :—

The festival began in 573 : its institution seems to be connected with the revolt of Cleonae from Sicyon, then under the tyrant Cleisthenes (Bury, Pindar, *Nemean Odes*, app., p. 250). But a festival of such importance could not have been managed by Cleonae unaided ; so small a city must have had behind her the resources of a stronger power, and that power can only have been Argos. This hypothesis of Bury's is indirectly confirmed by Eusebius' statement that the Argives "usurped" the conduct of the games in the 53rd Olympiad (567 B.C.). Actually, the games were administered by Cleonae under Argive patronage : cf. Pindar's reference (*Nem.* 4) to the Κλεωναῖος ἀγών and to Theaeus *of Argos* (*Nem.* 10) "receiving prizes from the men of Cleonae."

The Nemean festival was still held in Nemea in the year 323–2, for the Athenian ἀρχεθέωρος of that year had a Cleonaean proxenos ; and even as late as 310, for Apollonides, Cassander's general, returned to Macedon, παρελθὼν εἰς τὴν Ἀργείαν (not Ἄργος) καὶ θεὶς τὸν τῶν Νεμείων ἀγῶνα (Diod. 19, 64).

Not long afterwards, however, the Nemean games were transferred to Argos. [Vollgraff, *Mnemosyne* xliv, 1916 : Boethius, *Argiv. Kalender*, p. 58.] An inscription published by Vollgraff mentions Ἑλλανοδίκας τῶν Νεμέων καὶ Ἡραίων, and the ἀγών τῶν Ἡραίων καὶ Νεμέων. The Heraea was the pre-eminent *Argive* festival. The decree, which the form of the letters shows to belong to the third cent., refers to friendly relations between Argos and Corinth, which, however, must have been independent of one another at the time as there is no mention of an Achaean strategos. Hence the decree is to be dated before 243, for from 243 to 229 (when Argos entered the League) relations between Argos and Corinth were unfriendly.

The festival was now restored to Cleonae, but after 229, when Argos joined the League, it was once more transferred thither (cf. *Cleom.* 17).

ἐν Κλεωναῖς, i.e., in the Nemean valley four miles from the town (Boëthius, *op. cit.*, p. 4). Cf. the form of expression in *Cleom.* 14, 4 : στρατοπεδευσαμένων (τῶν Ἀχαιῶν) ἐν Δύμαις περὶ τὸ Ἑκατόμβαιον, although in the next sentence we learn that Cleomenes planted his army "*between* the city of Dyme and the Achaean army." Both ἐν Κλεωναῖς and ἐν Δύμαις mean in the territory of Cleonae and Dyme respectively.

29. For the first four sections the *Memoirs* are the obvious source. In sect. 5 Deinias is cited. Sections 7–8 are derived from a source or sources unsympathetic to Aratus.

29. 2. ὡς αὐτοῦ μὴ παρόντος : For gen. abs. where nom. would be regular cf. Xen., *Cyr.* 6, 1, 37.

29. 4. κατεῖχον, *pressed hard.* For this meaning Xen., *Cyr.* 6, 22, κατέχοντα κυνοδρομεῖν is cited, and *Cyr.* 1, 4, 22: τὴν φυγὴν τοῖς πολεμίοις ἰσχυρῶς κατέχων ἐποίει, if this is the true reading of the passage. **ἐκτροπάς**: here "bypaths" like the σκολιαὶ ἐκτροπαί of Diod. 3, 15, 26.

29. 5–8. This passage is one of the two extracts from the *Aratus* made by the patriarch Photius (*Bibliotheca*, p. 398). Photius' text differs from that of our MSS. by one omission, two additions, the reading Ἅγιν for Ἀγίαν in sect. 6, and a remarkable variation in the last clause of sect. 8, giving a text obviously inferior to ours. Ziegler is plainly right in accepting the additions found in Photius and rejecting the other variants.

29. 5. ἄχρι Μυκηνῶν: Mycenae lies slightly to the east of the road from Argos to Cleonae, being about 10 miles distant from each. Pausanias (2, 15, 2) states that "there are two roads from Cleonae to Argos. One, a short cut, is a mere footpath; the other lies over the pass of the Tretus, as it is called. Like the former, it is a narrow pass enclosed on all sides by mountains, but better adapted for driving."

29. 6. Agias was evidently the Macedonian commander.

29. 7. παρείλετο, sc. Ἄρατος.

κάρος, *torpor, drowsiness*, cf. *Ant.* 71, κάρον ὑπνώδη καὶ καταφοράν (heaviness); and in Galen, vol. ix, p. 196 (κάρος) κυρίως λέγεται ἡ παντὸς τοῦ σώματος αἰφνίδιος ἀναισθησία καὶ ἀκινησία.

30: Source, the *Memoirs*, except for sects. 2–3, which may represent Plutarch's impression of Lydiades after reading both Aratus and Phylarchus. Date 235.

30. 2. ῥυείς: *having been drawn into* this wrong-doing: so Plato, *Rep.* 495 B, οἱ μέγιστα κακὰ ἐργαζόμενοι καὶ οἱ τἀγαθά, οἳ ἂν ταύτῃ τύχωσι ῥυέντες.

ἅμα δὲ ζηλῶν ... καὶ δεδοικὼς τὸν Ἀ: Polyb. 2, 43, gives his reason in the words πάνυ πραγματικῶς καὶ φρονίμως προϊδόμενος τὸ μέλλον.

30. 4. στρατηγὸν εἵλοντο: B.C. 234–3.

30. 5. παρήγγελλεν στρατείαν: conative impf.: to declare war was the prerogative of a syncletos.

30. 6. ὡς εἴρηται, ch. 24, 5. **ᾑρέθη, ἀντιπρ.**: on the hiatus see App.

30. 7. κατηγορήσας, e.g., after Aristomachus in 228, at Aratus' instigation had declined battle at Pallantium, ch. 35, 7.

30. 8. The fable told how the hawk changed into a cuckoo and would become a hawk again. But the strange thing is that it was held by some among the Greeks as a fact in Natural History that cuckoos had been hawks earlier in the year. Dr. R. M. Henry has referred me to Arist., *Hist. Anim.* vi, 7, 563, B: ὁ δὲ κόκκυξ λέγεται μὲν ὑπό τινῶν ὡς μεταβάλλει ἐξ ἱέρακος διὰ τὸ ἀφανίζεσθαι τὸν ἱέρακα περὶ τοῦτον τὸν χρόνον ᾧ ὅμοιός ἐστιν· σχεδὸν δὲ καὶ τοὺς ἄλλους ἱέρακας οὐκ ἔστιν ἰδεῖν ὅτε θᾶττον φθέγγεται ὁ κόκκυξ πλὴν ὀλίγας ἡμέρας. ὁ δὲ κόκκυξ φαίνεται ἐπ' ὀλίγον χρόνον τοῦ θέρους τὸν δὲ χειμῶνα ἀφανίζεται. [See also Thompson, *Glossary of Greek Birds*, p. 88.]

ὑποψία βλάπτουσα τὴν πίστιν (MSS. φύσιν) **αὐτοῦ τῆς μεταβολῆς**: "suspicion spoiling men's confidence in his change." Perrin retains the reading φύσιν and translates: "a suspicion that did injustice to his real nature that he would change again"; but βλάπτουσα φύσιν cannot mean "doing injustice to his nature," and there is no word in the Greek answering to Perrin's "again."

We might, however, extract from the passage as given in the MSS. the meaning:—*suspicion seems to have attached to him, disabling his nature from changing.* But (1) if this means that L. feeling himself suspected remained at heart a tyrant, it is obviously not the idea which Plut. intends to convey ; and (2) the genitive after βλάπτω, though found in Homer, Tyrtaeus, and the imitative poets Nicander and Quintus Smyrnaeus, occurs but once in Attic, and then in a lyric passage, Aesch. *Agam.* 123, where hares in flight are described as βλαβέντα λοισθίων δρόμων.

Hence I think the anonymous scholar was right in his inference that φύσιν is nothing but a copyist's error for πίστιν.

31-32. Plutarch's account of the Aetolian incident is drawn from some other authority beside the *Memoirs.* This is almost certainly the *History* of Phylarchus, who liked the dramatic and marvellous and is fond of references to women. We find traces of Phylarchus in 31, 2 (taunts levelled at Aratus for cowardice). From 31, 4 to 32, 4 the whole narrative suggests that he was the authority. 32, 6 may come from Polemon (cf. 13, 2). The date of the Aetolian episode was early summer of 241 (*Intro.*, p. l).

Schulz has inferred that the Aetolians had separated into two divisions, one engaged in the sack of Pellene, the other, a smaller body, operating outside the walls. This latter was attacked by Aratus and fled into the town followed by the Achaeans. (For the story as told in Polyaen. 8, 59, see note on ch. 32.)

31. 1. On Agis' march to the isthmus, see *Ag.* 13 and 15. That we should read ἀφικομένου (Paris. 1673), not ἀφικνουμένου, is confirmed by the account in *Ag.* 15: συμμείξας δὲ τῷ 'Αράτῳ περὶ Κόρινθον ὁ Ἄγις ἔτι βουλευομένῳ . . . ἐπεδείξατο πολλὴν προθυμίαν . . . ἔφη γὰρ αὐτῷ μὲν δοκεῖν διαμάχεσθαι . . . ποιήσειν δὲ τὸ δοκοῦν 'Αράτῳ.

Aratus, however, preferred to let the Aetolians enter Peloponnesus, τοὺς καρποὺς σχεδὸν ἅπαντας συγκεκομισμένων ἤδη τῶν γεωργῶν. So he dismissed the Spartans with compliments.

31. 2. τὴν Γεράνειαν (Crane Mts.), between the Megarid and the Corinthia : cf. 31, 1, πρὸ τῆς Μεγαρικῆς. ἔμελλε, hesitated.

31. 5. πρὶν ἤ : an Ionic constr. common in post-classical Greek ; very rare in Att., but cf. the inscr. of B.C. 418, cited in Meisterhans *Gramm. Inschr.* 210, 13.

32. Frazer on Paus. 7, 27, 1 corrects his author's account of Pellene : " The summit of the mountain is neither rocky nor precipitous. It forms a sort of ridge which extends N. and S., sloping away in shelving plateaus both to E. and W. The ancient city would seem to have been clustered on both these slopes, and this is apparently what Pausanias means by saying that the city was divided into two parts by the peak which rises between them."

On this ridge we must place the temple of Artemis (cf. 32, 2, κατέβλεψε). Pausanias speaks (1) of a grove of Artemis above the temple of Athena and (2) of a temple of Artemis near the sanctuary of Apollo. The temple, we must suppose, was in or near the grove.

In Polyaen. 8, 59 the story of Epigethes' daughter appears in a different setting : " In front of Pellene is *a high hill opposite the acropolis*, on which the Pellenaeans had gathered and were arming. A priestess of Athena, *wearing a panoply that day according to custom* . . . looked across at the crowd of arming citizens . . . The Aetolians, thinking that Athena herself had appeared . . ., turned and fled."

Polyaenus' account is obviously very inferior to Plutarch's : (1) the topography is wrong, (2) the presence of the Aetolians in the city is ignored, (3) the scene is transferred from Artemis' to Athena's temple (Athena being normally the *pano-plied* goddess), and the daughter of Epigethes becomes Athena's priestess ; but from Paus. we know that the temple of Athena was *below* that of Artemis. Evidently the tale in Polyaenus is based on a blurred popular tradition.

Thus we have three accounts, that of 32, 1-2 (either from Phylarchus or the *Memoirs*) ; 32, 3-4 "what the Pellenaeans say," a mere miracle story doubtless from Phylarchus ; and the story in Polyaenus.

32. 1. ἐπιλεκτάρχης: "commander of a picked corps." The word is ἅπαξ εἰρημένον. It was evidently an Aetolian title: cf. Syll³ 421A, where ἐπιλεκταρ-χεόντων occurs in an Aetolian list of official titles (*c.* 272 B C.).

32. 3. ἀπαμβλίσκειν: *cast their untimely fruit*; the aor. ἀπήμβλωσε, "miscarried," occurs in *Pompey*, 53.

32. 6. On **Τιμάνθης**, see 12, 3, n.

ἐποίησεν ἐμφαντικῶς τὴν μάχην ἔχουσαν: "composed a vivid picture of the battle." The suggestion of Madvig to insert γραφήν before ἐποίησεν ("made of the battle a picture vividly composed ") is unnecessary. One could write, whether of a painter or a poet, such a sentence as Τιτανομαχίαν ἐποίησε, and add the words, τῇ διαθέσει ἐμπεφανισμένην : in the present passage the pf. part. is represented by ἐμφαντικῶς ἔχουσαν.

33. The facts are from the *Memoirs*, the criticism probably from Phylarchus.

33. 1. πολλῶν ἐθνῶν καὶ δυναστῶν: referring probably to the Aetolians and their Elean allies, and any Arcadian states which joined them on the break-up of the Arcadian League ; also the tyrants of Megalopolis, Argos, Hermione, Phlius, and Orchomenos.

Πανταλέοντι: Aetolian strategos in 238-7 (Mitylenean inscr. cited by Pomtow, P.-W, *Delphi*), and on several occasions afterwards (Pomtow, in Syll³ 522). **συμμαχίαν**: after the death of Gonatas—Spring 240.

33. 2-5. The criticisms are probably taken from Phylarchus. Note the simile ὥσπερ οἱ δυσέρωτες, as in his manner (Schulz).

33. 2. σπουδάς, B.C. 241-240.

33. 5. παρὰ μικρὸν ἀεὶ καὶ σύνεγγυς: "because he failed *just by a hair's breadth.*" σύνεγγυς = *vix* is unusual, elsewhere = *prope*.

Θριασίου (πεδίου), stretching N.E. of Eleusis, crossed by the road leading to Megara and on to the isthmus.

In general, cf. *Cleom.* 16, 5 : πολλὰ παθεῖν καὶ παραβαλέσθαι φησὶν αὐτὸς ὑπὲρ Ἀθηναίων ὅπως ἡ πόλις ἀπαλλαγείη φρουρᾶς καὶ Μακεδόνων.

34-35. Source, the *Memoirs*.

34. 2. Φυλακίαν: this name occurs here only and is generally held to stand for Phylace. Beloch, 4, 2, p. 529, rules out the Thessalian Phylace, and identifies the place with the Arcadian Phylace, "on the road between Tegea and Sparta, near *mod.* Kryavrysi," (Frazer on Paus. 8, 54, 2). The most probable date for the battle is 233. Two years previously Megalopolis was lost to the Macedonian connection. Walbank (p. 65) thinks the purpose of Bithys was to encourage the war party in Sparta to join in the struggle against the Leagues. We may recall that Lydiades wanted to fight Sparta in 234 (29, 5). But co-operation with Macedon and an Argive tyrant would have been contrary to Spartan tradition.

Βίθυς. In Athen. xiv, 3, p. 614, Phylarchus is cited for the story that Demetrius the Besieger once observed, "Lysimachus' court is just like the stage in a comedy; every one that comes out of it has a dissyllabic name (τόν τε Βίθυν χλευάζων καὶ τὸν Πάριν, μεγίστους ὄντας παρὰ τῷ Λυσιμάχῳ καί τινας ἑτέρους τῶν φίλων), while from my court come names like Peucestes, Menelaus, aye and Oxythemis!" This Bithys was probably grandfather of Plutarch's Bithys, for in *Syll.*³ 476, where Attic citizenship and other honours are conferred upon Demetrius' general, he is called Bithys of Lysimacheia.

Διογένης, Macedonian commander at Piraeus, which had apparently passed from Athens to Antigonus Gonatas c. 271 : see *Intro.*, p. xxi, note 2. In 229-8 he surrendered the fortress to the Athenians. Beloch (4, 2, p. 456) produces some evidence to show that he, like his predecessor Heraclitus of Athmonon, was an Athenian citizen. After his death he received heroic honours from the Athenians, and his priest was given a seat in the theatre in the fourth row behind that of the priest of Dionysus; it still bears the name Διογένους Εὐεργέτου.

ἐπειδή<περ>"Ἀρατος : the MSS. reading involves hiatus. The letters περ may well have fallen out before the first syllable of Ἀρατος. Benseler proposed to correct ἐπειδή to ἐπεί γ', a less obvious correction. For the irregular mood ἀπέθανεν, see note on 18, 7.

34. 3. διατρίβην, "amusement," as in *Timol.* 11. **ναῦν ἔπεμψεν :** hence Beloch argues that Plutarch's Phylacia was not the Thessalian Phylace.

34. 4. κολακείᾳ τῇ πρὸς . . . The MSS. read πᾶσαν δ' Ἀ. κουφότητα κολακείας τῆς πρὸς Μ. ὑπερβάλλοντες, which could mean only "the Athenians surpassing every frivolity of (i.e. characteristic of) their (previous) flattery towards Macedon . . ." But, as Madvig saw, what Plut. means is that on this occasion their flattery passed beyond the bounds of levity.

34. 4. Ἀκαδημείας : "Popular tradition gives this name to a place about ¾ mile N.W. of the Dipylon gate. The exact spot is a little S. of the rocky knoll on which are the graves of Lenormant and K. O. Müller, and which has been identified as the famous Colonus Hippios." Frazer on Paus. 1, 30, 4.

34. 5. πεισθείς, presumably by the Athenian magistrates. **Δημητρίου τελευτήσαντος,** towards the end of 230 (Dinsmoor).

34. 6. ἑτέρου ἄρχοντος, Lydiades strategos for 230–229 [Walbank, p. 189]. But Aratus was at Athens also in the early summer of 228, to clear off the financial business.

34. 7. Αἰγινήται. The island had been under Diogenes; being included among ἄλλα τὰ ταττόμενα μετὰ τοῦ Πειραιέως (IG. ii², 1, 1225)—Beloch 4, 1, 660 n. Ἑρμιονεῖς, the tyrant Xenon abdicated (Polyb. 2, 44). Μακεδόνων ἀσχόλων ὄντων : in their conflict with the Dardanians (c. 232-228 B.C.) ἡ πλείστη τῆς Ἀρκαδίας, i.e., all except Mantinea, Tegea, Orchomenos (*Cleom.* 3, 8). Caphyae probably ranked as a subject-district of Orchomenos.

35. 1. τὴν παλαιὰν ὑπόθεσιν. For the "old design" see ch. 25, 1. Beloch 4, 1, 640 n., however, takes it to mean that while A. was engaged on the liberation of *Athens* he sent to Aristomachus at Argos; thus the liberation of the two cities went on *pari passu*; which is more ingenious than convincing.

35. 2. διαλύσηται, satisfy, i.e., *pay off.* So in Demosth. 49, 29, διαλύεσθαι τὸν ναύκληρον.

35. 4. σύνεδροι, members of the council, σύνοδος, for which see *Intro.*, sect. 7.

35. 5. **Φλιασίους**: Cleonymus resigned the tyranny (Polyb. 2, 44).

ἐνιαυτῷ ὕστερον. The entry of Argos is treated as having taken place at the beginning of Aratus' strategia of 229–8. Aristomachus was elected strategos for 228-7.

35. 6. **βουλόμενος εἰς τὴν Λακωνικὴν ἐμβαλεῖν**: On the preliminaries of the Cleomenic war, see *Intro.*, p. lxv. [**καὶ**]: the clauses ἔγραφε τὴν στρατείαν ἀπαγορεύων and τῷ Κλεομένει . . . μὴ βουλόμενος are not co-ordinate, for the second gives the reason for the first.

παραβόλως: *in a dangerous manner*; cf. Polyb. 2, 47, Κλεομένους χρωμένου τῷ πολέμῳ παραβόλως: in these passages the danger was to Cleomenes' enemies, whereas in ch. 27 and *Cleom.* 25, τὸ ἐγχείρημα ἔδοξε τετολμῆσθαι παραβόλως καὶ μανικῶς, the danger was to the agent himself.

35. 7. **ὅτε δὴ**, "on which occasion"; like the simple ὅτε, often in Plut. at beginning of sentences or clauses where Attic prose would require τότε : also in Polyb., e.g., 30, 4, 6, ἐποιεῖτο τοὺς λόγους πρῶτον μὲν Φιλόφρων, μετὰ δὲ τοῦτον Αὐτομήδης· ὅτε δὴ ἔλαβον ἀποκρίσεις (Holden).

Παλλάντιον: "its position between Tegea and Megalopolis rules out Argos as a starting-point. An expedition from Megalopolis (the other alternative) against Laconia has the choice of two routes : (1) the direct road past Belbina, (2) by Asea and Kryavrysi and so by the Tegea road to Sparta. Since Pallantion lies on neither, there is reason to think that Aratus had persuaded Aristomachos to substitute a raid on the Arcadian corridor for the projected Laconian invasion," Walbank, p. 78. On the meeting of the armies Plutarch writes, *Cleom.* 4, 9: ἀπαντήσαντος δὲ περὶ Παλλάντιον Κλεομένους καὶ βουλομένου μάχεσθαι, φοβηθεὶς τὴν τόλμαν δ᾽ Ἄρατος οὐκ εἴασε διακινδυνεῦσαι τὸν στρατηγὸν ἀλλ᾽ ἀπῆλθε λοιδορούμενος μὲν ὑπὸ τῶν Ἀχαιῶν χλευαζόμενος δὲ καὶ καταφρονούμενος ὑπὸ τῶν Λακεδαιμονίων οὐδὲ πεντακισχιλίων τὸ πλῆθος ὄντων. The last sentence reveals Phylarchus whom Plut. evidently ignored when writing our present chapter.

χειροτονίᾳ. On the archairesiai, see *Intro.*, sect. 7.

δωδέκατον. The election was for 227-6. If Aratus was elected first in 245 (ch. 16, 1 n.) and eligible for re-election only every second year (ch. 24, 5), it follows that he was now elected not for the twelfth but the tenth time. Somebody —either Plut. or one of the innumerable scribes through whom his work has reached us—has blundered.

36. 1–3. These sections show no trace of any source except the *Memoirs*. *Cleom.* 5, 1 gives the main facts, the only differences being the emphasis on the magnitude of the Achaean defeat (ἅπαν μὲν (Κλεομένης) ἐτρέψατο καὶ διεπτόησεν αὐτῶν τὸ στράτευμα συχνοὺς δ᾽ ἀνεῖλε καὶ ζῶντας ἔλαβεν) and the omission (as irrelevant in a life of Cleomenes) of references to changes made by Aratus in the constitution of Mantinea.

On the other hand sections 4 and 5 impute motives of a self-regarding kind to Aratus for his refusal to engage his main body in the skirmish at Ladoceia, near Megalopolis. These criticisms are wanting in *Cleom.*, again, doubtless, as being irrelevant. Probably Phylarchus has been consulted.

On the events narrated in chapters 36–38, 1, see *Intro.*, p. lxvii.

36. 1. **Λύκαιον**, a mountain near the Elean frontier, about 20 miles N.W. of Megalopolis.

36. 3. Plut. records that after taking the town Aratus (1) introduced a garrison. (2) conferred the franchise on the μέτοικοι, and (3) acquired for the

τὸ τοῦ Ἀπόλλωνος ἱερόν : Paus. 2, 3, 5 has : ἐκ τῆς ἀγορᾶς τὴν ἐπὶ Σικυῶνα (ὁδόν) ἐρχομένοις ἔστιν ἰδεῖν ἐν δεξίᾳ ναὸν καὶ ἄγαλμα χαλκοῦν Ἀπόλλωνος. In 1896, when archaeologists of the American School at Athens discovered the site of the agora, it became possible to identify with the temple of Apollo the seven Doric columns which were the last remnant of ancient Corinth above ground. This sixth cent. temple was built on a hillock formed by an outcrop of rock rising to a height of from 20 to 40 ft. above the ground close by. In Aratus' time *this hillock was bounded W. by the Sicyon road, S. by the agora,* E. by the Lechaeum road. Seen from the agora the temple showed a line of fifteen columns surmounted by a sloping roof whose gable rose some 60 ft. above the spectator. The temple contained two main chambers, the western about 32. ft. square, the eastern about 52 × 32. The smaller contained the cult-statue. The foundation of the base has been found. [B. Powell, A. J. A. (1905), incorporating and correcting Dörpfeld's researches made in 1886. See the plan of Corinth.]

40. 4. περὶ θύρας : "bij de ingangen tot het tempelgebied" (Theunissen, p. 196) ; but θύραι must mean the *doors of a building* unless the context makes it clear that the word is a substitute for πύλαι. The natural explanation is that the partisans of Cleomenes thronged to the temple nominally for a conference with Aratus, actually to secure his person. In the Eastern, the larger of the two chambers, there might have been room for 800. The remainder gathered outside, and Aratus would have been effectually trapped had he not succeeded in making himself scarce at an early stage in the proceedings.

40. 5. Ἀπολλώνιον is the form found in all MSS. and is unobjectionable : see L. and S.

ὡς ἔλαθε πλήσιον τῆς ἄκρας γενόμενος : Aratus' route to the citadel was as follows : proceeding to the W. side of the temple hill he descended the slope leading to the Sicyon road, on reaching which he turned left, and so entered the agora at its N.W. corner to emerge at the S.W. corner, whence he took the ordinary route to the summit of Acrocorinthus. Descending by the same route he turned left when he reached the road leading to the Phlius gate, thus avoiding the city proper. The decree commanding "Aratus and the Achaeans to withdraw from the city" (Polyb. 2, 52) was subsequently passed by a regularly constituted assembly. From *Cleom.* 19 we learn that Aratus was in Corinth, ποιούμενός τινα τῶν λεγομένων λακωνίζειν ἐξέτασιν, when the news of Cleomenes' capture of Argos reached him, whereupon, διαταραχθεὶς καὶ τὴν πόλιν πρὸς τὸν Κλ. ἀποκλίνουσαν αἰσθόμενος, he himself summoned the citizens to the senate-house ; but instead of attending the meeting he slipped away to the gate, where his horse was brought to him, and so off to Sicyon. This must be Phylarchus' account, derived from hearsay. But though Plut. in *Cleom.* did not trouble to consult the *Memoirs* for this incident, he cites them (*Ibid.* 19) for what happened in Corinth *after Aratus had left!*

40. 6. μετεπέμψαντο τὸν Κ. καὶ παρέδοσαν τὴν πόλιν : in the second half of the sentence the omission of αὐτῷ is regular, since παρέδοσαν τὴν πόλιν relates to τὸν Κλεομένη in the former clause and there is no emphasis (Kühner-Gerth ii, p. 502). Less usual is it to find a participle (οὐδὲν οἰομένῳ) depending on the unexpressed pronoun.

In *Cleom.* 19, 4, Plut. adds : τῶν δὲ Κορινθίων ἁμιλλωμένων εἰς Ἄργος πρὸς τὸν Κλ. φησὶν ὁ Ἄρατος τοὺς ἵππους πάντας ῥαγῆναι, τὸν δὲ Κλ. μέμφεσθαι τοὺς Κορινθίους μὴ συλλαβόντας αὐτὸν ἀλλ' ἐάσαντας διαφυγεῖν.

διήμαρτεν ἀφέντων: the reading of the Aldine. The MSS. have διήμαρτον followed in PRL by ἀφέντων, in G. by ἀφέντες τὸν. If we suppose that the original reading was διήμαρτεν ἀφέντων and that διήμαρτεν became διήμαρτον, the alteration of ἀφέντων to ἀφέντες τὸν would readily be made by a careful copyist. Also, it is more natural that Cl. should compare what he himself had gained (Corinth) with what he had lost (Aratus), rather than with what the Corinthians had lost.

40. 7. περιετείχιζε: cf. *Cleom.* 19, 7, τὴν ἄκραν περιεχαράκωσε; but, as we learn from *Cleom.*, before this was done, the cities of the Acte had gone over to Cl. Before the king arrived at Corinth, he sent Megistonous as an envoy to Aratus: for this information the authority of the *Memoirs* is expressly claimed. In *Arat.* 41, 5, M.'s embassy is referred to out of its proper order.

41-44. 5. Critics are agreed in attributing the origin of these chapters to the *Memoirs*.

41. 1. οὐ πολλοί: the title οἱ πολλοί is regularly given in Polybius to the Achaean Syncletos. It is more likely that οὐ πολλοί (G L) was misread by the copyists of P R than vice versa.

στρατηγὸς αὐτοκράτωρ: the powers of the office may be illustrated by the account (Polyb. 38, 11) of the decree passed at the instance of Critolaus in B.C. 147-6: ὥστε κυρίους εἶναι τοὺς ἀνθρώπους οὓς ἐπὶ στρατηγίαν αἱρήσονται· διὸ τρόπον τινὰ μοναρχικὴν ἀνέλαβεν ἐξουσίαν.

41. 2. τριάκοντα ἔτη καὶ τρία πεπολιτευμένος ἐν τοῖς Ἀχαιοῖς: in *Cleom.* 16, 2, referring to the time of the abortive conference between the Achaeans and Cleomenes, Plut. uses similar words of Aratus, ἔτη τρία καὶ τριάκοντα πρωτευόντος αὐτοῦ. These figures are certainly wrong. As Freeman remarks: "The only marked period of 33 years in the life of Aratus is that between his first Generalship in 245 and his death in 213; this is probably what Plutarch was thinking of." Strangely enough Freeman catches out Fynes-Clinton (iii, 36) in a similar confusion.

41 3. οἱ περὶ Εὐρυκλείδην καὶ Μικίωνα: for the idiom οἱ περί see on 3, 4. In our extant literature there are only two references beside the present passage to the brothers. Polyb. 5, 106 states that after the establishment of their liberty, the Athenians under the leadership of E. and M. took no part in Hellenic affairs, but in accordance with their policy and aims, εἰς πάντας τοὺς βασιλεῖς ἐξεκέχυντο καὶ μάλιστα τούτων εἰς Πτολεμαῖον. Paus. ii, 9, 4, refers to them as ῥήτορας καὶ οὐκ ἀπιθάνους τῷ δήμῳ, who were poisoned by Philip V of Macedon. But inscriptions reveal that for some time before, and for nearly a generation after Athens regained her freedom, they guided the policy of the state. Their death probably occurred in 203, but the story of the poisoning is unsubstantiated. Their policy, although naturally it found no favour with either Aratus or Polybius, gave Athens peace and comparative prosperity for a quarter of a century. About the time of the Cleomenic war the Athenians instituted a new tribe, Ptolemais, in honour of Euergetes, and as the king in 226-5 had transferred his patronage and pension from Aratus to Cleomenes, Athens had all the more reason for refusing help to the Achaeans.

41. 5. Τρίπυλον is almost certainly a corruption of Τριτύμαλλον (*Cleom.* 19, 8) reduced by a copyist to Τρίτυλον, and then "emended" into something intelligible. It is clear from the citation of the *Memoirs* in the *Cleom.* passage that Megistonous' embassy came first, and that it was he who received Aratus' oracular response. T.'s embassy came immediately before C.'s investment of Sicyon, and may be dated *c.* Jan. 224.

ὑπερβαλλόμενοι τῷ ἡμίσει : this does not mean offering half as much again as Ptol., in which case the ἓξ τάλαντα would have been ὄκτω, but "doubling": cf. *Cleom.* 19, 3, τῷ Ἀράτῳ διπλῆν ἐπαγγελλόμενος τὴν σύνταξιν ἧς ἐλάμβανε παρὰ Πτολεμαίου.

41. 7. ὡς οὐκ ἔχοι τὰ πράγματα, μᾶλλον δ᾽ ὑπ᾽ αὐτῶν ἔχοιτο: a proverbial phrase : cf. Hdt. 7, 49, αἱ συμφοραὶ τῶν ἀνθρώπων ἄρχουσι καὶ οὐκὶ ὥνθρωποι τῶν συμφορέων ; Sallust, *Iug.* 1, neque regerentur magis quam regerent casus.

κατειρωνεύσασθαι : "since he seemed to have been mocking": cf. *Pomp.* 24, where pirates treat a Roman captive with deference when he mentions who he is ; they put his shoes on his feet and invest him with his toga (to avoid future mistakes), πολὺν δὲ χρόνον οὕτω κατειρωνευσάμενοι καὶ ἀπολαύσαντες τοῦ ἀνθρώπου, they make him walk the plank.

προσεκάθηντο τῇ πόλει τρεῖς μῆνας : mid-Jan. to mid-April 224 B.C.

42. 1–2. οἱ Ἀ. συνεληλυθότες εἰς Αἴγιον. In *Intro.*, p. lxxxii, it is argued that the date is April, 224. For the ratification of the treaty the synodos must have been turned into a syncletos ; the term ἐκκλησία is technically correct.

In *Cleom.* 19, 9 the story is told differently. The meeting of the Achaeans *preceded* and was responsible for Cleomenes' blockade of Sicyon. Certain details—the sending of the younger Aratus to Macedon, and the confiscation of Aratus' property—are common to both accounts. The *Aratus* account is confirmed by Polyb. 2, 52, which states that Cleomenes *relinquished* the siege of Sicyon, ἐπιγνοὺς τοὺς Ἀ. συντιθεμένους τὰ πρὸς τὸν Ἀντίγονον.

Ferrabino attempts to reconcile the *Aratus* and *Cleomenes* accounts by supposing that there was a synodos held at Aegium before the siege of Sicyon at which Antigonus' terms were accepted, and a syncletos, three months later, which ratified the treaty. The first is mentioned in *Cleom.* 19, the second in our chapter. But it seems inexplicable that a delay of three months should have occurred between the acceptance of the treaty and its ratification, and the passage quoted from Polybius makes against Ferrabino's hypothesis. I have no doubt that the Cleomenes version is due to Plutarch's carelessness in treating of matters which did not directly concern the hero of the biography.

43. 1. δημιουργῶν: see *Intro.*, sect. 7, p. ciii. οὐ πάνυ τι: see on 5, 3.

43. 2. ᾔδει γὰρ ηὐξημένον ἑαυτόν: this construction emphasises the identity between subj. and obj. Cf. with Kühner-Gerth, ii, 49, Xen. *Cyr.* 1, 4, 4: οὐχ ἃ κρείττων ᾔδει ὤν, ταῦτα προυκαλεῖτο τοὺς συνόντας ἀλλ᾽ ἅπερ εὖ ᾔδει ἑαυτὸν ἥττονα ὄντα, ἐξῆρχε. πρώτην, predicative : "and that it was originally in his feud with A. that he had found the principal starting-point (*occasio*) for his public policy." For ὑπόθεσιν, cf. ch. 15, 4, τούτους τοὺς λόγους ὑπόθεσιν λαβόντες, and Polyb. 15, 35 (of Dionysius), ἐκ δημοτικῆς καὶ ταπεινῆς ὑποθέσεως ὁρμηθεὶς ἧκε νέος ὢν εἰς τὰς Συρακούσας.

43. 2. ἐπικειμένην ⟨τὴν⟩ ἀνάγκην: the insertion of the article, proposed by Ziegler, greatly improves the sentence, especially as καιρόν has the article. "Homoioteleuton" might account for its disappearance.

43. 3. μετρίως καὶ κοινῶς)(τῇ τιμῇ περιττῶς, "in a simple ordinary style": cf. νόσον κοινὴν νοσῶν (ch. 52), and contrast Ant. 33, where κοινῶς καὶ φιλικῶς means "*in common like friends.*" καὶ τἆλλα πειρώμενος ἀνδρὸς ἀγαθοῦ καὶ νοῦν ἔχοντος: "and in other respects having experience of a good and sensible man," i.e. *proving him to be* such : cf. *Aem. Paul.* 8 (of Antigonus Doson), εἶτα (οἱ πρῶτοι τῶν Μακεδόνων) πειρώμενοι μετρίου καὶ κοινωφελοῦς βασιλέα προσηγόρευσαν. προσηγάγετο : aor. denoting simple occurrence in past time irrespective of duration. See examples in Kühner-Gerth i, 155.

43. 5. καίπερ ὢν νέος : born in 263-2 (Euseb. 1, 239). ἀργὸν, "ineffective" ; but the word seems hardly quite appropriate in this setting. οὐ μόνον Ἀχαιῶν <μᾶλλον> ἀλλὰ κ.τ.λ. : it is obvious that the text of the MSS. is defective. μᾶλλον might have fallen out after ἀλλά ; μᾶλλον Ἀχαιῶν is unexceptionable for μᾶλλον ἢ Ἀχαιοῖς. Transl., "not only in preference to Achaeans, but even to the Macedonians who were with him." πάντα χρώμενος : cf. εἰς ἅπαντα χρῆσθαι (15, 3); both are admissible phrases.

43. 6. δύο χολάς : "two gall bladders." χολαί as a rule = *a gall bladder*, but for sing. cf. Arist. *Part. An.* 4, 2, 2 : ζῶα οὐκ ἔχοντα χολήν ; also *Hist. An.* 2, 15, 9.

43. 8. συναγαγὼν ἑστίασιν : see on 17, 3, πότους συνῆγε. ἠρώτησεν : the aor. is rare in Attic, but found Xen. *Cyr.* 4, 5, 21, and in participle Soph. *Trach.* 403. ῥιγοῦν· ῥιγῶν Ἀττικῶς.

44. With this ch. are to be compared *Cleom.* 20-21 ; Polyb. 2, 53 : see *Intro.*, sect. 5, p. lxxxii.

44. 1. ἐν ταῖς Πηγαῖς. After the secession of Corinth the Achaeans had permitted Megara to join the Boeotian League (Polyb. 20, 6). The Boeotians, hostile to Antigonus some years before, had now entered into alliance with Macedon (Polyb. 20, 5, 7-11), and fought on the Macedonian side at Sellasia (Polyb. 2, 65, 4).

44. 2. Ἀριστοτέλης : see on ch. 3, 4. In *Cleom.* 20 Plut. adds : τὸ πλῆθος οὐ χαλεπῶς ἔπεισεν ἀγανακτοῦν ὅτι χρεῶν ἀποκοπὰς οὐκ ἐποίησεν αὐτοῖς ὁ Κλεομένης ἐλπίσασι.

44. 5. Ἄρατος στρατηγὸς αἱρεθεὶς ὑπ᾽ Ἀργείων : how Aratus qualified for this office and why it was given or accepted we have no means of explaining.

44. 6-**45.** We have here an anthology of charges against Aratus, collected beyond a doubt by Phylarchus.

44. 6. Ἀριστόμαχον . . . στρεβλώσαντες : see *Intro.*, sect. 5, p. lxxxiii, and the inconsistent statements of Polyb. 2, 60, there cited. The charge against A. according to Polybius was : "τήν τε πατρίδα καὶ τὴν ἑαυτοῦ προαίρεσιν ἀποσπάσας ἀπὸ τῶν Ἀχαιῶν." ἐφ᾽ ᾧ καὶ μάλιστα κακῶς ἤκουσεν ὁ Ἄρατος. Aratus, if both στρατηγὸς αὐτοκράτωρ and στρατηγός of the Argives, would be doubly responsible. (Antigonus had no special reason to seek vengeance on Aristomachus).

45. 1-4, contains an anacolouthon. The Achaeans τῶν ἄλλων ἐκείνῳ (Ἀράτῳ) τὰς αἰτίας ἐπέφερον οἷον ὅτι . . . (then follow five distinct charges made against Aratus) ; after which the idea contained in the introductory clause is repeated in the words, ᾐτιῶντο πάντων ἐκεῖνον.

Various corrections have been suggested to get rid of the anacolouthon, though in all probability it is due to Plut. himself. Thus Ziegler after οἷον reads ὅτε for ὅτι. But (1) after the words τῶν ἄλλων ἐπέφερον αἰτίας the conj. ὅτι would normally follow, (2) we should expect to be told explicitly what the Achaeans complained of, and (3) the words ᾐτιῶντο πάντων ἐκεῖνον would come somewhat awkwardly after clauses introduced by ὅτε.

'Ορχομενόν: this city, which had ceased to be a member of the League c. 230, was now permanently garrisoned by Macedon (Polyb. 4, 6), but in 199 it was offered by Philip to the League, with which it was in fact reunited soon afterwards; probably in 196 along with Heraea and Triphylia (Livy 33, 34; the text is defective in Polyb. 18, 30).

45. 2. ἐψηφίσαντο: on the constitution of the "symmachy," see *Intro.*, p. lxxxviii.

πρεσβεύειν = πρεσβεύεσθαι: cf. Polyb. 20, 2, 1; Plut. *Dion* 40; a post-classical use.

τρέφειν καὶ μισθοδοτεῖν: but only when the Macedonians were operating in Peloponnesus at the request of the Achaeans themselves.

θυσίας: Antigonus Gonatas refused deification (as Plut. implies in *Mor.* 360 D), but he was the only Hellenistic king that did so.

45. 4. ἐκείνῳ: *him* (emphatic), i.e. Antigonus Doson. ῥύμῃ: "impetus." οὐδενὸς ἤ: ἄλλου omitted as in Xen. *Cyr.* 2, 3, 10, οὐδὲ παρ' ἐνὸς οὐδὲ τοῦτο μαθὼν ἢ παρὰ τῆς φύσεως.

45. 5. The somewhat childish conduct attributed here to Doson was doubtless reported by Phylarchus, who eagerly absorbed any gossip prejudicial to the king of Macedon.

45. 6. τοὺς μὲν ἐνδοξοτάτους ἀπέκτειναν: Polyb. 2, 58 would have his readers believe that this is not true.

<ἐν> πέδαις: Greek practice favours the presence of the prep. (cf. Elmsley on Aristoph. *Ach.* 343), but the use is not absolute.

45. 7. ἐν ἀνάγκαις γλυκὺ γίνεται καὶ [οὐ] σκληρόν: the negative was inserted by a copyist who misunderstood the meaning of the quotation. What Simonides said was, "in time of stress even cruelty is sweet."

45. 8. θέσθαι: "one cannot assign on behalf of A. to any just or necessary cause . . ."

'Αχαιῶν: this correction of Curtius for 'Αργείων, as Bölte (P.-W., *Mantinea*) points out, is required by the logic of the passage. Plut. asserts that the Mantinean affair οὐχ Ἑλληνικῶς διῳκῆσθαι τοῖς Ἀχαιοῖς. Their "unhellenic conduct" was shown particularly in the change of the city's name to Antigoneia. It follows that the change was due to the Achaeans, not the Argives.

Antigoneia became a member of the League; league coins, silver and copper, are extant (Head, *Hist. Num.*, p. 418). The new community had been established before the death of Antigonus, for the base of a statue has been found honouring the king as σωτὴρ καὶ εὐεργέτης.

μέχρι νῦν: written before A.D. 125 when the Emperor Hadrian visited the town, and among other benefactions restored the old name (Paus. 8, 8, 12), which indeed had never passed completely out of use, for Bölte cites it from a list of Delphic θεαροδόκοι of 175 B.C.

45. 9. ἐρατεινὴ Μαντίνεια: Iliad 2, 607.

46. Source, the *Memoirs*.

46. 1. περὶ Σελλασίαν, July, 222 [*Intro.*, p. lxxv]. Ancient accounts of the battle: Polyb. 2, 65 ff.; Plut., *Philop.* 6, *Cleom.* 27; Paus. 2, 9, 2; 7, 7, 4; 8, 49, 5 f.

46. 2. νοσῶν ἤδη, autumn, 222: cf. Polyb. 2, 70.

οὔπω πάνυ μειράκιον: οὐ γὰρ εἶχε πλεῖον ἐτῶν τότε Φίλιππος ἑπτακαίδεκα (Polyb. 4, 5).

F

46. 3. φιλοτιμίας καὶ ὁρμῆς, *eagerness and inclination*: cf. τὴν τοῦ λαμβάνειν φιλοτιμίαν καὶ ἐπιθυμίαν, Xen., *Cyr.* 8, 1, 35.

47. The only known source for this ch. is Polybius (4, 6–11 and 15 f.). The divergences between Plut. and Polyb. have been studied by Schulz, supplemented by Stagl. The question is whether they point to the use by Plut. of another source than Polyb.

47. 1. Cf. Polyb. 4, 3. But whereas Plut. says that the Aetolians despised the Achaeans for their ἀργία and ἀταξία, Polybius says that they despised Philip ... ἅμα δὲ νομίζοντες ἀξιόχρεως εἶναι σφᾶς πρὸς τὸ πολεμεῖν αὐτοῖς Ἀχαιοῖς. Plut. has echoed Polybius' language while embodying some inferences of his own.

47. 2. Cf. Polyb. 4, 6, 9–12 : ποιούμενοι δὲ τὴν πορείαν διὰ τῆς Πατρέων καὶ Φαραιέων καὶ Τριταιέων χώρας, κ.τ.λ. If the Aetolians marched to Messenia, as Polyb. says, by Pharae and Tritaea, they would not have passed by Dyme. Stagl (p. 5) thinks it questionable whether in this passage Polybius was really Plutarch's source at all; more probably the discrepancy is due to carelessness on the part of Plutarch.

47. 3. **Τιμόξενον ὁρῶν ὀκνοῦντα**: the reason according to Polyb. 4, 7, 6 was : διὰ τὸ ῥαθύμως αὐτοὺς ἐσχηκέναι κατὰ τὸ παρὸν περὶ τὴν ἐν τοῖς ὅπλοις γυμνασίαν.

προέλαβεν : Polyb. 4, 7, 10 has παραλαβών.

47. 4. **ἡττᾶται περὶ Καφύας:** for a full account cf. Polyb. 4, 11–12.

47. 5. **θυμικώτερον:** so in Polyb. 4, 7, 8 θυμικώτερον ἐχρῆτο τοῖς πράγμασιν. For the criticisms of Aratus made at the midsummer synodos of 220 see Polyb. 4, 14.

ἀπημβλύνθη : cf. *Cic.* 5, Κικέρων ἀπημβλύνθη τὴν ὁρμήν. Polyb. 4, 19, 12 says that Aratus kept quiet until, after managing everything as they pleased, Dorimachus and Scopas proceeded to their own country, καίπερ διὰ τόπων ποιούμενοι τὰς πορείας εὐεπιθέτων καὶ στενῶν καὶ μόνου σαλπιγκτοῦ δεομένων.

47. 6. **κατῆγον τὸν Φ.** : cf. Polyb. 4, 19, 1. Philip declared war on Aetolia in autumn, 220, but did not come to Peloponnesus till autumn, 219.

48. See *Intro.*, sect. 7, pp. xci, xcii.

48. 1. "And then (i.e. on his arrival) in the first instance, moved by the prejudices raised against Aratus by A., M., and certain other courtiers, the king joined in the canvass with the opposition party, and showed anxiety that the Achaeans should elect Eperatus strategos." For the use of σπουδάζειν in reference to *canvassing*, cf. Plut. *Artax.* 21 ; Isocr. 1, 10. The date was Jan. 218 : see Polyb. 4, 82, 2–8. In Polybius Megaleas plays a subordinate part, and is not mentioned till later. In 4, 87, 9, Apelles τὸν Λεόντιον καὶ Μεγαλέαν ὑφ' αὑτὸν εἶχεν ὁλοσχερῶς. Probably Plut. had this passage in mind.

48. 2. **ἐκείνου καταφρονουμένου:** cf. Polyb. 5, 30, 1.

48. 4. **ἀγαθὸς παιδαγωγός:** referring to Philip's conciliatory treatment of Sparta in 219 Polybius (4, 24, 3) remarks : Ἀράτῳ τις ἐπιεικέστατ' ἂν προσάπτοι τὴν τότε ῥηθεῖσαν ὑπὸ τοῦ βασιλέως γνώμην.

48. 5. **ἡ πρὸς Κρῆτας ὁμιλία:** war had broken out in Crete between a league organised by Cnossus and Gortyn against Lyttos, Polyrheneia, Lappa, and some other towns. The Cnossians, who had received some support from Aetolia, had captured and burnt Lyttos during the absence of her citizen-soldiers, who, finding their city in ashes on their return, took refuge in Lappa. This town and Polyrheneia now obtained admission to the "Symmachy," and Philip sent to Crete a body of 700 troops. By their aid the Macedonian party became dominant in the W. half of Crete (Polyb. 4, 53–55). Soon afterwards we find, πάντας

response. T.'s embassy came immediately before C.'s investment of Sicyon, and may be dated *c.* Jan. 224.

ὑπερβαλλόμενοι τῷ ἡμίσει : this does not mean offering half as much again as Ptol., in which case the ἐξ τάλαντα would have been ὄκτω, but "doubling" : cf. *Cleom.* 19, 3, τῷ Ἀράτῳ διπλῆν ἐπαγγελλόμενος τὴν σύνταξιν ἧς ἐλάμβανε παρὰ Πτολεμαίου.

41. 7. ὡς οὐκ ἔχοι τὰ πράγματα, μᾶλλον δ' ὑπ' αὐτῶν ἔχοιτο : a proverbial phrase : cf. Hdt. 7, 49, αἱ συμφοραὶ τῶν ἀνθρώπων ἄρχουσι καὶ οὐκὶ ἄνθρωποι τῶν συμφορέων ; Sallust, *Iug.* 1, neque regerentur magis quam regerent casus.

κατειρωνεύσασθαι : "since he seemed to have been mocking": cf. *Pomp.* 24, where pirates treat a Roman captive with deference when he mentions who. he is ; they put his shoes on his feet and invest him with his toga (to avoid future mistakes), πολὺν δὲ χρόνον οὕτω κατειρωνευσάμενοι καὶ ἀπολαύσαντες τοῦ ἀνθρώπου, they make him walk the plank.

προσεκάθηντο τῇ πόλει τρεῖς μῆνας : mid-Jan. to mid-April 224 B.C.

42. 1–2. οἱ Ἀ. συνεληλυθότες εἰς Αἴγιον. In *Intro.*, p. lxxxii, it is argued that the date is April, 224. For the ratification of the treaty the synodos must have been turned into a syncletos ; the term ἐκκλησία is technically correct.

In *Cleom.* 19, 9 the story is told differently. The meeting of the Achaeans *preceded* and was responsible for Cleomenes' blockade of Sicyon. Certain details—the sending of the younger Aratus to Macedon, and the confiscation of Aratus' property—are common to both accounts. The *Aratus* account is confirmed by Polyb. 2, 52, which states that Cleomenes *relinquished* the siege of Sicyon, ἐπιγνοὺς τοὺς Ἀ. συντιθεμένους τὰ πρὸς τὸν Ἀντίγονον.

Ferrabino attempts to reconcile the *Aratus* and *Cleomenes* accounts by supposing that there was a synodos held at Aegium before the siege of Sicyon at which Antigonus' terms were accepted, and a syncletos, three months later, which ratified the treaty. The first is mentioned in *Cleom.* 19, the second in our chapter. But it seems inexplicable that a delay of three months should have occurred between the acceptance of the treaty and its ratification, and the passage quoted from Polybius makes against Ferrabino's hypothesis. I have no doubt that the Cleomenes version is due to Plutarch's carelessness in treating of matters which did not directly concern the hero of the biography.

43. 1. δημιουργῶν : see *Intro.*, sect. 7, p. ciii. οὐ πάνυ τι : see on 5, 3.

43. 2. ᾔδει γὰρ ηὐξημένον ἑαυτόν : this construction emphasises the identity between subj. and obj. Cf. with Kühner-Gerth, ii, 49, Xen. *Cyr.* 1, 4, 4 : οὐχ ἃ κρείττων ᾔδει ὤν, ταῦτα προυκαλεῖτο τοὺς συνόντας ἀλλ' ἅπερ εὖ ᾔδει ἑαυτὸν ἥττονα ὄντα, ἐξῆρχε. πρώτην, predicative : "and that it was originally in his feud with A. that he had found the principal starting-point (*occasiv*) for his public policy." For ὑπόθεσιν, cf. ch. 15, 4, τούτους τοὺς λόγους ὑπόθεσιν λαβόντες, and Polyb. 15, 35 (of Dionysius), ἐκ δημοτικῆς καὶ ταπεινῆς ὑποθέσεως ὁρμηθεὶς ἧκε νέος ὢν εἰς τὰς Συρακούσας.

43. 2. ἐπικειμένην <τὴν> ἀνάγκην : the insertion of the article, proposed by Ziegler, greatly improves the sentence, especially as καιρόν has the article. "Homoioteleuton" might account for its disappearance.

43. 3. μετρίως καὶ κοινῶς)(τῇ τιμῇ περιττῶς, "in a simple ordinary style": cf. νόσον κοινὴν νοσῶν (ch. 52), and contrast Ant. 33, where κοινῶς καὶ φιλικῶς means "*in common like friends.*" καὶ τἆλλα πειρώμενος ἀνδρὸς ἀγαθοῦ καὶ νοῦν ἔχοντος : "and in other respects having experience of a good and sensible man," i.e. *proving him to be* such: cf. *Aem. Paul.* 8 (of Antigonus Doson), εἶτα (οἱ πρῶτοι τῶν Μακεδόνων) πειρώμενοι μετρίου καὶ κοινωφελοῦς βασιλέα προσηγόρευσαν. προσηγάγετο: aor. denoting simple occurrence in past time irrespective of duration. See examples in Kühner-Gerth i, 155.

43. 5. καίπερ ὢν νέος: born in 263–2 (Euseb. 1, 239). ἀργὸν, "ineffective"; but the word seems hardly quite appropriate in this setting. οὐ μόνον Ἀχαιῶν <μᾶλλον> ἀλλὰ κ.τ.λ.: it is obvious that the text of the MSS. is defective. μᾶλλον might have fallen out after ἀλλά; μᾶλλον Ἀχαιῶν is unexceptionable for μᾶλλον ἢ Ἀχαιοῖς. Transl., "not only in preference to Achaeans, but even to the Macedonians who were with him." πάντα χρώμενος: cf. εἰς ἅπαντα χρῆσθαι (15, 3); both are admissible phrases.

43. 6. δύο χολάς: "two gall bladders." χολαί as a rule = *a gall bladder*, but for sing. cf. Arist. *Part. An.* 4, 2, 2: ζῶα οὐκ ἔχοντα χολήν; also *Hist. An.* 2, 15, 9.

43. 8. συναγαγὼν ἑστίασιν: see on 17, 3, πότους συνῆγε. ἠρώτησεν: the aor. is rare in Attic, but found Xen. *Cyr.* 4, 5, 21, and in participle Soph. *Trach.* 403. ῥιγοῦν· ῥιγῶν Ἀττικῶς.

44. With this ch. are to be compared *Cleom.* 20–21; Polyb. 2, 53: see *Intro.*, sect. 5, p. lxxxii.

44. 1. ἐν ταῖς Πηγαῖς. After the secession of Corinth the Achaeans had permitted Megara to join the Boeotian League (Polyb. 20, 6). The Boeotians, hostile to Antigonus some years before, had now entered into alliance with Macedon (Polyb. 20, 5, 7–11), and fought on the Macedonian side at Sellasia (Polyb. 2, 65, 4).

44. 2. Ἀριστοτέλης: see on ch. 3, 4. In *Cleom.* 20 Plut. adds: τὸ πλῆθος οὐ χαλεπῶς ἔπεισεν ἀγανακτοῦν ὅτι χρεῶν ἀποκοπὰς οὐκ ἐποίησεν αὐτοῖς ὁ Κλεομένης ἐλπίσασι.

44. 5. Ἄρατος στρατηγὸς αἱρεθεὶς ὑπ᾽ Ἀργείων: how Aratus qualified for this office and why it was given or accepted we have no means of explaining.

44. 6–45. We have here an anthology of charges against Aratus, collected beyond a doubt by Phylarchus.

44. 6. Ἀριστόμαχον . . . στρεβλώσαντες: see *Intro.*, sect. 5, p. lxxxiii, and the inconsistent statements of Polyb. 2, 60, there cited. The charge against A. according to Polybius was: "τήν τε πατρίδα καὶ τὴν ἑαυτοῦ προαίρεσιν ἀποσπάσας ἀπὸ τῶν Ἀχαιῶν." ἐφ᾽ ᾧ καὶ μάλιστα κακῶς ἤκουσεν ὁ Ἄρατος. Aratus, if both στρατηγὸς αὐτοκράτωρ and στρατηγός of the Argives, would be doubly responsible. (Antigonus had no special reason to seek vengeance on Aristomachus.)

45. 1–4, contains an anacolouthon. The Achaeans τῶν ἄλλων ἐκείνῳ (Ἀράτῳ) τὰς αἰτίας ἐπέφερον οἷον ὅτι . . . (then follow five distinct charges made against Aratus); after which the idea contained in the introductory clause is repeated in the words, ᾐτιῶντο πάντων ἐκεῖνον.

Various corrections have been suggested to get rid of the anacolouthon, though in all probability it is due to Plut. himself. Thus Ziegler after οἷον reads ὅτε for ὅτι. But (1) after the words τῶν ἄλλων ἐπέφερον αἰτίας the conj. ὅτι would normally follow, (2) we should expect to be told explicitly what the Achaeans complained of, and (3) the words ᾐτιῶντο πάντων ἐκεῖνον would come somewhat awkwardly after clauses introduced by ὅτε.

Achaeans in their defeat what they would not readily have obtained when victorious. According to Polyb. **2**, 57 after providing for the maintenance of order in the Achaean army, Aratus assembled the Mantineans and told them ὑπάρξειν αὐτοῖς τὴν ἀσφάλειαν πολιτευομένοις μετὰ τῶν Ἀχαιῶν. [Freeman (p. 348) infers from these words, that he simply called on the citizens to resume their old rights and their old duties as members of the Achaean League. Next, "Aratus at once raised to the rank of citizens a class of inhabitants who did not possess the full political franchise." Freeman's order of events seems strange. The manipulation of the franchise should have preceded the re-admission of the city into the League.

To return to Polybius: "The Mantineans (i.e., the new citizen-body) foreseeing intestine factions and Aetolian and Spartan intrigues, asked the Achaeans for a garrison; who accordingly selected by lot (ἀπεκλήρωσαν) 300 men from among themselves and added 200 mercenaries."

This statement of Polybius is represented in the *Aratus* by the words φρουρὰν ἐνέβαλεν.

In C.A.H. viii, p. 753, Tarn remarks: " As the majority ... were normally pro-Spartan he tried to safeguard the city by giving citizenship to metics and introducing Achaean *settlers*." Tarn may be right, but Polybius at any rate is careful to represent the Achaeans as a *garrison*.

μετοίκους: were these resident aliens as at Athens or "natives not possessing the full franchise," or a body composed of both these elements? Freeman notes that in 38, 4 we read: (Κλεομένης) πολλοὺς τῶν μετοίκων ἐμβαλὼν εἰς τὴν πολιτείαν, but in *Cleom*. 11 (of the same event), ἀναπληρώσας τὸ πολίτευμα τοῖς χαριεστάτοις τῶν περιοίκων. Perhaps Plut. makes no clear distinction between the μέτοικοι and περίοικοι.

36. 4. **αὖθις δὲ**, later on in the summer of 227. **ἀψιμαχοῦντι** has here the meaning, *enticing* [*him*] *to battle*, as in *Crassus* 10, *Dion*. 39.

36. 5. **λειπόμενος πλήθει**: Cleomenes had a large force of mercenaries.

37. The somewhat disrespectful tone adopted towards Aratus suggests, as Schulz remarks, that Phylarchus has been consulted.

37. 2. **ὡς αὐτόν**: the manuscripts have ὡς αὐτὸς ἀξιῶν, leaving the latter part of the sentence without construction.

ἐπιφανῆναι: urging them to *present themselves in support of* the pursuers. In 35 and 44 the word has the more usual suggestion, "present oneself to oppose." Reiske's αὐτόν is not required, for an oblique cause of αὐτός may be used instead of the reflexive, in order to indicate with emphasis opposition between one person and another, as here between Lydiades and Aratus: cf. Xen. *An*. 7, 4, 20, ὁ Ξ. δεῖται ἐπὶ τὸ ὄρος, εἰ βούλεται, συστρατεύεσθαι· εἰ δὲ μὴ αὐτὸν ἐᾶσαι.

37. 3. **ἐπιθεμένου τοῦ Κλεομένους**: *Cleom*. 6, 4, κατιδὼν Κλ. ἀνῆκε τοὺς Ταραντίνους καὶ τοὺς Κρῆτας (i.e. mercenaries) ἐπ' αὐτόν, ὑφ' ὧν ὁ Λυδιάδας ἀμυνόμενος εὐρώστως ἔπεσε . . . τὸν δὲ νεκρὸν ἀχθῆναι πρὸς αὐτὸν κελεύσας, κοσμήσας πορφυρίδι καὶ στέφανον ἐπιθεὶς πρὸς τὰς πύλας τῶν Μεγαλοπολιτῶν ἀπέστειλεν.

37. 5. **εἰς Αἴγιον**: the place prescribed for the meetings of the synodos. It looks as if the Achaeans nursed their wrath till the autumn, when they vented it by refusing funds for the payment of mercenaries and other expenses incurred by the strategos. If not rescinded, the veto would remain in force for some six months.

38. Aratus' victory at Orchomenos and capture of Megistonous is not mentioned in the *Cleomenes*. We cannot assume that Phylarchus ignored it, but should rather suppose that Plut. omitted it as having no special importance for Cleomenes' career. The account in sub-sections 1 and 2 of the present chap. (as Schulz infers) is derived from the *Memoirs*. The rest pretty obviously comes from Phylarchus.

38. 1. Μεγιστόνουν; stepfather of Cleomenes. As he assisted him in his coup d'état at Sparta (*Cleom.* 7), which took place about the autumn of 227, it is probable that the battle at Orchomenos was not fought till the following spring. Megistonous was probably released in return for the Achaean prisoners freed by Cleomenes after Hecatombaeum (i.e. towards the end of 226). A year later he appears as an envoy from Cleomenes to Aratus (*Arat.* 41; *Cleom.* 19).

πατρωόν, *stepfather*: a word found only here, in ch. 46 and in *Cleom.* 11. The usual word is μητρυιός.

38. 2–12. In autumn 227 Aratus *thought* of resigning his office, but changed his mind; when, however, his turn came he refused to be a candidate. But his turn did not come till Jan. 225. In the interval the battle of Hecatombaeum had been fought under Hyperbatas (226–5), and had turned out a disaster for the Achaeans.

38. 2. εἰωθώς: see on 24, 5.

ἐξωμόσατο: declared on oath his inability to accept office: cf. Arist. *Pol.* 1297ª 20, περὶ τὰς ἀρχὰς (σοφίζονται) τὸ τοῖς ἔχουσι τίμημα μὴ ἐξεῖναι ἐξόμνυσθαι.

38. 4. On Cleomenes' revolution at Sparta, see *Intro.*, sect. 5, p. lx *ad fin.*

38. 5. Cf. *Cleom.* 15, 1: οὕτω δὲ συντετριμμένοις τοῖς Ἀχαιοῖς ὁ μὲν ᾿Αρατ εἰωθὼς παρ᾿ ἐνιαυτὸν ἀεὶ στρατηγεῖν, ἀπείπατο τὴν ἀρχὴν καὶ παρῃτήσατο καλούντων καὶ δεομένων, οὐ καλῶς, οἷον ἐν χειμῶνι πραγμάτων μείζονι μεθεὶς ἑτέρῳ τὸν οἴακα καὶ προέμενος τὴν ἐξουσίαν.

καλῶς εἶχε. Cf. Thuc. 1, 38: καλὸν ἦν τοῖσδε, εἰ καὶ ἡμαρτάνομεν εἶξαι ἡμετέρᾳ ὀργῇ. In such expressions of unfulfilled demand the omission of ἄν is regular (Kuhner-Gerth ii, 1, p. 204). ἀκόντων takes the place of a protasis. q εἶξαι, sc. καλῶς εἶχε.

38. 6. ἐν τοῖς ὑπομνήμασι: in *Cleom.* 16, 4. Plut. remarks, τουτονὶ δ᾿ αὐτὸν ᾿Αντίγονον εἰρηκὼς κακὰ μυρία δι᾿ ὧν ἀπολέλοιπεν ὑπομνημάτων. More than one critic has suggested that Plut., although grammatically the reference must be to Doson, really had Gonatas in mind.

38. 7. ῾Ηρακλεῖδαι: cf. *Cleom.* 16, 6, τὸν ἀφ᾿ ῾Ηρακλέους γεγονότα.

38. 8. ὡς πολλὰ ποιήσων ἀγαθά: see *Intro.*, sect. 5, p. lxiv.

38. 9. ᾿Αντίγονος αὐτοκράτωρ ἡγεμών: cf. 24, 4, where a similar honour was conferred on Ptolemy Euergetes. After Hecatombaeum Ptolemy transferred his patronage to Cleomenes (Polyb. 2, 51). ἀναγορευθείς: Veitch, *Gk. Vbs. Irreg. and Defective*, p. 10, has corrected Cobet's dictum that ἀγορεύω and compounds were used only in pres. and impf. by classical writers.

τὸν Αἰσώπου μιμησάμενος κυνηγόν: among the fables that we know as Aesop's this story is not found. But in Arist. *Rhet.* 2, 20, it is said that when the people of Himera had made Phalaris *strategos autocrator* and it was proposed to allow him a bodyguard, Stesichorus told a fable of a horse which had been worsted in battle with a stag and called upon τὸν ἄνθρωπον for assistance, which led to the imposition of a bridle and the enslavement of the horse to its new ally. The same fable is repeated in Horace, *Epistles*, 1, 10. But why the ἄνθρωπος of Aristotle and *homo* of Horace appears as κυνηγός in Plutarch remains obscure.

38. 11. ἀπολογιζόμενος : *recounting,* as in Polyb. 4, 254, 4 ; 8, 24, 7 : 21, 3, 2. ὁ Πολύβιος : 2, 47, 4. προκαθιέναι, *put forward* : cf. *Crassus* 21, Σουρήναν ἐδόκει Ὑρώδης προκαθεῖναι πειρασόμενον μάχης.

39. This chapter resumes the narrative from 38, 1 : it shows no bias toward either Cleomenes or Aratus.

39. 1. ἀπέβαλον οἱ Ἀ. τὴν Μαντίνειαν : early summer of 226. A rising broke out in the city ; the Spartans were called in and the place surrendered to them (Polyb. 2, 58). In *Cleom.* 14 we have Phylarchus' account presumably : πρῶτον μὲν οἱ Μ. αὐτὸν (Κλεομένη) ἐπήγοντο, καὶ νύκτωρ παρεισπεσόντι τὴν φρουρὰν ὧν Ἀ. συνεκβαλόντες ἐνεχείρισαν αὐτούς. It looks as if the Achaeans were first ·tacked off their guard by an armed mob.

Εκατόμβαιον : a fortress S. of Dyme. Polyb. 2, 51 states that the Achaeans ʼe engaged πανδημεί (cf. *Cleom.* 14, 4). They had been summoned to protect cities of Achaea from the invader. From *Cleom.* 14 we discover that Hyper- s was the Achaean strategos, a fact not brought out either in the *Aratus* or olybius. Beloch dates the battle in the late summer of 226 : between the le and the peace negotiations no activity of Cleomenes is recorded except capture of the Elean town, Lasion.

πέμπειν εὐθύς : in *Cleom.* 15 Plut. adds : πρῶτον μὲν μέτρια τοῖς Ἀ. ἐδόκει ἐσθεσὶν ἐπιτάττειν, ἑτέρους δὲ πέμπων ἐκέλευσεν αὐτῷ παραδιδόναι τὴν ἡγεμονίαν ἀλλὰ μὴ διοισόμενος πρὸς αὐτούς, ἀλλὰ τοὺς αἰχμαλώτους εὐθὺς ἀποδώσων καὶ ωρία.

. 2. From *Cleom.* 15 we learn that there were *two* attempts to bring about nference. The first conference was to have met "at Lerna"—prob. a ʼe for Argos, Plut. being misled by the recollection that Cleomenes Lerna on the second occasion. [See next note.] This conference was ned on account of a sudden illness of the king, but Achaean prisoners released. Of this there is nothing in the *Aratus.* [See *Intro.*, sect. 5, . lxx.]

περὶ Λέρναν : if Lerna had been fixed as the place for the first conference, why, we may ask, should the venue have been changed to Argos for the second? Lerna was a locality on the west side of the Gulf of Nauplia, on the road from Tegea, whence C. started for the second conference.

39. 2. *Cleom.* 17 makes Aratus demand that C. should come to Argos *alone* (which is absurd, even if he had received hostages); or else the meeting might be held at the gymnasium of Cyllarabis outside the walls ; here he might come μετὰ τῆς δυνάμεως. The latter proposal may be authentic.

39. 3. ἀνέζευξεν : shifted his quarters.

ἐγκλήματα πολλὰ : in *Cleom.* 17 he complained, δεῖν εὐθὺς αὐτῷ τότε προειπεῖν οὐ νῦν ἥκοντος ἐπὶ τὰς θύρας ἀπιστεῖν καὶ ἀπελαύνειν. So in order to bring the Achaeans to a more trustful and unsuspicious state of mind, he sent them a declaration of war.

γέγραφε : the pf. for aor. is found occasionally in Plut., indicating apparently that the distinction between the tenses was becoming blurred. Cf. *Alex.* 22 (γέγραφε); *Mor.* 399 A (ἀνηγόρευκεν), 873 E (ἀπήγγελκεν), 48 C (ἐξέωκεν), 1113 F (κεκώλυκεν).

39. 4. κήρυκα πέμψας : *Cleom.* 17 adds : οὐκ εἰς Ἄργος ἀλλ' εἰς Αἴγιον (the " federal capital ") ὥς φησιν Ἄρατος, ὅπως φθάσῃ τὴν παρασκευὴν αὐτῶν.

Πελλήνη προσέβαλε καὶ τοῦ στρατηγοῦ τῶν 'Α. ἐκπεσόντος ἔσχε τὴν πόλιν :
On this incident we find in *Cleom.* 17, 6 : εἷλε Π. ἐξαπίνης ἐπιπεσὼν καὶ τοὺς
φρουροῦντας ἐξέβαλε μετὰ τῶν 'Αχαιῶν· μετὰ δὲ ταῦτα . . . where Blass
(followed by Ziegler) unwarrantably brackets the first μετά, remarking non-
chalantly, *das* μετά *enstanden aus dem Folgenden* : μετὰ δὲ ταῦτα. But it is
clear from our passage that Cleomenes did not get the city till the strategos
(Timoxenus) had been expelled, for the Greek cannot mean, as the corresponding
idiom in Latin might, that Cleomenes himself expelled him. The strategos
must have been expelled by the Pellenaeans (Achaeans) themselves.

Φενεὸν : a town in N. Arcadia, some thirty miles S.W. of Pellene : near
Pheneus, on the hill of Penteleia, was the fortress of Πεντέλειον.

εὐθὺς 'Αργεῖοι προσεχώρησαν : From *Cleom.* 17, 7 we learn that the
Achaeans, fearing treachery in Corinth and Sicyon, τοὺς ἱππεῖς καὶ τοὺς ξένους
ἀπέστειλαν ἐξ "Αργους ἐκεὶ παραφυλάξοντας· αὐτοὶ δὲ τὰ Νέμεια καταβάντες εἰς
"Αργος ἦγον ; but Cleomenes thinking the city would be unguarded during the
festival seized the Aspis, the citadel of Argos. According to Polyb. 2, 60
Aristomachus was largely responsible for the secession of Argos to Cleomenes :
ἐπεὶ μικρὸν ἐπικυδεστέρας εἶχε τὰς ἐλπίδας ὑπὲρ τοῦ μέλλοντος ἐν Κλεομένει τὴν
πατρίδα . . . ἀποσπάσας ἀπὸ τῶν 'Α. ἐν τοῖς ἀναγκαιοτάτοις καιροῖς προσένειμε τοῖς
ἐχθροῖς. [Late July, 225.]

39. 5-40. 1. "And in general none of the acquired territories (i.e., all
except old Achaea and Sicyon) remained constant to the A., but suddenly
Aratus found himself the centre of uproar as he saw Peloponnesus rocking
and the cities agitated by revolutionaries on every hand. For he was not at
all inclined to acquiesce in the present (defections), while in addition (καὶ)
it had become apparent that of the Sicyonians themselves and the Corinthians
many had been holding conversations with C. and, in their desire for personal
domination had been for a long time secretly disaffected towards the common-
wealth."

Both ἀτρεμεῖν ἐπὶ (*Dion* 44) and στέργειν ἐπὶ (Demosth. 996, 15) can bear
the meaning *acquiesce in*. (For ἀτρεμεῖν we find in Att. writers ἠρεμεῖν).

Perrin translates : " There was no quiet anywhere nor any contentment ...";
but there is no authority for the impersonal use of these verbs. The suggestion
that "Αρατος is to be supplied as the subject of both verbs is due to
Dr. R. M. Henry.

ὑπούλως has ceased to be felt as metaphorical; cf. *Dion* 54 : τῶν ὑπούλως
καὶ δυσμενῶς ἐχόντων.

40. Source, the *Memoirs.*

40. 2. ἐξουσίαν ἀνυπεύθυνον : one of the functions conferred upon A. by his
appointment as στρατηγὸς αὐτοκράτωρ. (*Intro.*, p. lxxviii.)

ἐν Σικυῶνι διεφθαρμένους : (Sintenis). MSS. give ἐν Σικυωνίαι ἐφθαρμένους.
The error arose by the misreading of δ as α. The false reading (incidentally)
introduces hiatus.

βαρυνόμενον τὴν . . . πολιτείαν : *feeling aggrieved against the administration.* Cf. *Cleom.* 17 : τῶν πρώτων βαρυνομένων "Αρατον. This use of the passive
of βαρύνω is common in post-classical Greek.

40. 3. συνδραμόντες : if a regular ecclesia this assembly should have met in
the theatre : in the temple there would be room for no more than seven or eight
hundred.

Κρηταιεῖς συμφρονήσαντας καὶ τῆς αὐτῆς μετασχόντας συμμαχίας ἕνα προστάτην ἑλέσθαι τῆς νήσου Φίλιππον (Polyb. 7, 12).

ἡ πρὸς Αἰτωλοὺς στρατεία: *Intro.*, pp. xcii, xciii.

The object of Plutarch here, as Schulz remarks (p. 48), is to collect and summarise laudatory references to Aratus scattered through Polybius' work in order to impress upon the reader the intellectual and moral superiority of Aratus to Philip.

48. 6. Schulz observes that Plutarch here unwarrantably generalises two incidents which he found in Polybius: (1) the Amphidamus affair (*Intro.*, p. xcii) and (2) the quarrel after the banquet (Pol. 5, 15).

48. 7. Cf. Polyb. 5; 15, 16, 25–29. As a matter of fact Megaleas alone was fined, Leontius was executed, Apelles and Megaleas committed suicide, Ptolemaeus was executed.

49. 1. The thought is Plutarch's, but the language is derived from Polyb. 10, 26, 8 : καί μοι δοκεῖ τὰ μὲν ἀγαθὰ φύσει περὶ αὐτὸν ὑπάρξαι, τὰ δὲ κακὰ προβαίνοντι κατὰ τὴν ἡλικίαν ἐπιγενέσθαι.

49. 2. τὸν νεώτερον Ἄρατον ἠδίκει περὶ τὴν γυναῖκα : cf. Livy 27, 31, 8, Uni etiam principi Achaeorum Arato adempta uxor nomine Polycratia ac spe regiarum nuptiarum in Macedoniam asportata fuerat ; the statement recurs in a speech of Aristaenus (32, 21). These passages are evidently derived from lost portions of Polybius. Philip had been Aratus' guest in 219. Beloch 4, 2, p. 140, thinks that Philip carried out his promise to marry Polycrateia, and that she was the mother of Perseus. He points out (1) that her name indicates her as belonging to the family of Polycrates, one of the oldest and most respected in Argos (Polyb. 5, 64, 6). [The name Polycrates survived in Aratus' family down to Plutarch's own time, *Arat.* 1, 5.] (2) The name of Perseus, who was born *c.* 213, connects him with Argos. (3) It is plain from Pol. 23, 7 (cf. 23, 3, 7; 40, 11) that Perseus was a legitimate son of Philip. (4) The slanderous allegation, that he was the son of an Argive sempstress Gnathaenion, preserves the fact that he was an Argive on his mother's side. Polycrateia seems to have died about 209.

50. 3. Ἰθωμάταν, Doric for Ἰθωμήτην: Polyb. 7, 11 (the source of the present passage) has Ἰθωμάτην. From its application to Zeus, whose temple was on the summit, the adj. apparently came to be used as the name of the mountain. For a description of Mt. Ithome see Frazer on Paus. 4, 3, 3.

50. 4. Apparently an insertion of Plutarch's own.

50. 5. τῷ Φαρίῳ Δημητρίῳ : Pharos was a small island in the Adriatic, off the Illyrian coast, colonised by the Parians in 385 B.C. According to Strabo 7, p. 315, the name was originally Paros, of which presumably Pharos is a corruption. By the third century the island had become subject to the Illyrians. When in 229, in spite of the combined efforts of the Achaeans and Aetolians, Corcyra was taken by the Illyrians, Demetrius, a native of Pharos, was appointed governor of the island. But when the Romans appeared he not only surrendered Corcyra but advised them on their campaign against Teuta, the Illyrian queen (Pol. 2, 11 ; 4, 16). In 225 he made himself independent of Rome and came to an understanding with Antigonus Doson, whom he assisted at Sellasia (Pol. 2, 65; 3, 16). At the beginning of the Hannibalic war Demetrius made a league with Philip and attacked Roman Illyria, but in 219 L. Aemilius captured Pharos, carried off Demetrius' partisans, and compelled him to flee to Philip's court (Polyb. 3, 16 ff.; 4, 37; 32, 23. In hope of recovering his dominions Demetrius supported the movement which led to the peace of Naupactus, and urged Philip against Rome. In Philip's treaty with Hannibal it was provided that Rome should be required to release the imprisoned Pharians (215 B.C.). Shortly afterwards Demetrius met his death in an attempt to surprise Messene.

51. 1. διαβαίνοντος εἰς Ἤπειρον αὐτοῦ: In the summer of 214, when besieging Apollonia on the Illyrian coast, Philip was routed by the praetor Laevinus, who, when called upon for help, hurried to Illyria and threw into Apollonia reinforcements which, together with the citizens, sacked the Macedonian camp (Livy 24, 40). Philip had to retire overland to Macedonia, and Laevinus established himself permanently in the Illyrian ports (C.A.H. viii, p. 122).

51. 2. τοὺς Μεσσηνίους αὖθις, κ.τ.λ.: Probably in the autumn of 214. "Little is known of this adventure, but two facts are certain. Demetrius of Paros was sent against the city, repulsed, and killed, and Philip in futile anger ravaged Messenian territory ... (His action) threw into the arms of Aetolia the Messenians, who, rich and poor alike, seceded from the League (Symmachy) and completed the rupture between Aratus and Philip." (Holleaux, C.A.H. viii, p. 122.) [Polyb. 3, 19, 11: 8, 10, 1: Paus. 4; 29, 1 and 32, 2: Livy 32, 21, 23.]

51. 3. διεβλήθη πρὸς, "was thoroughly incensed with," cf. Polyb. 30, 17 (20), 3, [the Roman Senate's attitude to Eumenes] διαβεβλημένοι πρὸς αὐτὸν οὐκ ἐβούλοντο ἐμφανίζειν αὐτούς.

51. 4. ἐξ ἡμέρου βασιλέως, κ.τ.λ.: cf. Polyb. 10, 26 and 18, 33, 6. **τὸ δ' οὐκ ἦν ἄρα μεταβολὴ:** cf. ch. 49, 1. **ἀγνοηθείσης,** *unrecognised.*

52. 1. "For that the feelings towards A. which had grown up in him from the beginning contained a mixture of shame and fear ..."

52. 2. Ταυρίωνα . . . ἐκέλευσεν . . . μάλιστα διὰ φαρμάκων . . . The story of the poisoning of Aratus, because he disapproved of Philip's proceedings at Messene, comes from Polyb. 8, 14. Modern opinion rightly regards the story with distrust. "It is doubtful," remarks Shuckburgh, "whether drugs acting in the manner described were known to the ancients, and certainly spitting blood would be no conclusive evidence of poison." Niese goes so far as to say, "*There is no slow poison of the kind*; Aratus seems to have succumbed to a disease the origin of which was unknown." Holleaux (*loc. cit.*) holds the same view.

It is to be noted that the younger Aratus developed some form of insanity, a condition which was also put down to poisoning. It is possible that father and son both suffered from tuberculosis, which attacked the lungs of the one and the brain of the other.

Taurion, the alleged poisoner, had been appointed governor of Corinth by Antigonus Doson in his will. He had remained loyal to Philip, and refused to associate with Apelles and the conspirators. During the social war he co-operated on several occasions with Aratus and Timoxenus. **[ἐν] ἀδήλῳ τρόπῳ:** the insertion of the preposition would be a solecism in prose, although ἐν τρόποις occurs in Aeschylus *Ag.* 918; *Eum.* 441.

52. 2-3. We find three statements here which have nothing corresponding in Polyb. 8, 14—(1) ἐκέλευσεν ἀδήλῳ τρόπῳ τοῦτο πρᾶξαι, (2) ὁ δὲ ποιησάμενος τὸν 'Α. συνήθη, (3) ἀλλὰ τῶν θέρμας ... εἰς φθορὰν περαινόντων. Schulz asks, Whence did Plut. derive them? It seems to me that (1) and (2) may well be the product of Plutarch's imagination working on Polybius' narrative, while (3) may represent a tradition which Plut. heard from his friend Polycrates, a lineal descendant of Aratus.

52. 4. ἑνός γε τῶν συνήθων)(Polyb. 8, 14, πρὸς ἕνα τῶν ὑπηρετῶν Κεφάλωνα.

53. 1. τὸ ἑπτακαιδέκατον : The date of his death is 213–12. On his strategiai see *Intro.*, lxxxi.

53. 2. δεισιδαιμονίας : Holden in his ed. of *Timoleon*, p. 214, points out that whereas this word = *religion* in writers of the classical period (Xen., *Cyr.* 3, 3, 58, Arist., *Pol.* 5, 2 (1315 a), in later Greek it acquired the meaning (first probably in Theophrastus, *Characters* 16) of *excessive dread of the gods*. Cf. Plutarch's definition in *Mor.* 165 B. (This being the current meaning in post-classical times it is clear, as observed by Hatch, *Essays in Biblical Greek* (p. 45), that in the *Acts of the Apostles* 17, 2 and 25, 19 no other sense is admissible.)

53. 3. "Art thou planning a requital in perpetuity of thy dead chief Aratus for his saving of life, O Sicyon, by means of a funeral rite and festival ? Since whatsoever in earth or sky or sea oppresses him or is by him oppressed is an offence against religion."

ζωάγριον = a reward for the saving of life. The word appears nowhere else in the sing. (cf. θρεπτήρια, τροφεῖα). If Apollo had followed the rule observed by Homer, he might have kept the customary form ζωάγρια, with hiatus after the bucolic diaeresis !

ἀμφί, "by means of" : cf. Pind. *Pyth.* 1, 12, (κῆλα) θέλγει φρένας ἀμφὶ Λατοΐδα σοφίᾳ.

ὁσίη : a word particularly used of tendance of the dead ; Wyttenbach on *Mor.* 375 e, cf. 585 D, De Soc. Genio, ὁσίως ὑπὸ τῶν φίλων κεκηδεῦσθαι; and Dion Chrysostom, *Or.* 37, p. 462 A (of a dead man, to whom a statue has been erected), τὰ τῆς ὁσίας περίκειται.

ὥσπερ οἰκιστήν κ.τ.λ. : so in Thuc. 5, 11, the people of Amphipolis honoured Brasidas with games and yearly sacrifices, καὶ τὴν ἀποικίαν ὡς οἰκιστῇ προσέθεσαν. Similarly the Sicyonians had heroized the elder Euphron, ἔθαψάν τε ἐν τῇ ἀγορᾷ καὶ ὡς ἀρχηγέτην τῆς πόλεως σέβωνται. The honours bestowed upon Demetrius Poliorcetes, and Antigonus Doson in their lifetime implied deification.

53. 5. 'Αράτιον: "the usual termination of buildings consecrated to some god or hero is -ιον as Διονύσιον 'Απολλώνιον Δημήτριον ; or -αιον as "Ηραιον 'Αθήναιον Νύμφαιον ; seldom -ειον or -εῖον as Θησεῖον 'Ηρακλεῖον Μαυσωλεῖον Μουσεῖον 'Ηφαιστεῖον."—Holden on *Tim.* 39, 4. Hence there seems no reason to change (with Reiske and Ziegler) the 'Αράτιον of the MSS. to 'Αράτειον. The latter form, however, is found in Paus. 2, 9, 4.

Δαισίου μηνός: correctly equated by Plut. with the Attic Thargelion (May–June) in *Cam.* 19, *Alex.* 16. Here by an error it is equated with 'Ανθεστηριῶν (February). Skalet (p. 85) supposes that Plut. has in mind here a Sicyonian Daisios, coming at a different time of the year from the Macedonian, but for this there is no evidence. In imperial times Δαίσιος was used in the Greek-speaking parts of the empire as the equivalent of mensis Iunius: cf. the *titulus* of the Nicene council, ἐν μηνὶ Δεσίῳ, ἐννεακαιδεκάτῃ, πρὸ δέκα τριῶν Καλανδῶν 'Ιουλίων.

53. 5. [τοῦ μηνός]: In the MSS. the passage runs, θύουσιν αὐτῷ θυσίαν, τὴν μὲν ᾗ ᾗ τὴν πόλιν ἀπήλλαξε τῆς τυραννίδος—ἡμέρᾳ πέμπτῃ Δαισίου μηνός ... τὴν δὲ τοῦ μηνὸς ἐν ᾗ γενέσθαι τὸν ἄνδρα διαμνημονεύουσι: "they offer him sacrifice, the first on the day on which he freed the city from the tyranny—the 5th of Daisios—the second on the day of the month, on which according to tradition he was born."

τοῦ μηνός causes difficulty. Grammatically it might mean "the month Daisios," but obviously this is not the sense Plutarch wishes to convey; or it might mean *every* month, but Plut. does not mean a *monthly* sacrifice.

Reiske emended to τοῦ μηνὸς ἐν ᾧ "the second sacrifice during the month in the course of which . . ." but, even if we are content with the sense, this emendation destroys the parallelism of the sentence.

I assume τοῦ μηνός to be a gloss which some one wrote on the margin to indicate that the antecedents of the two relative pronouns were *not* τὴν μὲν and τὴν δέ. If we delete the words, the two halves of the sentence balance, τὴν μὲν ᾗ . . . being answered by τὴν δ' ἐν ᾗ . . . "the second on the day in course of which . . ."

53. 6. τῶν περὶ τὸν Διόνυσον τεχνιτῶν : From the time of Alexander the Great onward we find literary and (more frequently) epigraphic references to these guilds, which were organised exactly as a democratic state, and negotiated independently with the cities. The guildsmen were freemen who kept their citizen rights in the communities from which they came. In virtue of their sacred functions they were immune from conscription. The object of the guilds was to maintain the celebration of sacred festivals ; they comprised poets, actors, and musicians. Most Greek cities had theatres and periodic festivals, but few maintained artists of their own ; of these few Sicyon seems to have been one (Bulletin de Correspondance hellénique xxiii, 1899, p. 54, no. 966).

53. 7. ταῖς ἡμέραις ἐκείναις : On those particular days.

αἱ δὲ πλεῖσται . . . ἐκλελοίπασιν : Pausanias (2, 8, 2 : 2, 7, 5) mentions the Arateum and Aratus' statue in the theatre but says nothing about the sacrifices. Polybius 8, 14 has ... θυσίας αὐτῷ καὶ τιμὰς ἡρωικὰς ἐψηφίσαντο καὶ συλλήβδην ὅσα πρὸς αἰώνιον ἀνήκει μνήμην . . .

54. 2. See on 52, 2 and 3.

54. 3. παρέτρεψεν, "he diverted him" : the active of this vb. is always transitive ; hence ὀρεγόμενος was emended in the Aldine to ὀρεγόμενον. **καίπερ ὄντι νέῳ καὶ ἀνθοῦντι :** The younger Aratus was strategos in 219-218, and therefore doubtless thirty years of age. He probably died shortly after his father. It appears at any rate that he was dead before 198 B.C. (Livy 32, 21). We must assume that the Aratus who was sent to Egypt in 181 B C. and to Rome in 179 (Pol. 24, 6) was his son Aratus III.

54. 5. καταπολεμηθείς, at Cynoscephalae, 197 B.C. (Plut., *Aemilius* 8, *Flamin.* 2-9). **τὸν υἱὸν ὁμηρεύσοντα παραδούς,** i.e., his younger son Demetrius, born *c.* 208, referred to below as ἀρετῇ διαφέροντα. He was apparently not only *persona grata* with the Romans but the favourite of the Macedonians.

54. 7. Γναθαινίου : see on 49, 2 where Beloch's grounds for rejecting the story of Perseus' illegitimacy are summarised. On the fate of the Antigonid family see *Aem. Paul.*, chaps. 8, 34, and 36.

APPENDIX ON THE TEXT.

The manuscripts now recognised as possessing independent authority for the *Aratus* are the following : —

1. G = codex Sangermanensis or Coislinianus (indicated by Sintenis as S^g), (Paris, Fonds Coislin, no. 319), a parchment MS. of the eleventh or twelfth century. The original writing was corrected by a second hand, not much later than the first. But while the corrector has removed minor blemishes, such as mistakes in spelling, he has far more frequently erased the genuine reading and introduced readings taken from an inferior MS. closely resembling the Laurentian [2, *below*]. The Sangermanensis was collated for the London edition of 1723–29 by Moïse du Soul (Solanus), but in many passages he failed to distinguish the original reading from the correction (collated again by Ziegler in 1908). Of the MSS. available for the *Aratus* G is easily the best.

2. L = cod. Laurentianus (Florence), 69, 6. This MS. dates from the year 997, as we learn from a note appended to it, but is full of careless mistakes, some of which have been corrected. Of correctors, three different hands have been observed (all alike cited by Ziegler as L^2). The correctors had the aid of a MS. closely resembling G, but may also have had recourse to conjecture. (Collated by Lindskog and Ziegler, the latter being responsible for the *Aratus*.)

3. P = codex Palatinus, 283 (Heidelberg), of the eleventh or twelfth century, collated by Sintenis, and again more accurately by Ziegler. For the *Aratus*, P ranks next in value to G.

4. R = codex Vaticanus Urbinas, 97, of the tenth or eleventh century. It is carefully written, and was corrected by a second hand shortly after it had been copied from its archetype. There are some notes in later hands. The correctors are indicated by Ziegler as R². The text of R is very closely connected with that of P. (Collated by Ziegler in 1908.)

The Paris MSS., 1671–4, are copies of L, a fact first discovered by Fuhr (see his *Agis and Cleomenes and the Gracchi*, 1882). None the less, these MSS. are occasionally useful, because, as Ziegler records, "doctorum virorum curae non expertes sunt qui et alios codices non nunquam adhibuerunt." Especially is this true of Paris. 1673.

The patriarch Photius in his *Bibliotheca* gives excerpts from the *Lives* derived from a MS. superior, generally, to ours. The superiority is not manifest, however, in the two short citations from the *Aratus* (28, 5 to end, and 53, 2–4).

EDITIONS OF *LIVES*.

Of these the most important are—

(1) The Editio Princeps, published by P. Junta, Florence, 1517. For the *Aratus*, Junta used cod. Laurentianus conv. suppr. 169, a copy, as is now known, of Paris. 1679, which itself was copied from R.

(2) The Aldine, Venice, 1519. In the *Aratus* it contains about half-a-dozen certain corrections of the text.

(3) Stephanus' edition of *Lives* and *Moralia*, Geneva, 1572, in thirteen volumes. In the last volume Stephanus published his own valuable conjectures on the *Lives* (pp. 390–466). In the text Stephanus incorporated readings from the Paris MSS., which resulted in a text far superior to the Juntine and Aldine. Stephanus' edition ranks as the Vulgate of Plutarch. The Frankfurt editions of 1599 and 1620 and the Paris edition of 1624 are re-impressions of Stephanus' edition.

(4) Bryan's edition, completed by Du Soul (Solanus), published in London (1723–29), is noted as the first to give the readings of the codex Sangermanensis.

(5) Reiske's edition of 1774–82 is chiefly valuable for Reiske's own emendations.

(6) Coraes' edition (Paris, 1809–14) "did great service in turning to account the readings of the MSS. published by his predecessors, in adopting a number of the best conjectures of Stephanus, Bryan, du Soul, and Reiske, in eliciting from the French version of Amyot the variants he had found in the MSS. of Rome and Venice, and in combining these with some excellent emendations of his own"—Holden, *Timoleon*, p. 161.

(7) Schaefer's edition, 1826–30, has given some valuable emendations, but is not otherwise important.

(8) Sintenis' edition of 1839–46 (revised for the Teubner series, 1852–5) was the first critical edition, in that Sintenis was the first to show on what MSS. the Vulgate was based.

(9) The edition of Lindskog and Ziegler, Teubner, 1914–35, is a great improvement on Sintenis. For instance, in the *Aratus*, Sentenis uses, in addition to G and P, the Paris MSS., 1671–4 and 1679, unaware that 1671–4 are copies of L, and 1679 of R. Further, Sintenis' "prava mendorum patientia defensioque" (Madvig) is a serious defect, though, as Madvig admits, there was a considerable improvement in this respect in his Teubner edition of 1852–5.

Ziegler's collation of L and R, and his adoption of a number of convincing conjectures, has provided a text which is not likely to be superseded unless a new and superior manuscript were to be discovered.

Apart from editors of the *Lives*, there are some scholars whose names occur constantly in the critical notes as contributing corrections of the text. For the *Aratus* the most important are—

> Xylander (Wilhelm Holtzman), Professor of Greek at Heidelberg, 1558–1576;
> Anon., i.e., *lectiones Anonymi*, conjectures of various Renaissance scholars, including Xylander;

and of nineteenth century scholars,

> Emperius (1806–41), whose *Opuscula* were published posthumously in 1847;
> Madvig (1804–1886), *Adversaria*, vol. i, pp. 565–677.
> Cobet (1813–89), *Novae* and *Variae Lectiones*, *Collectanea Critica* and *Mnemosyne*, vi, pp. 113–173.

PLUTARCH'S AVOIDANCE OF HIATUS.

It is admitted that Plutarch made it his practice not to write a word beginning with a vowel immediately after a word ending either with a long vowel or a
short vowel incapable of elision. This characteristic of his style was first observed
by Benseler, the editor of Isocrates, in 1841. Plutarch is, however, less strict in
observing this rule than Isocrates; certain exceptions are allowed, e.g. hiatus
may occur after the article, the words καί, ἥ, μή, prepositions, numerals, between
words expressing a single notion, or after a pause. Thus, as Sintenis remarks,
Plutarch allows ἡ ἀρετή, or καὶ ἀρετή, or οἱ ἵπποι, or ὄκτω ἵπποι, or ἕκτῃ ἐπὶ
δεκάτῃ, or Κιθαιρωνίᾳ Ἥρᾳ, or βορέᾳ ἀνέμῳ, or Φοιβίδου υἱός.

Hence among the instances of hiatus found in the MSS. of the Aratus no
suspicion attaches to Κλεινίου ἀδελφῷ (2, 4) or τοῦ καλουμένου Ὄρνιθος (20, 3).
In 30, 6, MSS. give στρατηγὸς ᾑρέθη ἀντιπράττοντος Ἀράτου, and though hiatus
after a comma is in general suspect, there are in the *Lives* a number of examples
of hiatus before a genitive absolute. In 19, 3, . . . τὰ πραττόμενα, ᾑρεῖτο the
text appears on other grounds to be corrupt (see crit. and explan. notes *ad loc.*).
Clear instances of illicit hiatus in the MSS. are: 2, 3, τὸν υἱὸν αὐτοῦ ἀνελεῖν
Ἄρατον: 5, 4, οὐ πάνυ ἀνέφικτον: 8, 3, ἀπὸ τοῦ πύργου αὐτὸν ἀντεφώνησε:
24, 2, ἐπειδὴ Ἄρατος ἀπέθανεν: 40, 3, ἐν Σικυωνίᾳ ἐφθαρμένοι: on which see
notes.

INDEX OF PROPER NAMES.

[*The figures refer to chapter and section. The addition of* n. *refers to note* ad loc.]

ʼΑβαντίδας, 2.

ʼΑβοιώκριτος, 16, 1n.

ʼΑγίας, 29, 6n.

Ἀγις, 31, 1n.

ʼΑθῆναι, 34, 3: 35, 2.

ʼΑθηναῖοι celebrate Aratus' defeat, 34, 4: seek his co-operation in negotiating for Piraeus, 34, 5: refuse help to Achaeans, 41, 3.

Αἰγίας, 18, 5–19, 2.

Αἰγινῆται, 34, 7n.

Αἴγιον, 37, 5: 42, 1–2n.: 53, 1.

Αἴγυπτος, 12, 6: 46, 1.

Αἰμίλιος, 54, 8.

Αἰσχύλος (Argive), 25, 2–3.

Αἴσωπος, *cited* 30, 8n.

Αἰτωλοί plot against Sicyon, 4, 1n.: defeat Boeotians, 16, 1n.: routed at Pellene, 31–32n.: allied with Achaeans, 33, 1: refuse aid to Achaeans, 41, 3; defeat Achaeans at Caphyae, 47: Philip's campaign against, 48, 5.

ʼΑκαδημεία, 34, 4.

ʼΑκροκόρινθος, 16, 5n.: seized by Antig. Gonatas, 17: by Aratus. 18–22: ceded to Antig. Doson, 44, 5.

ʼΑλέξανδρος (of Corinth), 17, 2n.: 18, 2n.

ʼΑκαρνᾶνες, 50, 7.

ʼΑλκμαίων, 3, 5.

ʼΑμοιβεύς, 17, 4n.

ʼΑμφιάρεως, 3, 5.

ʼΑνδρία (MSS. ʼΑδρία), 12, 2n.

ʼΑνθεστηριών, 53, 5n.

ʼΑντιγόνεια, 45, 8n.

(1) ʼΑντίγονος (Gonatas), his promise to Aratus, 4, 3: displeasure, 9, 5: holds Andros, 12, 2n.: eulogises Aratus, 15n.: surprises Acrocorinthus, 17: co-operates against Aratus with Aristippus, 25, 6: death, 34, 1.

(2) ʼΑντίγονος (Doson) offers to aid Achaeans in return for Acrocorinthus, 38, 9: Aratus' conversations with, 38, 11: his terms accepted, 41, 2: meets Aratus, 43, 1–3: honoured by Achaeans, 45: returns to Macedon, 46: death, 47.

(1) ʼΑπελλῆς (the painter), 13, 1–2n.

(2) ʼΑπελλῆς, Maced. courtier, 48, 1.

ʼΑπόλλων, 7, 1.

ʼΑπολλώνιον, 40, 5n.

ʼΑράτιον, 53, 5n.

Ἀρατος, early days, 2: characterisation of, 3: frees Sicyon, 4, 1–9, 3: restores exiles, 9, 4: persuades Sicyon to join Ach. League, 9, 6: further characterisation of, 10: serves in Ach. army, 11, 1: receives gift from "the king," 11, 2: sails for Egypt, 12: honoured at Sicyon, 14: eulogised by Antigonus, 15: appointed strategos (i), 16, 1: supports Boeotians, *ib.*: as strategos (ii) plans attack on Acrocorinthus, 16, 2: a previous attempt by, 18, 1: captures Acrocorinthus, 18, 2–24, 1: raids Attica, 24, 3–4: is appointed strategos in alternate years, 24, 5: conflict with Argive tyrants, Aristomachus I and Aristippus, 25; 27–29: relations with Lydiades, 30: routs Aetolians at Pellene, 30–31: forms alliance with Aetolians, 33, 1: invades Attica, 33: defeated at Phylacia, 34, 1: takes part in negotiations for Piraeus, 34, 6–7: treats with Aristomachus II for entry of Argos into Ach. League, 35, 1–5: appointed strategos (xii?), 35, 7: defeated by Cleomenes at Lycaeum, 36, 1–3: and near Megalopolis, 36, 5–37, 10: refused supplies by Achaeans,

GREEK INDEX TO NOTES.

(Exclusive of proper names.)

ENGLISH INDEX TO NOTES.

(Grammatical entries in italics.)

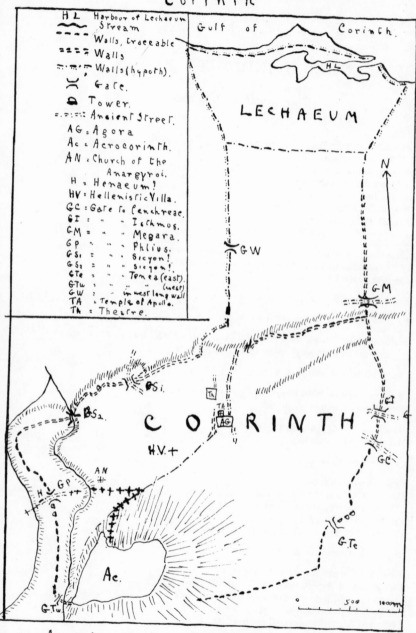

Corinth

Legend:
- H L = Harbour of Lechaeum
- ~~~ Stream
- - - - Walls, traceable
- ===== Walls
- ⌐⌐⌐ Walls (hypoth).
- ⋑⋐ Gate.
- ⬤ Tower.
- ∷∶∶∷ Ancient Street.
- AG = Agora
- Ac = Acrocorinth.
- AN = Church of the Anargyroi.
- H = Heraeum?
- HV = Hellenistic Villa.
- GC = Gate to Cenchreae.
- GI = " " Isthmus.
- GM = " " Megara.
- Gp = " " Phlius.
- GS₁ = " " Sicyon?
- GS₂ = " " Sicyon?
- GTe = " " Tenea (east)
- GTw = " " (west)
- GW = " in west long wall
- TA = Temple of Apollo.
- Th = Theatre.

Gulf of Corinth.

LECHAEUM

N

CORINTH

GW

GM

GS₁

Th

TA
AG

HV. +

AN

GP

H

Ac.

GTw

GI

GC

G.Te

0   500   1000m

++++ Aratus' route in 243 B.C. (adapted from Theunissen)
-·-·- Usual path to citadel.

GREEK TEXTS AND COMMENTARIES
An Arno Press Collection